D0952165

STYLE GUIDE

OTHER ECONOMIST BOOKS

Guide to Analysing Companies
Guide to Business Modelling
Guide to Business Planning
Guide to Economic Indicators
Guide to the European Union
Guide to Financial Management
Guide to Financial Markets
Guide to Hedge Funds
Guide to Investment Strategy
Guide to Management Ideas and Gurus
Guide to Organisation Design
Guide to Project Management
Guide to Supply Chain Management
Numbers Guide

Book of Obituaries
Brands and Branding
Business Consulting
The City
Coaching and Mentoring
Dealing with Financial Risk
Economics
Emerging Markets
The Future of Technology
Headhunters and How to Use Them
Mapping the Markets
Marketing
Successful Strategy Execution
The World of Business

Directors: an A–Z Guide
Economics: an A–Z Guide
Investment: an A–Z Guide
Negotiation: an A–Z Guide

Pocket World in Figures

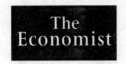

STYLE GUIDE

THE ECONOMIST IN ASSOCIATION WITH
PROFILE BOOKS LTD

Published by Profile Books Ltd,
3A Exmouth House, Pine Street, London EC1R OJH
www.profilebooks.com

The greatest care has been taken in compiling this book.
However, no responsibility can be accepted by the publishers or compilers
for the accuracy of the information presented.

Typeset in EcoType by MacGuru Ltd
info@macguru.org.uk

Printed in Great Britain by
Clays, Bungay, Suffolk

A CIP catalogue record for this book is available
from the British Library

ISBN 978 1 84668 175 2

The paper this book is printed on is certified by the © 1996 Forest
Stewardship Council A.C. (FSC). It is ancient-forest friendly. The printer holds
FSC chain of custody SGS-COC-2061

FSC
Mixed Sources
Product group from well-managed
forests and other controlled sources

Cert no. SGS-COC-2061
www.fsc.org
© 1996 Forest Stewardship Council

Contents

Preface

Every newspaper has its own style book, a set of rules telling
journalists whether to write e-mail or email, Gadaffi or Qaddafi,
judgement or judgment. *The Economist's* style book does this and a bit
more. It also warns writers of some common mistakes and encourages
them to write with clarity and simplicity.

All the prescriptive judgments in the style guide are directly
derived from those used each week in writing and editing *The
Economist.*

This tenth edition of the "The Economist Style Guide" is in three
parts. The first is based on the style book used by those who edit
The Economist; it is largely the work of John Grimond, who has over
the years been Britain, American and foreign editor. The second, on
American and British English, describes some of the main differences
between the two great English-speaking areas, in spelling, grammar and
usage.

To make the style guide of greater general interest, Part 3 consists of
handy reference material that might appeal to readers of *The Economist.*

Throughout the text, italic type is used for examples except where
they are presented in lists, when the type is Roman, as this text is.
Words in **bold** indicate a separate but relevant entry, that is, a cross-
reference. Small capitals are used only in the way *The Economist* uses
them, for which see the entry **abbreviations**.

Many people have been involved in this book as it has
developed and changed over the years. Thanks are due to all
of them, with special thanks to Penny Butler, who has played a
crucial role from the start.

John Grimond, *January 2010*

Introduction

On only two scores can *The Economist* hope to outdo its rivals consistently. One is the quality of its analysis; the other is the quality of its writing. The aim of this book is to give some general advice on writing, to point out some common errors and to set some arbitrary rules.

The first requirement of *The Economist* is that it should be readily understandable. Clarity of writing usually follows clarity of thought. So think what you want to say, then say it as simply as possible. Keep in mind George Orwell's six elementary rules:

1 Never use a metaphor, simile or other figure of speech which you are used to seeing in print (*see* **metaphors**).
2 Never use a long word where a short one will do (*see* **short words**).
3 If it is possible to cut out a word, always cut it out (*see* **unnecessary words**).
4 Never use the passive where you can use the active (*see* **grammar and syntax**).
5 Never use a foreign phrase, a scientific word or a jargon word if you can think of an everyday English equivalent (*see* **jargon**).
6 Break any of these rules sooner than say anything outright barbarous (*see* **iconoclasm**).

Readers are primarily interested in what you have to say. By the way in which you say it you may encourage them either to read on or to give up. If you want them to read on:

Catch the attention of the reader Then get straight into the article. Do not spend several sentences clearing your throat, setting the scene or sketching in the background. Introduce the facts as you tell the story and hold the reader by the way you unfold the tale and by a fresh but unpretentious use of language.

In starting your article, let your model be the essays of Francis Bacon. His "Of Marriage" begins, "He that hath wife and children hath given hostages to fortune; for they are impediments to great enterprises, either of virtue or mischief." "Of Riches" he starts with "I cannot call riches better than the baggage of virtue." "Of

Cunning" opens with "We take cunning for a sinister or crooked wisdom." "Of Suspicion" is instantly on the wing with "Suspicions amongst thoughts are like bats amongst birds, they ever fly by twilight." "Of Ambition" wastes no time in asserting, "Ambition is like choler; which is an humor that maketh men active, earnest, full of alacrity, and stirring, if it be not stopped. But if it be stopped, and cannot have his way, it becometh adust, and thereby malign and venomous."

Each of these beginnings carries implicitly within it an entire essay. Each seizes the reader by the lapels and at once draws him into the subject. No gimmickry is needed, no flowery language, no literary contrivance. Plain words on their own carry enough meaning to provoke an intriguing thought, stir the reader's curiosity and thus make him want to continue.

You must strive for a similar effect. Articles in *The Economist* are like essays, in that they have a beginning, a middle and an end. They should not be mere bits of information stitched together. Each should be a coherent whole, a series of paragraphs that follow logically in order and, ideally, will suffer if even one sentence should be cut out. If the article is a report, the facts must be selected and presented as a story. If it is a leader or more analytical article, it should also have a sense of sequence, so that the reader feels he is progressing from a beginning to a conclusion.

Either way, it is up to you to provide the ideas, analysis and argument that bind the elements of the article together. That is the difficult part. Once you have them, though, you need only plain, straightforward words to express them. Do not imagine that you can disguise the absence of thought with long words, stale metaphors or the empty jargon of academics. Do not imagine, either, that you can make an intrinsically dull subject more interesting by using a series of hackneyed phrases. In moderation, however, you can enliven your writing with a fresh metaphor, an occasional exuberance or an unusual word or phrase that nicely suits your purpose.

Read through your writing several times Edit it ruthlessly, whether by cutting or polishing or sharpening, on each occasion. Avoid repetition. Cut out anything superfluous. And resist any temptation to achieve a literary effect by making elliptical remarks or allusions to unexplained people or events. Rather, hold your reader's attention by keeping the story moving. If the tale begins to flag, or the arguments seem less than convincing, you can rescue it only by the sharpness of your mind. Nothing is to be gained by resorting to orotundities and grandiloquence, still less by calling on clichés and vogue expressions. Unadorned, unfancy prose is usually all you need.

Do not be stuffy "To write a genuine, familiar or truly English style", said Hazlitt, "is to write as anyone would speak in common conversation who had a thorough command or choice of words or who could discourse with ease, force and perspicuity setting aside all pedantic and oratorical flourishes."

Use the language of everyday speech, not that of spokesmen, lawyers or bureaucrats (so prefer *let* to *permit, people* to *persons, buy* to *purchase, colleague* to *peer, way out* to *exit, present* to *gift, rich* to *wealthy, show* to *demonstrate, break* to *violate*). Pomposity and long-windedness tend to obscure meaning, or reveal the lack of it: strip them away in favour of plain words.

Do not be hectoring or arrogant Those who disagree with you are not necessarily *stupid* or *insane*. Nobody needs to be described as silly: let your analysis show that he is. When you express opinions, do not simply make assertions. The aim is not just to tell readers what you think, but to persuade them; if you use arguments, reasoning and evidence, you may succeed. Go easy on the *oughts* and *shoulds*.

Do not be too pleased with yourself Don't boast of your own cleverness by telling readers that you correctly predicted something or that you have a scoop. You are more likely to bore or irritate them than to impress them.

Do not be too chatty *Surprise, surprise* is more irritating than informative. So is *Ho, ho* and, in the middle of a sentence, *wait for it*, etc.

Do not be too didactic If too many sentences begin *Compare, Consider, Expect, Imagine, Look at, Note, Prepare for, Remember* or *Take*, readers will think they are reading a textbook (or, indeed, a style book). This may not be the way to persuade them to renew their subscriptions.

Do your best to be lucid ("I see but one rule: to be clear", Stendhal) Simple sentences help. Keep complicated constructions and gimmicks to a minimum, if necessary by remembering the *New Yorker*'s comment: "Backward ran sentences until reeled the mind."

Mark Twain described how a good writer treats sentences: "At times he may indulge himself with a long one, but he will make sure there are no folds in it, no vaguenesses, no parenthetical interruptions of its view as a whole; when he has done with it, it won't be a sea-serpent with half of its arches under the water; it will be a torch-light procession."

Long paragraphs, like long sentences, can confuse the reader. "The paragraph", according to Fowler, "is essentially a unit of thought, not of length; it must be homogeneous in subject matter and sequential in treatment." One-sentence paragraphs should be used only occasionally.

Clear thinking is the key to clear writing. "A scrupulous writer", observed Orwell, "in every sentence that he writes will ask himself at least four questions, thus: What am I trying to say? What words will express it? What image or idiom will make it clearer? Is this image fresh enough to have an effect? And he will probably ask himself two more: Could I put it more shortly? Have I said anything that is avoidably ugly?"

Scrupulous writers will also notice that their copy is edited only lightly and is likely to be used. It may even be read.

A note on editing

Editing has always made a large contribution to *The Economist*'s excellence. It should continue to do so. But editing on a screen is beguilingly simple. It is quite easy to rewrite an article without realising that one has done much to it at all: the cursor leaves no trace of crossings-out, handwritten insertions, rearranged sentences or reordered paragraphs. The temptation is to continue to make changes until something emerges that the editor himself might have written. One benefit of this is a tightly edited newspaper. One cost is a certain sameness. The risk is that the newspaper will turn into a collection of 70 or 80 articles which read as though they are the work of but a few hands.

The Economist has a single editorial outlook, and it is anonymous. But it is the work of many people, both in London and abroad, as its datelines testify. If the prose of our Tokyo correspondent is indistinguishable from the prose of our Nairobi correspondent, readers will feel they are being robbed of variety. They may also wonder whether these two people really exist, or whether the entire newspaper is not written in London.

The moral for editors is that they should respect good writing. That is mainly what this style guide is designed to promote. It is not intended to impose a single style on all *The Economist*'s journalists. A writer's style, after all, should reflect his mind and personality. So long as they are compatible with *The Economist*'s editorial outlook, and so long as the prose is good, editors should exercise suitable self-restraint. Remember that your copy, too, will be edited. And even if you think you are not guilty, bear in mind this comment from John Gross:

> Most writers I know have tales to tell of being mangled by editors and mauled by fact-checkers, and naturally it is the flagrant instances they choose to single out - absurdities, outright distortions of meaning, glaring errors. But most of the damage done is a good deal less spectacular. It consists of small changes (usually too boring to describe to anyone else) that flatten a writer's style, slow down his argument, neutralise his irony; that ruin the rhythm of a sentence or the balance of paragraph; that deaden the tone that makes the music. I sometimes think of the process as one of "desophistication".

John Grimond

part 1

the essence of style

a or the *see* **grammar and syntax**.

abbreviations

Write words in their full form on first appearance:

Trades Union Congress (not TUC), *Troubled Asset Relief Programme* (not TARP)

unless an abbreviation or acronym is so familiar that it is used more often in full:

AIDS BBC CIA EU FBI HIV IMF NATO NGO OECD UNESCO

or unless the full form would provide little illumination – AWACS, DNA. If in doubt about its familiarity, explain what the organisation is or does. After the first mention, try not to repeat the abbreviation too often; so write *the agency* rather than *the* IAEA, *the party* rather than *the* KMT, to avoid spattering the page with capital letters. There is no need to give the initials of an organisation if it is not referred to again. This clutters both the page and the brain.

Do not use spatterings of abbreviations and acronyms simply in order to cram more words in; you will end up irritating readers rather than informing them. An article in a recent issue of *The Economist* contained the following:

CIA DCI DNI DOD DVD FBI NCTC NSA

The article immediately following had:

CTAC CX DIS FCO GCHQ IT JIC JTAC MI5 MI6 MP SCOPE WMD

Some of these are well known to most readers and can readily be held in the mind. But unfamiliar abbreviations may oblige the reader to constantly refer back to the first use. Better to repeat some names in full, or to write *the agency, the committee, the party*, etc, than to allow an undisciplined proliferation. And prefer *chief executive* or *boss* to CEO.

ampersands should be used:

1.   when they are part of the name of a company:
Procter & Gamble Pratt & Whitney

2.   for such things as constituencies where two names are linked to form one unit:
The rest of Brighouse & Spenborough joins with the Batley part of Batley & Morley to form Batley & Spen.
The area thus became the Pakistani province of Kashmir and the Indian state of Jammu & Kashmir.

3.   in R&D and S&L.

definite article If an abbreviation can be pronounced – COSATU, NATO, UNESCO – it does not generally require the definite article. Other organisations, except companies, should usually be preceded by *the*:

the BBC the KGB the NHS the NIESR the UNHCR

elements do not take small caps when abbreviated:

carbon dioxide is CO_2
lead is Pb
methane is CH_4

However:

chlorofluorocarbons are CFCS
the oxides of nitrogen are generally NOX

Different isotopes of the same element are distinguished by raised (superscript) prefixes:

carbon-14 is ^{14}C
helium-3 is ^3He

Do not sprinkle chemical symbols unnecessarily: they may put readers off. But common abbreviations such as CO_2 may sometimes be used for variety.

headings, cross-heads, captions, etc In headings, rubrics, cross-heads, footnotes, captions, tables, charts (including sources), use ordinary caps, not small caps.

initials in people's and companies' names take points (with a space between initials and name, but not between initials). In general, follow the practice preferred by people, companies and organisations in writing their own names, for example:

I.M. Pei J.C. Penney J. Sainsbury A.N. Wilson

junior and senior Spell out in full (and lower case) *junior* and *senior* after a name:

George Bush junior George Bush senior

lower case Abbreviate:

kilograms (*not* kilogrammes) to kg (or kilos)
kilometres per hour to kph
kilometres to km
miles per hour to mph

Use lower case for *kg, km, lb* (never *lbs*), *mph* and other measures, and for *ie, eg,* which should both be followed by commas. When used with figures, these lower-case abbreviations should follow immediately, with no space:

11am 4.30pm 15kg 35mm 100mph 78rpm

Two abbreviations together, however, must be separated: *60m b/d.* Use *b/d* not *bpd* as an abbreviation for *barrels per day.*

MPs Except in British contexts, use *MP* only after first spelling out member of Parliament in full (in many places an *MP* is a military policeman).

Members of the *European Parliament* are *MEPs* (not Euro-*MPs*). Members of the *Scottish Parliament* are *MSPs*. Members of the *Welsh Assembly* are *AMs* (Assembly Members).

organisations

EFTA is the *European Free Trade Association.*
The *FAO* is the *Food and Agriculture Organisation.*
The *FDA* is the *Food and Drug Administration.*
The *IDA* is the *International Development Association.*
NAFTA is the *North American Free-Trade Agreement.*
The *PLO* is the *Palestine Liberation Organisation.*

pronounceable abbreviations

Abbreviations that can be pronounced and are composed of bits of words rather than just initials should be spelt out in upper and lower case:

Cocom	Mercosur	Unicef
Frelimo	Nepad	Unisom
Kfor	Renamo	Unprofor
Legco	Sfor	

Trips (trade-related aspects of intellectual property rights)

There is generally no need for more than one initial capital letter, unless the word is a name: *ConsGold, KwaZulu, McKay, MiG.*

ranks and titles Do not use *Prof, Sen, Col*, etc. *Lieut-Colonel* and *Lieut-Commander* are permissible. So is *Rev*, but it must be preceded by *the* and followed by a Christian name or initial: *the Rev Jesse Jackson* (thereafter *Mr Jackson*).

scientific units named after individuals Most scientific units, except those of temperature, that are named after individuals should be set in small capitals, though any attachments denoting multiples go in lower case:

watt is w
kilowatt, 1,000 watts, is kw
milliwatt, one-thousandth of a watt, is mw
megawatt, 1m watts, is mw
megahertz is mh

small caps usage

In body text, use small capitals for abbreviations, acronyms and proper names spelt in capitals, whether they can be pronounced as words or not, with no points:

CIF EU FOB GDP IKEA NATO

Single letters, whether or not attached by hyphens to words, should also be set in small caps:

A-level T-shirt U-turn X-ray Y chromosome

Abbreviations that include upper-case and lower-case letters must be set in a mixture of small capitals and roman: BPhil, BSkyB, PhD. The same rule applies if an abbreviation is linked to a number: AK-47, MiG-25, M1, SALT-2.

Brackets, apostrophes and all other typographical furniture accompanying small capitals are generally set in ordinary roman, with a lower-case s (also roman) for plurals and genitives: IOUs, MPs' salaries, SDRs, etc. Ampersands should also be set as small caps: R&D.

Do not use small caps for:

the elements of the periodic table, eg H, Pb, Sn, NaCl

degrees of temperature, eg °C, °F, °R

currencies, eg Nkr, Sfr

roman numerals, eg C, D, I, L, M, V, X. So Richard III, Louis XIV, Pope John XXIII and so on. But do not adorn popes, monarchs, etc, with numerical postscripts unless they are needed to differentiate, for example, Benedict XVI from Benedict XV, or Elizabeth II from her 16th-century namesake.

anything in captions, charts (including sources), footnotes, headings, rubrics or tables

writing out upper-case abbreviations Most upper-case abbreviations take upper-case initial letters when written in full. The LSO is the London Symphony Orchestra. However, there are exceptions:

CAP *but* common agricultural policy
EMU *but* economic and monetary union
GDP *but* gross domestic product
PSBR *but* public-sector borrowing requirement
VLSI *but* very large-scale integration

miscellaneous Spell out:

page pages hectares miles

Remember, too, that the V of HIV stands for virus, so do not write HIV virus.

See **measures** in Part 3.

absent In Latin *absent* is a verb meaning *they are away*. In English it is either an adjective (*absent friends*) or a verb (*to absent yourself*). It is not a preposition meaning *in the absence of*.

accents On words now accepted as English, use accents only when they make a crucial difference to pronunciation:

café cliché communiqué éclat exposé façade soupçon

But: *chateau decor elite feted naive*

The main accents and diacritical signs are:

acute	république
grave	grand-mère
circumflex	bête noire
umlaut	Länder, Österreich (Austria)
cedilla	français
tilde	señor, São Paulo

If you use one accent (except the tilde – strictly, a diacritical sign), use all:

émigré mêlée protégé résumé

Put the accents and diacritical signs on French, German, Spanish and Portuguese names and words only:

José Manuel Barroso	cafèzinho
Federico Peña	coñac
Françoise de Panafieu	déjeuner
Wolfgang Schäuble	Frühstück

See also **italics**.

acronym A pronounceable word, formed from the initials of other words, like *radar* or *NATO*. It is not a set of initials, like the *BBC* or the *IMF*.

actionable means *giving ground for a lawsuit*. Do not use it to mean *susceptible of being put into practice*: prefer *practical* or *practicable*. Do not use *action* as a verb.

adjectives and adverbs *see* **grammar and syntax, punctuation.**

adjectives of proper nouns *see* **grammar and syntax, punctuation.**

address What did journalists and politicians do in the days, not so long ago, when *address* was used as a verb only before objects such as *audience, letter, ball, haggis* and, occasionally, *themselves*? Questions can be *answered*, issues *discussed*, problems *solved*, difficulties *dealt with. See* **clichés.**

aetiology is the *science of causation*, or *an inquiry into something's origins. Etiolate* is to *make* or *become pale for lack of light.*

affect (verb) means to have an influence on, as in *the novel affected his attitude to immigrants. See also* **effect.**

affirmative action is a euphemism, uglier even than *human-rights abuses* and more obscure even than *comfort station*, with little to be said for it. It is too late to suppress it altogether and perhaps too soon to consign it to the midden of civil-rights studies, but try to avoid it as much as possible. If you cannot escape it, put it in quotation marks on first mention and, unless the context makes its meaning clear, explain what it is. You may, however, find that *preferential treatment, job preferment* or even *discrimination* serve just as well as alternatives. *See* **euphemisms.**

affordable By whom? Avoid *affordable housing, affordable computers* and other unthinking uses of advertising lingo.

Afghan names *see* **names.**

aggravate means *make worse*, not *irritate* or *annoy*.

aggression is an unattractive quality, so do not call a *keen* salesman an *aggressive* one (unless his foot is in the door).

agony column Remember that when Sherlock Holmes perused this, it was a *personal column*. Only recently has it come to mean *letters to an agony aunt*.

agree Things are agreed *on, to* or *about*, not just agreed.

aircraft *see* **hyphens** and **italics.**

alibi An *alibi* is the fact of being elsewhere, not a false explanation.

alternate, alternative *Alternate* (as an adjective) means *every other*. As a noun, it has now come to mean a *stand-in* for a director or delegate. *Alternative* (as a noun), strictly, means one of two, not one of three, four, five or more (which may be *options*). As an adjective, *alternative* means *of two* (*or, loosely, more*) *things, or possible as an alternative*.

Americanisms If you use Americanisms just to show you know them, people may find you a *tad* tiresome, so be discriminating. Many American words and expressions have passed into the language; others have vigour (*scofflaw*), particularly if used sparingly, or charm (*discombobulate*). Some are short and to the point, so, for example, prefer *lay off* to *make redundant*.

Spat and *scam*, two words beloved by some journalists, have the merit of brevity, but so do *row* and *fraud*; *squabble* and *swindle* might sometimes be used instead. But many words favoured in American English usage are unnecessarily long, or unusual, so use:

and *not* additionally
the army *not* the military (noun)
car *not* automobile
company *not* corporation
court *not* courtroom or courthouse
district *not* neighborhood
normality *not* normalcy
oblige *not* obligate
property *not* real estate
rocket *not* skyrocket
speciality *not* specialty
stocks *not* inventories (unless there is the risk of confusion with
    stocks and shares)
transport *not* transportation

Other Americanisms are euphemistic or obscure, so avoid:

ball games	rookies
end runs	stand-off
point men	

Back-formations are common in English, so *curate*, the verb meaning *organise* or *superintend* exhibitions of pictures, sculptures and so on formed from *curator*, is now acceptable in British English. But it is still too soon for *gallerist* (prefer *dealer* or, if appropriate, just *gallery*).

adverbs Put adverbs where you would put them in normal speech, which is usually after the verb (not before it, which usually is where Americans put them).

avoiding nouning adjectives Similarly, do not noun adjectives such as:

advisory – prefer *warning*
centennial – prefer *centenary*
inaugural – prefer *inauguration*
meet (noun) – *meeting* is better
spend (noun) – *spending* is preferable

avoiding verbing and adjectiving nouns Try not to verb nouns or to adjective them. So do not:

access files (except electronically)
action proposals
author books (still less *co-author* them)
critique style guides
gun someone down, use *shoot*
haemorrhage red ink (haemorrhage is a noun)
let one event *impact* another
loan money
pressure colleagues (*press* will do)
progress reports
source inputs
trial programmes

Avoid *parenting* (or using the word) and *parenting skills*.
(*See also* **grammar and syntax**.)
And though it is sometimes necessary to use nouns as adjectives, there is no need to call:

an *attempted coup* a *coup attempt*
a *suspected terrorist* a *terrorist suspect*
the *Californian legislature* the *California legislature*

Vilest of all is the habit of throwing together several nouns into one ghastly adjectival reticule:

Texas millionaire real-estate developer and failed thrift entrepreneur Hiram Turnipseed ...

coining words Avoid coining verbs and adjectives unnecessarily.

Instead of:

dining experiences and *writing experiences*: use *dining* and *writing*
downplaying criticism, you can *play* it *down* (or perhaps *minimise* it)
upcoming and *ongoing* are better put as *forthcoming* and *continuing*
Why *outfit* your children when you can *fit* them *out*?

Hosting has now entered the language (often to mean *acting as host at an event paid for by someone else*, otherwise *giving* would be the right word), but *guesting* (*appearing as a guest* on a programme) should be kept at bay.

old-fashioned terms Some American expressions that were once common in English English (and some still used in Scottish English) now sound old-fashioned to most British ears. So prefer:

clothes or *clothing* to *apparel* or *garments*
doctors to *physicians*
got to *gotten*
lawyers to *attorneys*
often to *oftentimes*
over or *too* to *overly*
stick to *cane*

overuse of American words Do not feel obliged to follow American fashion in overusing such words as:

constituency – try *supporters*
gubernatorial – this means *relating to a governor*
perception – try *belief* or *view*
rhetoric (of which there is too little, not too much) – try *language* or *speeches* or *exaggeration* if that is what you mean

some differences In an American context you may *run* for office (but please *stand* in countries with parliamentary systems) and your car may sometimes run on *gasoline* instead of *petrol*. But if you use *corn* in the American sense you should explain that this is *maize* to most people (unless it is an *old chestnut*).
Slate can also mean *abuse* (as a verb) but does not, in Britain, mean *predict, schedule* or *nominate*. And if you must

use American expressions, use them correctly (a *rain-check* does not imply checking on the weather outside).

In Britain:

Cars are *hired*, not *rented*, and are left in *car parks*, not *parking lots*.

City centres are not *central cities*.

Companies: *call for* a record profit if you wish to exhort the workers, but not if you merely predict one. And do not *post* it if it has been achieved. If it has not, look for someone new to *head*, not *head up*, the company.

Countries, nations and states: London is the *country's* capital, not the *nation's*. If you wish to build a *nation*, you will *bind its peoples together*; if you wish to build a *state*, you will forge its *institutions*.

Deep: make a *deep* study or even a study *in depth*, but not an *in-depth* study.

Ex-servicemen are not necessarily *veterans*.

Football for most people is a *game* – you do not have to call it a *sport* – that Americans call *soccer*.

Do not *figure out* if you can *work out*.

Fresh should be used of vegetables, not teenagers.

Grow a beard or a tomato but not a company (or indeed a salesman: the *Financial Times* reported on August 8th 2003 that BMW was "to grow its own car salesmen").

Hikes are *walks*, not *increases*.

Hospital: when we are seriously ill we are *in hospital*, not *in the hospital*, still less *hospitalised*.

Do not use *likely* to mean *probably*.

Make a *rumpus* rather than a *ruckus*, be *rumbustious* rather than *rambunctious*, and *snigger* rather than *snicker*.

On-site inspections are allowed, but not *on-train teams* or *in-ear headphones*.

Outside America, nowadays, you stay *outside* the door, not *outside of* it.

Programme: you may *program* a computer but in all other contexts the word is *programme*.

Use *power cut* or *blackout* rather than *outage*.

Keep a promise, rather than *deliver on* it.

Raise cattle and pigs, but children are (or should be) *brought up*.

Regular is not a synonym for *ordinary* or *normal*: Mussolini brought in the *regular* train, All-Bran the *regular* man; it is quite *normal* to be without either.

A *religious group* sounds better than a *faith-based organisation*.
Scenarios are best kept for the theatre, *postures* for the gym,
     parameters for the parabola.
School: children are *at* school, not *in* it.
Do not *task* people, or *meet with* them.
Throw *stones*, not *rock*.
Trains run from *railway stations*, not *train stations*. The people
     in them, and on buses, are *passengers*, not *riders*.
Use *senior* rather than *ranking*.

And only the speechless are *dumb*, the well-dressed (and a
few devices) *smart* and the insane *mad*.

tenses Choose tenses according to British usage, too. In particular,
do not fight shy – as Americans often do – of the perfect tense,
especially where no date or time is given. Thus:

Mr Obama has woken up to the danger is preferable to *Mr
Obama woke up to the danger*, unless you can add *last week* or
when he heard the explosion.
Do not write *Your salary just got smaller* or *I shrunk the
kids*. In British English *Your salary has just got smaller* and *I've
shrunk the kids*.

See also **adjectives of proper nouns, euphemisms, grammar and
syntax,** and Part 2.

among and between Some sticklers insist that, where division
is involved, *among* should be used where three or more are
concerned, *between* where only two are concerned. So:

*The plum jobs were shared among the Socialists, the Liberals and
the Christian Democrats, while the president and the vice-president
divided the cash between themselves.*

This distinction is unnecessary. But take care with *between*. *To
fall between two stools*, however painful, is grammatically acceptable;
to fall between the cracks is to challenge the laws of physics.
Prefer *among* to *amongst*.

an should be used before a word beginning with a vowel sound (*an
egg, an umbrella, an MP*) or an h if, and only if, the h is silent (*an
honorary degree*). But *a European, a university, a U-turn, a hospital,
a hotel. Historical* is an exception: it is preceded by *an*, the h
remaining silent.

anarchy means the *complete absence of law* or *government*. It may be harmonious or chaotic.

animals For the spelling of the Latin names of animals, plants, etc, *see* **Latin names.**

annus horribilis, annus mirabilis *Annus horribilis* is often used, presumably in contrast to *annus mirabilis*, to describe an *awful year*, for example by Queen Elizabeth in 1992 (the year of her daughter's divorce, the separation of the Duke and Duchess of York and a fire at Windsor Castle) and by Kofi Annan in 2004 (a year of scandal and controversy at the United Nations). It serves its purpose well, but it should be noted that *annus mirabilis* originally meant much the same thing: 1666, of which it was first used, was the year of the great fire of London and the second year of the great plague in England. Physicists, however, have latterly used the term to describe 1932, the year in which the neutron was discovered, the positron identified and the atomic nucleus first broken up artificially. And Philip Larkin, more understandably, used it to describe 1963, the year in which sexual intercourse began.

anon means *soon*, though it once meant *straight away*. *Presently* also means *soon*, though it is increasingly misused to mean *now*. (*See* also **presently**.)

anticipate does not mean *expect*. Jack and Jill expected to marry; if they anticipated marriage, only Jill might find herself expectant.

apostasy, heresy If you abandon your religion, you commit *apostasy*. If that religion is the prevailing one in your community and your beliefs are contrary to its orthodoxy, you commit *heresy*.

apostrophes *see* **punctuation**.

appeal is intransitive nowadays (except in America), so appeal *against decisions*.

appraise means *set a price on*. *Apprise* means *inform*.

Arabic The Arabic alphabet has several consonants that have no exact equivalents in English: for example, a hard *t* as well as a normal soft one, a hard *s* as well as a soft one, two different (one vocalised, the other not) *th* sounds. Moreover, there are three sounds: a glottal stop like a hiccup, a glottal sound akin to strangulation and a uvular trill. Ultra-fastidious transliterators try to reproduce these subtleties with a profusion of apostrophes and *h*s which yield spellings like Mu'ammar al-Qadhdhafi. The risk of error and the sheer ugliness on the page are too great to justify the effort, so usually ignore the differences.

Vowels present a lesser problem. There are only three – *a*, *u*, *i* – but each can be lengthened. Do not bother to differentiate between the short and the long *a*. Occasionally, a spelling is established where the *u* has been lengthened by using oo, as in *Sultan Qaboos*. In such instances, follow that convention, but in general go for *ou*, as in *murabitoun* or *Ibn Khaldoun*. For a long *i* you should normally use *ee* (as in *mujahideen*).

Muhammad is the correct spelling unless it is part of the name of someone who spells it differently. (*See also* **names**.)

as of say, April 5th or April. Prefer *on* (or *after*, or *since*) April 5th, in April.

assassinate is, properly, the term used not just for any old killing, but for the murder of a prominent person, usually for a political purpose. (*See* **execute**.)

as to There is usually a more appropriate preposition, eg *about*. Or rewrite the sentence.

autarchy, autarky *Autarchy* means absolute sovereignty. *Autarky* means self-sufficiency.

avocation An *avocation* is a distraction or *diversion from your ordinary employment*, not a synonym for *vocation*.

bail, bale In the hayfield, *bale*; otherwise *bail, bail out* and *bail-out* (noun).

Bangladeshi names *see* **names**.

-based A *Paris-based group* may be all right, if, say, that group operates abroad (otherwise just say a *group in Paris*). But avoid *community-based, faith-based, knowledge-based*, etc. A *community-based organisation* is perhaps a *community organisation*; a *faith-based organisation* is probably a *church*; a *knowledge-based industry* needs explanation: all industries depend on knowledge.

beg the question means neither *raise the question, invite the question* nor *evade the answer*. To *beg the question* is to adopt an argument whose conclusion depends upon assuming the truth of the very conclusion the argument is designed to produce.

All governments should promote free trade because otherwise protectionism will increase. This begs the question.

Belarusian names *see* **names**.

bellwether This is the leading sheep of a flock, on whose neck a bell is hung. It is nothing to do with climate, prevailing winds or the like, but the term is used in the stockmarket.

between *see* **among and between**.

biannual, biennial *Biannual* can mean twice a year or once every two years. Avoid. Since *biennial* also means once every two years, that is best avoided too. So are *bimonthly* and *biweekly*, which also have two meanings. Luckily, *fortnightly* is unambiguous.

bicentennial Prefer bicentenary (as a noun).

black *In the black* means *in profit* in Britain, but *making losses* in some places. Use *in profit*.

blond, blonde *Blond* is an adjective and, unusually, in its adjectival use it retains its two genders (see **grammar and syntax**, masculine or feminine). Use *blonde* as a noun, referring to a woman with blond hair: *the blonde in the corner of the room.* Use *blond* for everything else, including the hair of a blonde.

blooded, bloodied *Blooded* means *pedigreed* (as in *blue-blooded*) or *initiated. Bloodied* means *wounded.*

bon vivant not *bon viveur.*

born, borne are both past participles of the verb *bear. Born* is used in the sense of giving birth: *She was born in April. Borne* is used for *supporting* or *putting up with* (*The victims had borne enough pain*) and for giving birth in active constructions (*She had already borne six children*).

both ... and A preposition placed after *both* should be repeated after *and.* Thus *both to right and to left;* but *to both right and left* is all right.

brackets *see* **punctuation**.

British titles *see* **titles**.

brokerage is what a stockbroking firm does, not what it is.

by contrast, in contrast Use *by contrast* only when you are comparing one thing with another: *Somalia is a poor country. By contrast, Egypt is rich.* This means Egypt is rich by comparison with Somalia, though by other standards it is poor. If you are simply noting a difference, say *in contrast: The Joneses spend their holidays in the south of France. In contrast, the Smiths go to south Wales.*

cadre Keep this word for the *framework of a military unit* or the *officers of such a unit*, not for a *communist functionary*.

calibres *see* **hyphens.**

Cambodian names *see* **names.**

Canute's exercise on the seashore was designed to persuade his courtiers of what he knew to be true but they doubted, ie, that he was not omnipotent. Don't imply he was surprised to get his feet wet.

capitals A balance has to be struck between so many capitals that the eyes dance and so few that the reader is diverted more by our style than by our substance. The general rule is to dignify with capital letters organisations and institutions, but not people; and full names, but not informal ones. More exact rules are laid out below. Even these, however, leave some decisions to individual judgment. If in doubt use lower case unless it looks absurd. And remember that "a foolish consistency is the hobgoblin of little minds" (Ralph Waldo Emerson).

avoiding confusion Use capitals to avoid confusion, especially with no (and therefore yes). *In Bergen no votes predominated* suggests a stalemate, whereas *In Bergen No votes predominated* suggests a triumph of noes over yeses. In most contexts, though, yes and no should be lower case: "*The answer is no.*"

cities *City* with a capital, even though *City* is not an integral part of their names:

Guatemala City	New York City
Ho Chi Minh City	Panama City
Kuwait City	Quebec City
Mexico City	

City also takes a capital when it is part of the name:

Dodge City   Quezon City
Kansas City   Salt Lake City
Oklahoma City

compass points Lower case for:

east west north south

except when part of a name (*North Korea, South Africa, West End*) or part of a thinking group: *the South, the Mid-West, the West* (but lower case for vaguer areas such as the American *north-east, north-west, south-east, south-west*).

If you are, say, comparing regions some of which would normally be upper case and some lower case, and it would look odd to leave them that way, put them all lower case:

House prices in the north-east and the south are rising faster than those in the mid-west and the south-west.

The regions of Africa are *southern, east, west* and *north Africa*. But *South Africa* is the name of the country.

Europe Europe's divisions are no longer neatly political, and are now geographically imprecise, so use lower case for *central, eastern* and *western Europe*.

Use *West Germany* (*West Berlin*) and *East Germany* (*East Berlin*) only in historical references. They are now *west* or *western Germany* (*Berlin*) and *east* or *eastern Germany* (*eastern Berlin*).

The *Basque country* (or *region*) is ill-defined and contentious, and may include parts of both France and Spain, so lower case for country (or region).

See also **Euro-**.

finance In finance there are particular exceptions to the general rule of initial capitals for full names, lower case for informal ones. There are also rules about what to do on second mention.

Deutschmarks are still known just as *D-marks*, even though all references are historical.
Special drawing rights are lower case but are abbreviated as *SDRs*, except when used with a figure as a currency (SDR500m).

The *Bank of England* and its foreign equivalents have initial caps when named formally and separately, but collectively they are central banks in lower case, except those like Brazil's, Ireland's and Venezuela's, which are actually named the *Central Bank*. The *Bank of England* becomes the *bank* on second mention.

The *IMF* may become the *fund* on second mention.

The *World Bank* and the *Fed* (after first spelling it out as the *Federal Reserve*) take initial upper case, although these are shortened, informal names. The *World Bank* becomes the *bank* on second mention.

Treasury bonds issued by America's Treasury should be upper case; *treasury bills* (or *bonds*) of a general kind should be lower case. Avoid *T-bonds* and *t-bills*.

food and drink Lower case should be used for most common or familiar wines, cheeses, grape varieties, for example:

barollo	dim sum	piesporter
bordeaux	emmental	pinotage
brunello	gorgonzola	pont-l'évêque
burgundy	hock	primitivo
champagne	merlot	rioja
chardonnay	moselle	syrah
cheddar	parmesan	zinfandel

But the proper names of particular wines take upper case:

Cheval Blanc Lafite Marqués de Riscal Pontet-Canet

as do some foods and drinks that would look odd lower case:

Bombay duck Nuits St George Parma ham

historical terms

Allies (in the second world war)	New Deal
Black Death	Prohibition
Cultural Revolution	Reconstruction
D-Day	Reformation
the Depression (1930s)	Renaissance
Enlightenment	Restoration
Holocaust (second world war)	Thirty Years War
Industrial Revolution	Year of the Dog, Horse, Rat,
Middle Ages	etc (*but* new year)

organisations, institutions, acts, etc

1 Organisations, ministries, departments, institutions, treaties, acts, etc, generally take upper case when their full name (or something pretty close to it, eg, *State Department*) is used.

Amnesty International
Arab League
Bank of England (the bank)
Central Committee
Court of Appeal
the Crown (Britain)
Department for Environment, Food & Rural Affairs (DEFRA)
Department of State (the department)
European Commission
Forestry Commission
Health and Safety at Work Act
High Court
House of Commons
House of Lords
House of Representatives
Household Cavalry
Metropolitan Police
Ministry of Defence
New York Stock Exchange
Oxford University
Politburo
Scottish Parliament (the parliament)
Senate
St Paul's Cathedral (the cathedral)
Supreme Court
Treasury
Treaty of Rome
Welsh Assembly (the assembly)
World Bank (the bank)

2 Organisations with unusual or misleading names, such as the *African National Congress* and *Civic Forum*, may become the *Congress* and the *Forum* on second and subsequent mentions.

3 But most other organisations – agencies, banks, commissions (including the *European Commission* and the *European Union*), etc – take lower case when referred to incompletely on second mention.

4 Informal names

Organisations, committees, commissions, special groups, etc, that are impermanent, ad hoc, local or relatively insignificant should be lower case:

international economic subcommittee of the Senate Foreign
    Relations Committee
Market Blandings rural district council
Oxford University bowls club
subcommittee on journalists' rights of the National Executive
    Committee of the Labour Party

5 Rough descriptions or translations

Use lower case for rough descriptions (*the safety act*, the *American health department*, the *French parliament*, as distinct from its *National Assembly*). If you are not sure whether the English translation of a foreign name is exact or not, assume it is rough and use lower case.

6 Congress and Parliament

Congress and *Parliament* are upper case, unless parliament is used not to describe the institution but the period of time for which it sits.

This bill will not be brought forward until the next parliament.

But *congressional* and *parliamentary* are lower case, as is the *opposition*, even when used in the sense of *her majesty's loyal opposition*.

The *government*, the *administration* and the *cabinet* are always lower case.

After first mention, the *House of Commons* (or *Lords*, or *Representatives*) becomes the *House*.

7 Acts

In America acts given the names of their sponsors (eg, *Glass-Steagall*, *Helms-Burton*) are always rough descriptions (*see above*) and so take a lower-case *act*.

people

1 Ranks and titles

Use upper case when written in conjunction with a name, but lower case when on their own:

Colonel Qaddafi, *but* the colonel

Pope Benedict, *but* the pope
President Obama, *but* the president
Queen Elizabeth, *but* the queen
Vice-President Ansari, *but* the vice-president

Do not write *Prime Minister Brown* or *Defence Secretary Gates*; they are *the prime minister, Mr Brown*, and *the defence secretary, Mr Gates*. You might, however, write *Chancellor Merkel*.

2 Office-holders
When referred to merely by their office, not by their name, office-holders are lower case:

the chairman of Marks & Spencer
the chancellor of the exchequer
the foreign secretary
the president of the United States
the prime minister
the speaker
the treasury secretary

The only exceptions are a few titles that would look unduly peculiar without capitals:

Black Rod
Chancellor of the Duchy of Lancaster
Lord Chancellor
Lord Privy Seal
Master of the Rolls

and a few exalted people, such as:

the *Dalai Lama*, the *Aga Khan*. Also *God* and *the Prophet*.

3 Some titles serve as names, and therefore have initial capitals, though they also serve as descriptions: *the Archbishop of Canterbury, the Emir of Kuwait*. If you want to describe the office rather than the individual, use lower case: *The next archbishop of Canterbury will be a woman. Since the demise of the ninth duke, there has never been another duke of Portland*.

places Use upper case for definite geographical places, regions, areas and countries (*The Hague, Transylvania, Germany*), and for vague but recognised political or geographical areas (but *see* **Europe** above):

Central, South and South-East Asia
East Asia (which is to be preferred to the Far East)
the Gulf
Highlands (of Scotland)
Middle East
Midlands (of England)
North Atlantic
North, Central and South America
South Atlantic
the West (as in the decline of the West)
West Country

Use capitals for particular buildings even if the name is not strictly accurate, eg, the *Foreign Office*.

And if in doubt use lower case (*the sunbelt*).

The *third world* (an unsatisfactory term now that the communist second world has disappeared) is lower case.

Avoid the *western hemisphere*. Unlike the *southern hemisphere* and the *northern hemisphere*, it is not clear where the *western hemisphere* begins or ends. The *Americas* will usually serve instead.

political terms

1 The full name of political parties is upper case, including the word party:

Communist (if a particular party)
Labour Party
Peasants' Party
Republican Party

2 But note that some parties do not have party as part of their names, so this should therefore be lower case:

Greece's New Democracy party
India's Congress party
Indonesia's Golkar party
Turkey's Justice and Development party

3 Note that usually only people are:

Democrats	Liberal Democrats
Christian Democrats	Social Democrats

Their parties, policies, candidates, committees, etc, are:

Democratic   Liberal Democratic
Christian Democratic   Social Democratic

But a committee may be Democrat-controlled, and use Christian democratic, etc, if not referring to a party of that name.

The exceptions are Britain's *Liberal Democrat Party* and Thailand's *Democrat Party*.

4 When referring to a specific party, write *Labour*, the *Republican nominee*, a prominent *Liberal*, etc, but use lower case in looser references to *liberals, conservatism, communists*, etc. *Tories*, however, are upper case, as is *New Labour*.

proper names When forming nouns, adjectives and verbs from proper names, retain the initial capital:

Buddhism   Leninist
Christian   Luddite
Finlandisation   Maronite
Gaullism   Marxist
Hindu   Napoleonic
Hobbesian   Paisleyite
Islamic   Russify
Jacobite   Thatcherism

Exceptions are: *platonic, pyrrhic.*

Note that Indian castes are lower-case italic, except for *brahmin*, which has now become an English word and is therefore lower-case roman (unless it is mentioned along with several other less familiar caste names in italic).

province, county, river, state Lower case when not strictly part of the name:

Cabanas province   New York state
Limpopo river   Washington state

Exceptions are: *Mississippi River, River Thames.*

trade names Use capitals:

BlackBerry Google Hoover Teflon Valium

miscellaneous (lower case)

19th amendment (*but* Article 19)
aborigines
amazon (female warrior)
angst
blacks (and whites)
cabinet
civil servant
civil service
civil war (even America's)
cold war
common market
communist (generally)
constitution (even America's)
cruise missile
draconian
first world war
french windows
general synod
gentile
government
Gulf war
gypsy
internet
junior (as in George Bush junior)
Kyoto protocol
the left
mafia (any old group of criminals)
mecca (when used as a *mecca for tourists*)
new year (*but* New Year's Day)
Olympic games (and Asian, Commonwealth, European)
opposition
philistine
the pope
the press
the queen
quisling
realpolitik
republican
revolution (everyone's)
the right
second world war
senior (as in George Bush senior)
six-day war
the speaker
state-of-the-union message
titanic (*not* the ship)
white paper
wild west
world wide web
young turk

miscellaneous (upper case)

Anglophone (*but* prefer English-speaking)
Antichrist
anti-Semitism
Atlanticist
the Bar
the Bible
Catholics
CD-ROM (should be set in small capitals)
Christ
Christmas Day
Christmas Eve
Coloureds (in South Africa)
the Cup Final
the Davis Cup
Earth (when, and only when, it is being discussed as a planet like Mars or Venus)
Francophone (*but* prefer French-speaking)
Hispanics

House of Laity
Koran
Labour Day
Mafia (the genuine article)
May Day
Mecca (in Saudi Arabia,
  California and Liberia)
Memorial Day
New Year's Day
New Year's Eve
Pershing missile (because it
  is named after somebody)
Protestants
the Queen's Speech

Semitic (-ism)
Social Security (in American
  contexts only, where it is
  used to mean pensions;
  what is usually understood
  by social security
  elsewhere is welfare in the
  United States)
Stealth fighter, bomber
Teamster
Ten Commandments
Test match
Tube (London Underground)
Utopia (-n)

See also **abbreviations**.

captions *see* **headings and captions**.

cartel A *cartel* is a group that restricts supply in order to drive up prices. Do not use it to describe any old syndicate or association of producers – especially of drugs.

case "There is perhaps no single word so freely resorted to as a trouble-saver", says Gowers, "and consequently responsible for so much flabby writing." Often you can do without it. *There are many cases of it being unnecessary* is better as *It is often unnecessary. If it is the case that* simply means *If. It is not the case* means *It is not so.*

Cassandra Do not use *Cassandra* just as a synonym for a prophet of doom. The most notable characteristic about her was that her predictions were always correct but never believed.

catalyst A *catalyst* is something that speeds up a chemical reaction while itself remaining unchanged. Do not confuse it with one of the agents.

Central Asian names *see* **names**.

centred on not *around* or *in*.

challenge Although duels and gauntlets have largely disappeared into history, modern life seems to consist of little else but *challenges*. At every turn, every president, every minister, every government, every business, everyone everywhere is faced with *challenges*. No one nowadays has to face a *change*, *difficulty*, *task* or *job*. Rather these are *challenges* – fiscal challenges, organisational challenges, structural challenges, regional challenges, demographic challenges, etc. Next time you grab the word *challenge*, drop it at once and think again.

charge If you *charge* intransitively, do so as a bull, cavalry officer or some such, not as an *accuser* (so avoid *The standard of writing was abysmal, he charged*).

charts and tables should, ideally, be understandable without reading the accompanying text. The main point of the heading should therefore be to assist understanding, though if it does so amusingly, so much the better. If the subject of the chart (or table) is unambiguous (because, say, it is in the middle of a story about Germany), the title need not reflect the subject. In that case, however, the subtitle should clearly state: *Number of occasions on which the word angst appears in German company reports, 2005–10.*

cherry-pick If you must use this cliché, note that *to cherry-pick means to engage in careful rather than indiscriminate selection*, whereas *a cherry-picker is a machine for raising pickers (and cleaners and so on) off the ground.*

Chinese is a language. It may be either *Mandarin* or *Cantonese*.

Chinese names *see* **names**.

circumstances stand around a thing, so it is *in*, not *under*, them.

civil society pops up a lot these days, often in the company of *citizenship skills*, *community leaders*, *good governance*, the *international community*, *social capital* and the like ("Development of civil society is social-reality specific" is a typical example). That should serve as a warning. It can, however, be a useful, albeit ill-defined term to describe collectively all non-commercial organisations in between the family and the state. But do not use it as a euphemism for NGOs (non-governmental organisations), which is how it is usually employed.

clerical titles *see* **titles**.

clichés weren't always clichéd. The first person to use *window of opportunity* or *level playing-field* or *accident waiting to happen* was justly pleased with himself. Each is a strong, vivid expression – or was. The trouble is that such expressions have been copied so often that they have lost their vividness. Mass printing made constant repetition easy, which explains how the word cliché came into being: it is the French term for a *stereotype printing plate*. Careful writers since Flaubert, who was so obsessive in his search for freshness that he insisted on anything approaching a cliché being printed in italics, have tried to avoid hackneyed phrases.

In "A Dictionary of Clichés" (1940), Eric Partridge wrote: "Clichés range from fly-blown phrases (*much of a muchness; to all intents and purposes*), metaphors that are now pointless (*lock, stock and barrel*), formulas that have become mere counters (*far be it from me to ...*) – through sobriquets that have lost all their freshness and most of their significance (*the Iron Duke*) – to quotations that are nauseating (*cups that cheer but not inebriate*), and foreign phrases that are tags (*longo intervallo, bête noire*)."

In truth, many of yesterday's clichés have become so much a part of the language that they pass unnoticed; they are like Orwell's dead metaphors. The ones most to be avoided are the latest, the trendiest. Since they usually appeal to people who do not have the energy to pick their own words, they are often found in the wooden prose of bureaucrats, academics and businessmen, though journalese is far from immune.

Clichés numb, rather than stimulate, the reader's brain. Many of the clichés in *The Economist* are phrases like *bite the bullet, confirmed bachelor, eye-watering sums, grinding to a halt, high-profile, honeymoon period, incurable optimist, road maps, tax packages, too close to call, toxic debt, whopping bills*. They serve merely to bore. Far worse are some of those placed in its pages by its managers, which probably induce terminal despair. The following appeared in an advertisement in May 2009: *world-class analysis, key industries, proven track record, strategic, transformative thinking, decisive goal-driven leader, consummate collaborator within a team framework, impactful programmes, strategic and consultative approach, professional in all internal and external interactions, results-driven, relationship-building and communication skills*.

Many of these expressions are meaningless. All are ugly. All are borrowed unthinkingly from the language of other advertisers,

and since they appear so often they fail to make an impact.
Similar horrors are perpetrated by, for example, the United Nations
Development Programme, looking for an *economic recovery
cluster leader and governance cluster leader* to *play a dynamic and
pivotal role in the key programmatic areas of UNDP*; the University
of Birmingham, seeking *an academic practice advisor skilled
in collaborating with academic staff on pedagogic development
initiatives ... The role is multi-faceted and challenging ... You will be
expected to prioritise and effectively manage the complexities of your
own workload*; and the Royal Society of Arts, anxious to recruit
a *dynamic, high-calibre director of education to lead and deliver
its flagship education programme*, who will *deliver a progressive,
innovative portfolio of projects and seminars*, and *lead and grow
its education programme*, which, not surprisingly, has *cutting-edge
research and policy development*. The society also takes pride in
its *inclusive design resource*, which *draws together key contextual
information* with, among other things, *inspirational design concepts*.

Bureaucrats are inveterate offenders. They delight in posts like
*service improvement managers for lifelong disabilities service, heads of
offending services* and *human-resources officers*. Their work is always
challenging, exciting, key, strategic and often *multi-disciplinary*. They
are inevitably *committed, creative, dynamic, innovative* and *proactive*.
Sometimes, however, they go wild. Britain's Ministry of Justice, for
instance, advertising for a *director of estate capacity* to *lead a team of
150 people through a period of dynamic change to create a significant
increase in capacity* (ie, help build three new Titan prisons), sought
candidates with *strong influencing skills within the context of multi-
layered internal and external stakeholder management with experience
of developing business-as-usual results*.

Here is part of a letter from a large London think-tank,
explaining that it might be slow in updating members' details
because it was improving its computer system. This simple
message was conveyed in 125 words, of which these are some:

"The organisation is upgrading its IT infrastructure by
introducing a new database which will enable us to store and
share information more effectively internally. We embarked upon
this major project when it became clear that the current system
no longer adequately supported our requirements. When the new
system is fully implemented in the autumn it will enable us to
more effectively manage our relationship with members and other
stakeholders ... We kindly ask for your patience while we resolve
any issues over the next two weeks."

Language such as this is so common that its authors have stopped asking themselves whether it means anything, whether the message might make more impact if it were expressed in 20 words rather than 125 or whether anyone will even bother to read it.

Even publishers are capable of writing drivel. *The book introduces the SpeakOut*, writes one, *an innovative, interactive drop-in engagement process. It provides hands-on, systematic guidance and detailed checklists for managing community engagement processes, as well as targeted advice on facilitation, recording and training.*

Do not add to such tosh. Be specially careful not to borrow the empty phrases of politicians who constantly invoke *paradigm shifts, wake-up calls, supply-side solutions, blue-sky thinking* and *social inclusion*, while asserting their desire to *go the extra mile, push the envelope* and *kick-start the economy. Making a difference* is one of the most fatuous favourites. Thus a former director of communications for the Labour Party could assert that the prime minister, Gordon Brown, was being criticised only because he wanted to *make a difference*, as though the same plea could not have been made for A. Hitler or J. Stalin.

Not all clichés, however, are used unthinkingly. Politicians often resort to hackneyed language to give the impression that they are saying something when they are doing their best to avoid it.

This is Harriet Harman, who was solicitor-general at the time, ruling out a prosecution because there was, she said, *an evidential deficiency related to the prosecution's inability within the current statutory framework to disprove the defence raised on the particular facts of the case.* Here the language chosen is deliberately numbing, chosen precisely to obscure the fact that the prosecution had no evidence.

Treat all such stuff as a caution. ("Political language is designed to ... give an appearance of solidity to pure wind." George Orwell)

Nothing betrays the lazy writer faster than fly-blown phrases used in the belief that they are snappy, trendy or cool. Some of these clichés are deliberately chosen, usually from a film or television, or perhaps a politician. Others come into use less wittingly, often from social scientists. If you find yourself using any of the following vogue words, you should stop and ask yourself whether it is the best word for the job, would you have used it in the same context five or ten years ago, and if not why not:

address, meaning *answer, deal with, attend to, look at*

Brits
care for and all caring expressions – how about *look after*?
commit to meaning *commit yourself to*
famously: usually redundant, nearly always irritating
focus: all the world's a stage, not a lens
historic: let historians, not contemporary commentators, be the judge
individual: fine as an adjective and occasionally as a noun, but
　　increasingly favoured by the wooden-tongued as a longer
　　synonym for *man, woman* or *person*
inform, when used as a pretentious alternative to *influence*
metrosexual
overseas – inexplicably, and often wrongly, used to mean *abroad* or
　　foreign
participate in – use *take part in*, with more words but fewer
　　syllables
process – a word properly applied to *attempts to bring about peace*,
　　because they are meant to be evolutionary, but now often
　　used in place of *talks*
relationship – *relations* can nearly always do the job
resources, especially *human resources*, which may be *personnel*,
　　staff or just *people*
supportive – *helpful*?
target – if you are tempted to *target your efforts*, try to *direct* them
　　instead
transparency – *openness*?
wannabes

Such words should not be banned, but if you find yourself
using them only because you hear others using them, not because
they are the most appropriate ones in the context, you should
avoid them. Overused words and off-the-shelf expressions make
for stale prose.

See also **euphemisms, horrible words, journalese and slang**.

co- This prefix is sometimes useful but now overdone. In the sentences
He co-founded the company with Sir Alan or *He co-wrote "The Left
Nation" with Adrian Windback*, the *co-* is unnecessary. *Co-author*
and *Co-sleep* are worse than that. "We want parents ... not to
co-sleep with their baby," said Professor Peter Fleming. This was
because "the majority of the co-sleeping deaths occurred in a
hazardous sleeping environment." (The *Times*, October 14th 2009.)

coiffed not *coiffured*.

collapse (verb) is not transitive. You may *collapse*, but you may not *collapse something*.

colons *see* **punctuation**.

come up with Try *suggest, originate* or *produce.*

commas *see* **punctuation**.

commit Do not *commit to*, but by all means *commit yourself to* something.

community is a useful word in the context of religious or ethnic groups. But in many others it jars. Not only is it often unnecessary, it also purports to convey a sense of togetherness that may well not exist:

The *black community* means *blacks* (or *African-Americans*, etc).
The *business community* means *businessmen* (who are supposed to be competing, not colluding).
The *homosexual community* means *homosexuals* or *gays.*
The *intelligence community* means *spies.*
The *online community* means *geeks and nerds.*
The *migration and development communities* means *NGOs.*
The *international community*, if it means anything, means *other countries, aid agencies* or, just occasionally, *the family of nations.*
What the *global community* (*Financial Times*, July 12th 2005) means is a mystery.

Community is a word that crops up in the company of the meaningless jargon and vacuous expressions beloved of bombastic bureaucrats. Here is John Negroponte, appearing before the American Senate:

"Teamwork will remain my north star as director of national intelligence – not just for my immediate office but for the entire intelligence community. My objective will be to foster proactive co-operation ... The Office of Director of National Intelligence should be a catalyst for focusing on the hardest, most important questions ... Some argue that there are three intelligence communities ... a military intelligence community ... a foreign intelligence community ... and a domestic intelligence community ..."

company names Call companies by the names they call themselves. Here is a selection of names that are sometimes spelt incorrectly.

ABN AMRO
ACNeilsen
Allied Domecq
AOL
AstraZeneca
AT&T (American Telephone and Telegraph)
AXA (French insurance company)
BAE Systems
Benetton
Berkshire Hathaway
Bertelsmann
BHP Billiton (Australian mining group)
BlackBerry
BNP Paribas
BP (which no longer refers to itself as British Petroleum)
BSkyB
BT (British Telecom)
Cadbury Schweppes
Capgemini
Citigroup (Citibank in some countries)
Coca-Cola
ConocoPhillips
DaimlerChrysler
DuPont
E.ON (German utility company)
easyJet (but EasyJet at start of sentence)
eBay
Eli Lilly
Ericcson (Swedish telecoms company)

Exxon Mobil
GlaxoSmithKline
HarperCollins
Hewlett-Packard (HP)
JPMorgan (investment banking arm of JPMorgan Chase)
J. Sainsbury (Sainsbury's is the name above the shop)
L'Oréal
Marks & Spencer
Merrill Lynch
Moody's, rating agency
NASDAQ
News Corporation (News Corp)
Nielsen/NetRatings
Pfizer
Philip Morris
Philips (Dutch electronics multinational)
Pillsbury
PricewaterhouseCoopers
Procter & Gamble
QinetiQ
Rolls-Royce
Sears, Roebuck
ThyssenKrupp
Toys "R" Us
Vivendi Universal
Vodafone Group
Wal-Mart
WH Smith
Xstrata
Yahoo!
ZenithOptimedia

comparatives Take care. One thing may be *many times more expensive* than another. It cannot be *many times cheaper*. Indeed, it can be cheaper only by a proportion that is less than one. A different but similar mistake is to say that *people grew twice as poor during a given period*. Instead, say *people's incomes fell by half during that period* (if that is what you mean, which, since it confuses income with wealth, it may not be).

compare A is compared *with* B when you draw attention to the difference. A is compared *to* B only when you want to stress their similarity.

Shall I compare thee to a summer's day?

compound (verb) does not mean *make worse*. It may mean *combine* or, intransitively, it may mean to *agree* or *come to terms*. To *compound a felony* means to *agree for a consideration not to prosecute*. (It is also used, with different senses, as a noun and adjective.)

comprise means *is composed of. NATO's force in Afghanistan comprises troops from 42 countries. America's troops make up (not comprise) nearly half the force.* Alternatively, *Nearly half NATO's force in Afghanistan is composed of American troops.*

confectionary is a sweet; *confectionery* is sweets in general.

contemporary *see* **current**.

continuous describes something uninterrupted. *Continual* admits of a break. If your neighbours play loud music every night, it is a *continual* nuisance; it is not a *continuous* one unless the music is never turned off.

contract *see* **subcontract**.

contrast, by or **in** *see* **by contrast, in contrast**.

convince should be followed by a noun or, in the passive, *that* or *of*. Do not *convince* people *to* do something. If you want to write *to*, the verb you need is *persuade*. *The prime minister was persuaded to call a June election; he was convinced of the wisdom of doing so only after he had won.*

coruscate means *sparkle* or *throw off flashes of light*, not *wither, devastate* or *reduce to wrinkles* (that's *corrugate*).

could is sometimes useful as a variant of *may* or *might*: *His coalition could* (or *might*) *collapse*. But take care. Does *He could call an election in June* mean *He might call an election in June* or *He would be allowed to call an election in June*?

council, counsel A *council* is a *body of people*, elected or appointed, that advises, administers, organises, legislates, etc. *Counsel* (noun) means *advice* or *consultation*, or *lawyers who give legal advice and fight cases in court*.

crescendo Not an acme, apogee, peak, summit or zenith but a *passage of increasing loudness*. You cannot therefore *build to a crescendo*.

crisis A *decisive event* or *turning-point*. Many of the economic and political troubles wrongly described as *crises* are really *persistent difficulties*, *sagas* or *affairs*.

critique is a noun. If you want a verb, try *criticise*.

currencies Use $ as the standard currency and, on first mention of sums in all other currencies, give a dollar conversion in brackets.

Apart from those currencies that are written out in full (*see below*), write the abbreviation followed by the number. Currencies are not set in small capitals unless they occur as words in text without figures attached: "*Out went the D-mark, in came the euro.*"

Britain
> pound, abbreviated as £
> pence, abbreviated as p
> 1p, 2p, 3p, etc to 99p (not £0.99)
> £6 (*not* £6.00), £6.47
> £5,000-6,000 (*not* £5,000-£6,000)
> £5m-6m (*not* £5m-£6m)
> £5 billion-6 billion (*not* £5-6 billion), £5.2 billion-6.2 billion

America
> dollar, abbreviated as $, will do generally; *US$* if there is a mixture of dollar currencies (*see below*)
> cents, spell out, unless part of a larger number: $4.99

other dollar currencies

A$	Australian dollars	NT$	Taiwanese dollars
C$	Canadian dollars	NZ$	New Zealand dollars

HK$	Hong Kong dollars	S$	Singaporean dollars
M$	Malaysian dollars	Z$	Zimbabwean dollars

Europe

euro, plural euros, abbreviated as €, for those countries that have adopted it.

cents, spell out, unless part of a larger number.

€10 (*not* 10 euros), €10.75

DM, BFr, drachmas, FFr, Italian lire, IR£ (punts), markkas, Asch, Ptas and other currencies of the euro area have all been replaced by €, but may turn up in historical references.

DKr Danish krone (plural kroner)

IKr Icelandic krona (plural kronur)

NKr Norwegian krone (plural kroner)

SFr Swiss franc, SFr1m (*not* 1m Swiss francs)

SKr Swedish krona (plural kronor)

sums in all other currencies are written in full, with the number first.

Brazil, *real*	100m *reais* (*see below*)
China, yuan	100m yuan (*not* renminbi) (*see below*)
India, rupee	100m rupees
Nigeria, naira	100m naira
peso currencies	100m pesos
South Africa, rand	100m rand (*not* rands)
Turkey, Turkish lira	100m liras
But Japan, yen	¥, ¥1,000 (*not* 1,000 *yen*)

Brazil Because of the risk of confusion with its English homonym, the *real* (plural *reais*) – but no other currency – is italicised in all text.

China Properly, Chinese sums are expressed as, eg, 1 yuan RMB, meaning 1 yuan renminbi. *Yuan*, which means *money*, is the Chinese unit of currency. *Renminbi*, which means the *people's currency*, is the description of the yuan, as sterling is the description of the pound. Use *yuan*.

See also **figures**; and **currencies** and **measures** in Part 3.

current, contemporary *Current* and *contemporary* mean *at that time*, not necessarily *at this time*. So a series of current prices from 1960 to 1970 will not be in *today's prices*, just as *contemporary art* in 1800 was not *modern art*. *Contemporary history* is a contradiction in terms.

cusp is a *pointed end* or a *horn* of, for example, the moon, or *the point at which two branches of a curve meet*. So it is odd to write, say, "Japan is on the cusp of a recovery" unless you think that recovery is about to end.

cyber-expressions Most cyber-terms are lower case: *cyber-attack*, *cyber-soccer*, etc, but *cybernetics*, *cyberspace* and *cyberwars*.

dashes *see* **punctuation**.

dates month, day, year, in that order, with no commas:

July 5th	1996-99
Monday July 5th	2005-10
July 5th 2009	1998-2009
July 27th-August 3rd 2010	1990s
July 2002	

Do not write *on June 10th-14th*; prefer *between June 10th and 14th*. If, say, ministers are to meet over two days, write *on December 14th and 15th*.

Do not burden the reader with dates of no significance, but give a date rather than just *last week*, which can cause confusion. *This week* and *next week* are permissible.

Dates are often crucial to an account of events, but sentences (and, even more, articles) that begin with a date can be clumsy and off-putting. *This week Congress is due to consider the matter* is often better put as *Congress is due to consider the matter this week*. The effect is even more numbing if a comma is inserted: *This week, Congress is due to consider the matter*, though this construction is sometimes merited when emphasis is needed on the date.

Dates that require *AD* or *BC* should be set as one unhyphenated word (*76AD*, *55BC*), with the letters in small capitals after the number. The same applies to *CE* (common era) and *BCE* (before common era), which also go after the number (*76CE*, *55BCE*).

deal (verb) Transitively, *deal* means distribute: "He was dealt two aces, two kings and a six." Intransitively, *deal* means *engage in business*. Do not *deal* drugs, horses, weapons, etc; *deal in* them.

decimate means to destroy a proportion (originally a tenth) of a group of people or things, not to destroy them all or nearly all.

demographics is no more a word than *geographics* is; it should be *demography*.

deprecate, depreciate To *deprecate* is to *argue* or *plead against* (by prayer or otherwise). To *depreciate* is to *lower in value*.

different from not *to* or *than*.

dilemma Not just any old awkwardness but one with horns, being, properly, a form of argument (the horned syllogism) in which you find yourself committed to accept one of two propositions each of which contradicts your original contention. Thus a *dilemma* offers the choice between two alternatives, each with equally nasty consequences.

discreet, discrete *Discreet* means *circumspect* or *prudent*. *Discrete* means *separate* or *distinct*. Remember that "Questions are never indiscreet. Answers sometimes are." (Oscar Wilde)

disinterested means *impartial*; *uninterested* means *bored*. "Disinterested curiosity is the lifeblood of civilisation." (G.M. Trevelyan)

Dominicans Take care. Do they come from Dominica? Or the Dominican Republic? Or are they friars?

douse, dowse *Douse* means to *throw water over something* or *extinguish a light or a fire*. *Dowse* means to *search for underground water with a divining rod*.

down to *down to earth* yes, but "Occasional court victories are not down to human rights." (*The Economist*) No: *down to* does not mean *attributable to*, *the responsibility of* or even *up to* (*It's up to you*).

due process is a technical term, or piece of **jargon**, which was first used in England in 1355. It comes in two forms, *substantive due process*, which relates to the duties of governments to act rationally and proportionally when doing anything that affects citizens' rights, and *procedural due process*, which relates to the need for fair procedures. If you use the expression, make sure it is clear what you mean by it.

due to when used to mean *caused by* must follow a noun, as in *The cancellation, due to rain, of* ... Do not write *It was cancelled due to rain*. If you mean *because of* and for some reason are reluctant to say it, you probably want *owing to*. *It was cancelled owing to rain* is all right.

Dutch names *see* **names**.

earnings Do not write *earnings* when you mean *profits* (try to say if they are *operating, gross, pre-tax* or *net*).

-ee *employees, evacuees, detainees, divorcee, referees, refugees* but, please, no *attendees* (those attending), *draftees* (conscripts), *enrollees* (participants), *escapees* (escapers), *indictees* (the indicted), *retirees* (the retired), or *standees*. A *divorcee* may be male or female.

e-expressions Except at the start of a sentence, the *e-* is lower case and hyphenated:

e-business
e-commerce
e-mail

   Computer terms are also usually lower case:

dotcom
home page
laptop
online
the net (and internet)
the web, website and world wide web

   When giving *websites*, do not include *http://*. Just *www* is enough: *www.economist.com*. But it should be included for websites that do not use *www*, eg *http://twitter.com*.

See also **cyber-expressions**.

effect the verb, means to *accomplish*, so *The novel effected a change in his attitude. See also* **affect**.

-effective, -efficient *Cost-effective* sounds authoritative, but does it mean *good value for money, gives a big bang for the buck* or just plain *cheap*? If *cheap*, say *cheap. Energy-efficient* is also dubious. Does it mean *thrifty, economical* or something else? *Efficiency* is the *ratio of energy put out to energy put in.*

effectively, in effect *Effectively* means with *effect*; if you mean *in effect*, say it. *The matter was effectively dealt with on Friday* means it was *done well* on Friday. *The matter was, in effect, dealt with on Friday* means it was *more or less attended to* on Friday. *Effectively leaderless* would do as a description of the demonstrators in East Germany in 1989 but not those in Tiananmen Square, also in 1989. The devaluation of the Slovak currency in 1993, described by some as *an effective 8%*, turned out to be a rather ineffective 8%. The Philippine economy, it has been said, is *effectively managed* by a mere 60 families. Some would be less complimentary about their stewardship.

either ... or *see* **none.**

elections *see* **grammar and syntax.**

elite, elitist Once a neutral word meaning a *chosen group* or *the pick of the bunch*, *elite* is now almost always used pejoratively. *Elitist* and *elitism* are even more reprehensible. No matter that the words have their roots in the French verb *élire*, to elect, and the Latin *eligere*, to pick out, if you believe in government by a chosen group, or are a member of such a group, you are a reprobate. Only *elite forces* seem to escape censure. Though scornful of elites in education and politics, most people, when taken hostage, are happy to be rescued by elite troops. Use these words with care.

enclave, exclave An *enclave* is a piece of territory or territorial water entirely surrounded by foreign territory (Andorra, Ceuta, Kaliningrad, Melilla, Nagorno-Karabakh, Nakhichevan, San Marino). An *exclave* is the same thing, viewed differently, if, and only if, it belongs to another country. Alaska is is part of the United States, but is separated from it by Canada, with which it shares a boundary. It is also accessible by sea, since its other boundaries are the Arctic and Pacific Oceans and the Bering Sea.

enormity means a *crime, sin* or *monstrous wickedness*. It does not mean *immensity*.

environment is often unavoidable, but it's not a pretty word. Avoid *the business environment, the school environment, the work environment*, etc. Try to rephrase the sentence – *conditions for business, at school, at work*, etc. *Surroundings* can sometimes do the job. In a *writing* *environment* you may want to make use of your correction fluid, rubber (or American eraser) or delete key.

epicentre means *that point on the surface* (usually the Earth's) *above the centre of something below* (usually an earthquake). So Mr Putin was not at the *epicentre* of the dispute, he was at its *centre*.

The *hypocentre*, in contrast, is *the place on the surface* (usually of the earth) *below something above* (usually an explosion). It is the same as *ground zero*. At Hiroshima in 1945, it was 580 metres above the ground.

eponymous is the adjective of *eponym*, which is *the person or thing after which something is named*. So George Canning was the *eponymous hero* of the Canning Club, Hellen was the *eponymous ancestor* of the Hellenes (Greeks), Ninus was the *eponymous founder* of Nineveh. Do not say *John Sainsbury, the founder of the eponymous supermarket*. Rather he was the *eponymous founder of J. Sainsbury's*.

ethnic groups Your first concern should be to avoid giving offence. But also avoid mealy-mouthed **euphemisms** and terms that have not generally caught on despite promotion by pressure-groups. *Ethnic* meaning *concerning nations or races*, or even something ill-defined in between, is a useful word. But do not be shy of *race* and *racial*. After several years in which *race* was seen as a purely social concept, not a scientific one, the term is coming back among scientists as a shorthand way of speaking about genetic rather than cultural or political differences. *See also* **political correctness**.

> **Africans** may be descended from Asians, Europeans or black Africans. If you specifically mean the last, write *black Africans*, not simply *Africans*.

> **Anglo-Saxon** is not a synonym for *English-speaking*. Neither the United States nor Australia is an Anglo-Saxon country; nor is Britain. Anglo-Saxon capitalism does not exist.

> **Asians** In Britain, but nowhere else, *Asians* is often used to mean *immigrants and their descendants from the Indian subcontinent*. Many such people are coming to dislike the term, and many foreigners must assume it means people from all over Asia, so take care. Note that, even in the usage peculiar to Britain, *Asian* is not synonymous with *Muslim*.

blacks In many countries, including the United States, many
black people are happy to be called *blacks*, although some
prefer to be *African-Americans*. *Black* is shorter and more
straightforward, but use either. Both *Native American* and
Indian are acceptable as terms for indigenous Americans.

mixed race Do not call people who are neither pure white nor
pure black *browns*. People of mixed race in South Africa are
Coloureds.

other groups The inhabitants of *Azerbaijan* are *Azerbaijanis*, some
of whom, but not all, are *Azeris*. Those *Azeris* who live in
other places, such as Iran, are not *Azerbaijanis*. Similarly, many
Croats are not Croatian, many Serbs not Serbian, many Uzbeks
not Uzbekistanis, etc.

Spanish-speakers in the United States When writing about
Spanish-speaking people in the United States, use either
Latino or *Hispanic* as a general term, but try to be specific (eg,
Mexican-American). Many Latin Americans (eg, those from
Brazil) are not Hispanic.

euphemisms Avoid, where possible, euphemisms and
circumlocutions, especially those promoted by interest-groups
keen to please their clients or organisations anxious to avoid
embarrassment. This does not mean that good writers should
be insensitive to giving offence: on the contrary, if you are to be
persuasive, you would do well to be courteous. But a good writer
owes something to plain speech, the English language and the
truth, as well as to manners. **Political correctness** can be carried
too far.

So, in most contexts, *offending* behaviour is probably *criminal*
behaviour. *Female teenagers* are *girls*, not *women*. *Living with
mobility impairment* probably means *wheelchair-bound*. *Developing*
countries are often *stagnating* or even *regressing* (try *poor*)
countries. The *underprivileged* may be *disadvantaged*, but are more
likely just *poor* (the very concept of *underprivilege* is absurd, since
it implies that some people receive less than their fair share of
something that is by definition an advantage or prerogative).

Remember that euphemisms are the stock-in-trade of people
trying to obscure the truth. Thus Enron's *document-management
policy* simply meant *shredding*. France's proposed *solidarity*

contribution on airline tickets was a *tax*. Bankers' *guaranteed bonuses* are *salaries* (or fractions thereof).

Take particular care if you borrow the language of politicians, especially when they are trying to justify a war. "They make a wilderness and call it peace," wrote Tacitus nearly 2,000 years ago, quoting Calgalus, a British chief whose people had suffered at the hands of the Romans. Orwell was equally acute in pointing out 60 years ago how terms like *transfer of population* and *rectification of frontiers* put names on things without calling up mental pictures of them. *Friendly fire, body count, prisoner abuse, smart bombs, surgical strike, collateral damage* have been coined more recently with the same ends in mind. The Reagan administration spoke of its airborne invasion of Grenada in 1983 as a *vertical insertion*. The butchers of the Balkans produced *ethnic cleansing*, and the jihadists of al-Qaeda have offered *sacred explosions* in place of Islamically incorrect *suicide bombs*. The Bush administration, with its all-justifying *war on terror*, provided more than its fair share of bland misnomers. Its practice of *enhanced interrogation* was *torture*, just as its practice of *extraordinary rendition* was probably *torture contracted out to foreigners* and its *self-injurious behaviour incidents* at Guantánamo Bay were *attempted suicides*. The president's ensuing *reputational problem* just meant he was *mistrusted*.

Orwell would surely have put *human-rights abuses* in the same category of nerve-deadening understatement as *pacification* and *elimination of unreliable elements*. The term may occasionally be useful, but try to avoid it by rephrasing the sentence more pithily and accurately. *The army is accused of committing numerous human-rights abuses* probably means *The army is accused of torture and murder. Decommissioning weapons* means *disarming*. A *high-net-worth individual* is a *rich man* or *rich woman. Zero-percent financing* means an *interest-free loan. Quantitative easing* means *increasing the money supply. Non-observable inputs* are *assumptions used in self-serving guesswork. Intimate apparel* is *underwear*.

See also **affirmative action**.

Euro- is the prefix for anything relating to the European Union; *euro-* is the prefix for anything relating to the currency. The usual rules apply for the full, proper names (with informal equivalents on the right below). Thus:

European Commission	the commission
European Parliament	the parliament

European Union	the Union
Treaty of Rome	the Rome treaty
Treaty on European Union	the Maastricht treaty
Treaty of Lisbon	the Lisbon treaty

The EU grouping may be called *EU-15*, *EU-27*.

When making *Euro-* or *euro-words*, always introduce a hyphen. Exceptions are:

Europhile Europhobe Eurosceptic Eurobond Euroyen bond

Prefer *euro zone* or *euro area* (two words, no hyphen) to *euro-land.*

CAP is the *common agricultural policy.*
EMU stands for *economic and (not European) monetary union.*
ERM is the *exchange-rate mechanism.*
IGC is an *inter-governmental conference.*

ex- (and former) Be careful. A *Labour Party ex-member* has lost his seat; an *ex-Labour member* has lost his party.

execute means *put to death by law.* Do not use it as a synonym for *murder.* An *extra-judicial execution* is a contradiction in terms. (*See* **assassinate.**)

existential Often used, seldom understood, even it seems by those who use it, *existential* means *of* or *pertaining to existence.* In logic it may mean *predicating existence*, and in other philosophical contexts, *relating to existentialism.* It is sometimes used in such phrases as *existential threat* or *existential crisis*, where the author wants it to mean a threat to the existence (of Israel, say) or a crisis that calls into the question the existence of something (eg, NATO). But in most instances, including most in *The Economist*, it seems to serve no purpose other than to make authors believe they are impressing readers.

fact *The fact that* can often be reduced to *that*.

factoid A *factoid* is something that sounds like a fact, is thought by many to be a fact (perhaps because it is repeated so often), but is not in fact a fact.

fed up *with*, not *of*.

federalist in Britain, someone who believes in centralising the powers of associated states; in the United States and Europe, someone who believes in decentralising them.

fellow Often unnecessary, especially before *countrymen* ("*Friends, Romans, fellow-countrymen*"?).

feral can mean *brutish* or *uncultivated*, but is best used of plants, animals, children, etc, that were once tamed or domesticated but have *run wild*.

ferment, foment When you *ferment*, what you are doing is to cause something to effervesce, like yeast. But you *foment* trouble, sedition, revolution.

fewer than, less than *Fewer* (not *less*) *than seven speeches, fewer than seven samurai.* Use *fewer*, not *less*, with numbers of individual items or people. *Less than £200, less than 700 tonnes of oil, less than a third*, because these are measured quantities or proportions, not individual items.

fief not *fiefdom*.

figures Never start a sentence with a figure; write the number in words instead.

Use words for simple numerals from one to ten inclusive,

except: in references to pages; in percentages (eg, 4%); and in sets of numerals, some of which are higher than ten.

Deaths from this cause in the past three years were 14, 9 and 6.

Always use numbers with units of measurement, even for those less than ten:

4 metres, 9 miles, but *four cows*

It is occasionally permissible to use words rather than numbers when referring to a rough or rhetorical figure (such as *a thousand curses, a hundred years of solitude*).

In all other cases, though, use figures for numerals from 11 upwards.

first to tenth centuries, the 11th century	a 29-year-old man
20th century, 21st century	a man in his 20s
20th-century ideas	20th anniversary
in 100 years' time	

The *Thirty Years War* is an exception.

decimal point Use figures for all numerals that include a decimal point (eg, 4.25).

fractions Figures may be appropriate for fractions, if the context is either technical or precise, or both:

Though the poll's figures were supposed to be accurate to within 1%, his lead of 4¹/₄ points turned out on election day to be minus 3¹/₂.

Where precision is less important but it is nonetheless impossible to shoot off the fraction, words may look better:

Though the beast was sold as two-year-old, it turned out to be two-and-a-half times that.

Fractions should be hyphenated (one-half, three-quarters, etc) and, unless they are attached to whole numbers (8¹/₂, 29³/₄), spelled out in words, even when the figures are higher than ten:

He gave a tenth of his salary to the church, a twentieth to his mistress and a thirtieth to his wife.

fractions and decimals Do not compare a fraction with a decimal. So avoid:

The rate fell from 3¹/4% to 3.1%.

Fractions are more precise than decimals (3.33 neglects an infinity of figures that are embraced by ¹/3), but your readers probably do not think so. You should therefore use fractions for rough figures:

Kenya's population is growing at 3¹/2% a year. A hectare is 2¹/2 acres.

and decimals for more exact ones:

The retail price index is rising at an annual rate of 10.6%.

But treat all numbers with respect. That usually means resisting the precision of more than one decimal place, and generally favouring rounding off. Beware of phoney over-precision.

hyphens and figures Do not use a hyphen in place of *to* except with figures:

He received a sentence of 15-20 years in jail but He promised to have escaped within three to four weeks.

Latin usage It is outdated to use Latin words. So, with figures, do not write *per caput*, *per capita* or *per annum*. Use:

a head or per head
a person or per person
a year or per year
2 litres of water per person
prices rose by 10% a year

See also **per caput**.

measurements In most non-American contexts prefer:

hectares to acres
kilometres (or km) to miles
metres to yards
litres to gallons
kilos (kg) to lb
tonnes to tons

Celsius to Fahrenheit, etc

1   In American contexts, you may use the measurements
    more familiar to Americans (though remember that
    American pints, quarts, gallons, etc, are smaller than
    imperial ones).
        Regardless of which you choose, you should give an
    equivalent, on first use, in the other units:

    *It was hoped that after improvements to the engine the car
    would give 20km to the litre (47 miles per American gallon),
    compared with its present average of 15km per litre.*

2   Remember that in only a few countries do you now
    buy petrol in imperial gallons. In America it is sold in
    American gallons; in most other places it is sold in litres.

3   Note that a four-by-four vehicle can be a 4×4.

million, billion, trillion, quadrillion Use *m* for million. Spell out
billion and trillion (though their conventional abbreviations
are *bn* and *trn*).

8m   8 billion
£8m   €8 billion

A *billion* is a thousand million, a *trillion* a thousand
billion, a *quadrillion* a thousand trillion.

per cent, percentage points
Use the sign % instead of *per cent*. But write *percentage*, never *%age*
(though in most contexts *proportion* or *share* is preferable).
    A fall from 4% to 2% is a drop of two percentage points, or of
50%, but not of 2%. (*See also* **per cent**.)

ranges Write:

5,000-6,000
5-6%
5m-6m (*not* 5-6m)
5 billion-6 billion

But:

*Sales rose from 5m to 6m (not 5m-6m); estimates ranged between
5m and 6m (not 5m-6m).*

ratios Where *to* is being used as part of a ratio, it is usually best to spell it out.

> *They decided, by nine votes to two, to put the matter to the general assembly, which voted, 27 to 19, to insist that the ratio of vodka to tomato juice in a bloody mary should be at least one to three, though the odds of this being so in most bars were put at no better than 11 to 4.*

Where a ratio is being used adjectivally, figures and hyphens may be used, but only if one of the figures is greater than ten:

a 50-20 vote
a 19-9 vote

Otherwise, spell out the figures and use *to*:

a two-to-one vote
a ten-to-one probability

finally Do not use *finally* when you mean *at last. Richard Burton finally marries Liz Taylor* would have been all right second time round but not first.

firm Accountants', consultants', lawyers' and other partnerships are *firms*, not *companies*. Huge enterprises, like GE, GM, Ford, Microsoft and so on, should, by contrast, normally be called *companies*, although such outfits can sometimes be called *firms* for variety.

flaunt, flout *Flaunt* means display; *flout* means disdain. If you *flout* this distinction, you will *flaunt* your ignorance.

focus can be a useful word. It is shorter than *concentrate* and sharper than *look at*. But it is overused.

footnotes, sources, references *see* **footnotes, sources, references** in Part 3.

foreign languages and translation Occasionally, a foreign language may provide the *mot juste*. But try not to use foreign words and phrases unless there is no English alternative, which is unusual. So:

a year *or* per year, *not* per annum
a head *or* per head, *not* per caput *or* per capita

beyond one's authority, *not* ultra vires

(*See also* **italics.**)

names of foreign companies, institutions, groups, parties, etc should usually be translated. So:

the Dutch People's Party for Freedom and Democracy (*not* the Volkspartij voor Vrijheid en Democratie
the German Christian Democratic Union (*not* the Christlich Demokratische Union)
the Shining Path (*not* Sendero Luminoso)
the National Assembly (*not* the Assemblée Nationale)

But if an abbreviation is also given, that may be the initials of the foreign name:

UMP for France's Union for a Presidential Majority
SPD for the Social Democratic Party of Germany
PAN for Mexico's National Action Party

Break this rule when the name is better known untranslated:

Forza Italia
Médecins Sans Frontières
Parti Québécois (Canada)
yakuza (*not* 8-9-3)

placenames Some placenames are better translated if they are well known in English:

St Mark's Square in Venice (*not* Piazza San Marco)
the French Elysée Palace (*not* the Palais de l'Elysée)

titles of foreign books, films, etc The titles of foreign books, films, plays, operas and TV programmes present difficulties. Some are so well known that they are unlikely to need translation:

"*Das Kapital*" "*Mein Kampf*" "*Le Petit Prince*" "*Die Fledermaus*"

And sometimes the meaning of the title may be unimportant in the context, so a translation is not necessary:

"*Hiroshima, Mon Amour*"

But often the title will be significant, and you will want to translate it. One solution, easy with classics, is simply to give the English translation:

"*One Hundred Years of Solitude*" "*The Leopard*" "*War and Peace*" "*The Tin Drum*"

This is usually the best practice to follow with pamphlets, articles and non-fiction, too.

But sometimes, especially with books and films that are little known among English-speakers or unobtainable in English (perhaps you are reviewing one), you may want to give both the original title and a translation, thus:

"*11 Septembre 2001: l'Effroyable Imposture*" ("*September 11th 2001: the Appalling Deception*")
"*La Règle du Jeu*" ("*The Rules of the Game*")
"*La Traviata*" ("*The Sinner*")

Foreign titles do not need to be set in italics. Treat them as if they were in English.

Note that book publishers follow different rules here. (*See* **italics**.)

translating words and phrases If you want to translate a foreign word or phrase, even if it is the name of a group or newspaper or party, just put it in brackets without inverted commas, so:

Arbeit macht frei (work makes free)
jihad (struggle)
Médecins Sans Frontières (Doctors Without Borders)
Pravda (Truth)
zapatero (shoemaker)

forensic means *pertaining to courts of law* (held by the Romans in the forum) or, more loosely, *the application of science to legal issues*. *Forensic medicine* is *medical jurisprudence*. *Forensic* does not mean *very careful* or *very detailed*.

forgo, forego *Forgo* means do without; it forgoes the *e*. *Forego* means go before. A *foregone conclusion* is one that is predetermined; a *forgone conclusion* is non-existent.

former *see* **ex-**.

former and latter Avoid the use of *the former* and *the latter* whenever possible. It usually causes confusion.

Frankenstein was not the monster, but its creator.

free is an adjective or an adverb (and also a transitive verb), so you cannot have or do anything *for free*. Either you have it *free* or you have it *for nothing*.

French names *see* **names**.

fresh is not a synonym for *new* or *more*. "A few hundred fresh bodies are being recovered every day," reported *The Economist* improbably, two months after a tsunami had struck. Use with care.

full stops *see* **punctuation**.

fulsome is an old word that Americans generally use only to mean *cloying, insincere* or *excessively flattering*. In British English it can also mean *copious, abundant* or *lavish*.

fund (verb) is a technical term, meaning to convert floating debt into more or less permanent debt at fixed interest. Try to avoid it if you mean to *finance* or to *pay for*.

garner means *store*, not *gather*.

gearing is an ugly word which, if used, needs to be explained. It may be either the *ratio of debt to equity* or the *ratio of debt to total capital employed*. (*See also* **leverage**.)

gender is nowadays used in several ways. One is common in feminist writing, where the term has a technical meaning. "One is not born a woman, one becomes one," argued Simone de Beauvoir: in other words, one chooses one's gender. In such a context it would be absurd to use the word *sex*; the term must be *gender*. But, in using it thus, try to explain what you mean by it. Even feminists do not agree on a definition.

   The primary use of *gender*, though, is in grammar, where it is applied to words, not people. If someone is female, that is her *sex*, not her *gender*. (The gender of *Mädchen*, the German word for girl, is neuter, as is *Weib*, a wife or woman.) So do not use *gender* as a synonym for *sex*. *Gender studies* probably means *feminism*.

generation Take care. You can be a *second-generation Frenchman*, but if you are a *second-generation immigrant* it means you have left the country your parents came to.

gentlemen's agreement not *gentleman's*.

German names *see* **names**.

get is an adaptable verb, but it has its limits. A man does not *get* sacked or promoted, he *is* sacked or promoted. Nor does a prize-winner *get to* shake hands with the president, or spend the money all at once; he *gets the chance to*, *is able to*, or *allowed to*.

global Globalisation can go to the head. It is not necessary to describe, eg, the head of Baker & Mackenzie as the *global head* of that firm.

And what is a *global vacancy* (as advertised by The Economist Group)? And avoid saying "now that we're all part of a global world", unless you have hitherto believed the Earth to be flat.

good in parts is what the curate said about an egg that was wholly bad. He was trying to be polite.

gourmet, gourmand *Gourmet* means *epicure*; *gourmand* means *greedy-guts*.

governance *Corporate governance* has now entered the language as a useful, albeit ugly and ill-defined, term to describe the rules relating to the conduct of business. The popularity of *governance* in other contexts is more difficult to understand. An old word, it had largely fallen into suitable disuse until Harold Wilson chose it in 1976 for the title of his memoirs ("The Governance of Britain"), presumably to dignify an undistinguished prime ministership. It means simply *government*, a word that serves the same purpose without any of the pretensions or pomposity of *governance*.

grammar and syntax Take care in the construction of your sentences and paragraphs. A single issue of *The Economist* contained the following:

When closed at night, the fear is that this would shut off rather than open up part of the city centre.

Unlike Canary Wharf, the public will be able to go to the top to look out over the city.

Only a couple of months ago, after an unbroken string of successes in state and local elections, pollsters said ...

Some hints are provided here on avoiding pitfalls, infelicities and mistakes; this is not a comprehensive guide to English grammar and syntax.

a or the Strictly, *Barclays* is *a British bank*, not *the British bank*, just as *Toyota* is *a car company*, not *the car company*, and *Angela Gheorghiu* is *an opera singer*, not *the opera singer*. If it seems absurd to describe someone or something thus – that is, with the indefinite article – you can probably dispense with the description altogether or insert an extra word or two that may be useful to the reader: *Toyota, the world's biggest car company in 2009.*

active or passive? Be direct. Use the active tense. *A hit B* describes the event more concisely than *B was hit by A*.

adjectives and adverbs Adjectives qualify nouns, adverbs modify verbs. If you have a sentence that contains the words *firstly, secondly, more importantly*, etc, they almost certainly ought to be *first, second, more important*.

adjectives of proper nouns If proper nouns have adjectives, use them.

Crimean war (*not* the Crimea war)
Dutch East India Company (*not* the Holland East India
    Company)
Lebanese (*not* Lebanon) civil war
Mexican (*not* Mexico) problem
Pakistani (*not* Pakistan) government
Scottish Office (*not* the Scotland Office)

It is permissible to use the noun as an adjective if to do otherwise would cause confusion.

An *African initiative* suggests the proposal came *from Africa*, whereas an *Africa initiative* suggests it was *about Africa*.

Californian, Texan Do not feel you have to follow American convention in using words like *Californian* and *Texan* only as nouns. In British English, it is quite acceptable to write a *Californian* (not *California*) *judge*, *Texan* (not *Texas*) *scandal*, etc.

"Mr Gedge ... was not fond of St Rocque, and this morning it would have seemed less attractive to him than ever, for three of his letters bore Californian postmarks and their contents had aggravated the fever of his home-sickness." (P.G. Wodehouse, "Hot Water")
"The local avant-garde was in one of its 'painting is dead' phases, and was automatically dismissive of things Californian anyway." (Peter Schjeldahl, *The New Yorker*, May 9th 2005)

collective nouns – singular or plural? There is no firm rule about the number of a verb governed by a singular collective noun. It is best to go by the sense – that is, whether the collective noun stands for a single entity:

The council was elected in March.
The me generation has run its course.
The staff is loyal.

or for its constituents:

The council are at sixes and sevens.
The preceding generation are all dead.
The staff are at each other's throats.

Do not, in any event, slavishly give all singular collective nouns singular verbs: *The couple are now living apart* is preferable to *The couple is now living apart.*

majority When it is used in an abstract sense, it takes the singular; when it is used to denote the elements making up the majority, it should be plural.

A two-thirds majority is needed to amend the constitution but *A majority of the Senate were opposed.*

number Rule: *The number is ...; A number are ...*

pair and couple Treat both a *pair* and a *couple* as plural.

comparisons Take care, too, when making comparisons, to compare like with like:

The Belgian economy is bigger than Russia should be *Belgium's economy is bigger than Russia's.*

An advertisement for *The Economist* declared,

Our style and our whole philosophy are different from other publications.

contractions Don't overdo the use of *don't, isn't, can't, won't,* etc.

false possessive An *'s* at the end of a word, in the possessive or genitive case, does the job of *of*. An increasingly common practice, especially among broadcasters and sometimes in *The Economist,* is to use it to do the job of *in*. Thus places or buildings are described as, eg, *New York's Chrysler Building, Edinburgh's Usher Hall* or *Belfast's Shankill Road.* Do not commit this sin. The Chrysler Building is *in* New York, not of it, just as Shankill Road is *in* Belfast and the Usher Hall is *in* Edinburgh. *London's South Bank* is a particularly idiotic formulation since the *Bank* is that of the River Thames. *London's National Gallery* is similarly absurd: the gallery is the UK's, not London's, hence the *National* in its name.

genitive Take care with the genitive. It is fine to say a *friend of Bill's*, just as you would say *a friend of mine*, so you can also say *a friend of Bill's and Carol's*. But it is also fine to say a *friend of Bill*, or *a friend of Bill and Carol*. What you must not say is Bill *and Carol's friend*. If you wish to use that construction, you must say *Bill's and Carol's friend*, which is cumbersome.

gerunds Respect the gerund. Gerunds look like participles – *running, jumping, standing* – but are more noun-like, and should never therefore be preceded by a personal pronoun. So the following are wrong: *I was awoken by him snoring, He could not prevent them drowning, Please forgive me coming late.*

Those sentences should have ended:

his snoring, their drowning, my coming late.

In other words, use the possessive adjective rather than the personal pronoun.

indirect speech If you use indirect speech in the past tense, you must change the tense of the speaker's words appropriately:

Before he died, he said, "I abhor the laziness that is commonplace nowadays" becomes *Before he died, he said he abhorred the laziness that was commonplace nowadays.*

masculine and feminine Several English nouns have both a masculine and a feminine form, for example:

alumnus, alumna	man, woman
compère, commère	prince, princess
Filipino, Filipina	testator, testatrix
Latino, Latina	widow, widower

nouns acting as verbs Do not force nouns or other parts of speech to act as verbs: *A woman who was severely brain-damaged in 2000* would be better put as *A woman whose brain* *was severely damaged in 2000* (unless, remarkably, she was no longer brain-damaged at some later date).

participle Do not use a participle unless you make it clear what it applies to. Here are some examples of confused construction:

Proceeding along this line of thought, the cause of the train crash becomes clear.

Looking out from the city's tallest building, the houses stretch for miles and miles.

It is hard to beat this statement by a "retired public relations/ communications practitioner" standing for election as a trustee of the Royal Society of Arts:

Committed to invigorating perspectives in pursuit of the manifesto, and assisted by an active Scottish committee, programme diversity is deepening Scottish engagement across a wider range of more visible joint partner and sponsorship-assisted events.

plural nouns

1   The -ics words on page 69 (abstract nouns) are plural when preceded by *the*, or *the* plus an adjective, or with a possessive. For example:

The dynamics of the dynasty were dysfunctional.
The complicated politics of Afghanistan have a logic all their own.
The athletics take place in London.

2   These are plural:

antics	histrionics
atmospherics	hysterics
basics	tactics
graphics	statistics

Specifics are discouraged (try *details*), as are **demographics**.

3   *Data* and *media* are plural. So are *whereabouts* and *headquarters*.

4   *Elections* are not always plural. If, as in the United States, several votes (for the presidency, the Senate, the House of

Representatives, etc) are held on the same day, it is correct to talk about *elections*. But in, say, Britain parliamentary polls are usually held on their own, in a single *general election*.

The *opposition demanded an election* is often preferable to *The opposition demanded fresh elections*. And to write *The next presidential elections are due in 2015* suggests there will be more than one presidential poll in that year.

5   The *Taliban* are plural. The singular is *Talib*.

Make sure that plural nouns have plural verbs. Too often, in the pages of *The Economist*, they do not.

Kogalym today is one of the few Siberian oil towns which are [not is] *almost habitable.*

What better evidence that snobbery and elitism still hold [not holds] *back ordinary British people? –* and this in a leader on education.

quoting If you wish to quote someone, either give a date or use the present tense:

"He leaves a legacy of wisdom," said John Smith the next day or *... says Mr John Smith.*

The following paragraph is all too typical:

What next for Mistekistan? This week an uneasy peace broke out on the streets of Erati, the capital, after angry crowds besieged the palace of President Iyas Abikhernozthanayev. The president, who was head of the local communist party when Mistekistan was a Soviet republic called Sumistekia, fled to neighbouring Flyspekistan, where he was seeking asylum. However, fighting broke out between the Dabtchiks and the Bifsteks, two minorities in the south. The president of nearby Itznojokistan might try to broker a peace. "It looks a mess," said Professor Eniole Kwote of Meganostril University, whose centre for autocratic studies recently published a study saying the entire region is a shambles.

It would be better as:

What next for Mistekistan? An uneasy peace broke out this week on the streets of Erati, the capital, after angry crowds had besieged the palace of President Iyas Abikhernozthanayev. The president, who had been head of the local communist party when Mistekistan was a Soviet republic called Sumistekia, has fled to neighbouring Flyspekistan, where he is seeking asylum. However, fighting has broken out between Dabtchiks and Bifsteks, two minorities in the south. The president of nearby Itznojokistan may try to broker a peace. "It looks a mess," says Professor Eniole Kwote of Meganostril University, whose centre for autocratic studies recently published a study saying the entire region was a shambles.

singular nouns

1 *A government,* a *party,* a *company* (whether Tesco or Marks & Spencer) and a *partnership* (Skidmore, Owings & Merrill) are all it and take a singular verb.

2 *Brokers* are singular.

   Legg Mason Wood Walk is preparing a statement.

      So avoid:

   stockbrokers Morgan Stanley Smith Barney, bankers JPMorgan Chase or accountants Ernst & Young.

3 *Chemical, drug, pension:* prefer the singular when referring to:

   chemical (*not* chemicals) companies
   drug- (*not* drugs) traffickers
   pension (*not* pensions) systems

4 Countries are singular, even if their names look plural.

   The Philippines has a congressional system, as does the United States; the Netherlands does not.

      The *United Nations* is also singular.

5 Abstract nouns that look plural when being used generally, without the definite article, an adjective or a possessive, are singular. For example:

acoustics	economics
athletics	kinetics
ballistics	mathematics
dynamics	mechanics

physics	propaganda
politics	statics

when being used generally, without the definite article, are singular. For example:

"Economics is the dismal science" (Carlyle).
"Politics is the art of the possible" (Bismarck).
Statics is a branch of physics.

6   Some games are singular:

billiards	darts
bowls	fives

But teams that take the name of a town, country or university are plural, even when they look singular:

England were bowled out for 56.

7   *Law and order* defies the rules of grammar and is singular.

split infinitives Happy the man who has never been told that it is wrong to split an infinitive: the ban is pointless. Unfortunately, to see the rule broken is so annoying to so many people that you should observe it. To never split an infinitive is quite easy.

subjunctive Use the subjunctive properly. If you are posing a hypothesis contrary to fact, you must use the subjunctive. *If I were you ...* or *If Hitler were alive today, he could tell us whether he kept a diary.*

If the hypothesis may or may not be true, you do not use the subjunctive. *If this diary is not Hitler's, we shall be glad we did not publish it.*

If you have *would* in the main clause, you must use the subjunctive in the *if* clause. *If you were to disregard this rule, you would make a fool of yourself.*

It is common nowadays to use the subjunctive in such constructions as:

He demanded that the Russians withdraw.
They insisted that the Americans also move back.
The referee suggested both sides cool it.
In soccer it is necessary that everyone remain civil.

This construction is correct, and has always been used

in America, whence it has recrossed the Atlantic. In Britain, though, it fell into disuse some time ago except in more formal contexts:

I command the prisoner be summoned, I beg that the motion be put to the house.

In British English, but not in American, another course would be to insert the word *should*:

He demanded that the Russians should withdraw.
The Americans should also move back.
Both sides should cool it.
Everyone should remain civil.

Alternatively, some of the sentences could be rephrased:

He asked the Russians to withdraw.
It is necessary for everyone to remain civil.

See also **may and might**.

tenses Any account of events that have taken place must use a past tense. Yet newspaper articles may have greater immediacy if they use the present or future tenses where appropriate.

The perfect and pluperfect tenses also serve a purpose, often making accounts more pointed, and so more interesting. Here are a few rough rules:

1 If you use the past simple (aorist) tense, put a time or date to the event: *He died on April 11th.*
2 If you cannot, or do not want to, pin down the occasion in this way, use the perfect tense: *He has died*, or the present, *He is dead*. These imply continuance.
3 The pluperfect should be used for events that punctuate past continuance: *He grew up in post-war Germany, where he had seen the benefits of hard work.*
   So does the imperfect tense: *He was a long time dying.*

See also **may and might**.

ground rules Just as *house rules* are the rules of the particular house, so *ground rules* are *the rules of the particular ground* (or *grounds*). They are not *basic* or *general rules*.

halve is a transitive verb, so deficits can double but not *halve*. They must *be halved* or *fall by half*.

haver means to *talk nonsense*, not *dither*, *swither* or *waver*.

headings and captions set the tone: they are more read than anything else, especially in a newspaper. Use them, therefore, to draw readers in, not to repel them. That means wit (where appropriate), not bad puns; sharpness (ditto), not familiarity (call people by their last names, not their first names); originality, not clichés.

Writers and editors, having laboured over an article, are too often ready to yank a well-known catchphrase, or the title of a film, from the front of their mind without giving the matter any more thought. They do so, presumably, in the belief that the heading is less important than the words beneath it. If you find yourself reaching for any of the following, think again:

back to the future	kinder, gentler
bridges (or anything else) too far	hearts and minds
	mind the gap
China syndromes	new kids on the block
could do better (a favourite with education stories)	perfect storms
	shaken, not stirred
deal or no deal	$64,000 questions
empires striking back	southern discomfort
French connections	taxing times (tax stories)
F-words	thirty-somethings
flavours of the month	where's the beef?
generation X	windows of opportunity

On October 18th 2004, for instance, an *Economist* reader wrote as follows:

SIR – Your newspaper this week contains headlines derived from the following film titles: "As Good As It Gets", "Face-Off", "From

Russia With Love", "The Man Who Planted Trees", "Up Close and Personal" and "The Way of the Warrior". Also employed are "the Iceman Cometh", "Measure for Measure", "The Tyger" and "War and Peace" – to say nothing of the old stalwart, "Howard's Way".

Is this a competition, or do your sub-editors need to get out more?

Tom Braithwaite,
London

See also **clichés**, **journalese and slang**.

health care The American system of *health care* (adjective, *health-care*) for the poor is *Medicaid*, and for the elderly is *Medicare*. Canada's national health-care system is also called *Medicare*.

healthy If you think something is *desirable* or *good*, say so. Do not call it *healthy*.

heresy *see* **apostasy**.

heteronym *see* **homograph, homophone**.

hoards, hordes Few secreted treasures or stashes of things like food and money being kept to guard against privation (*hoards*) are multitudes on the move (*hordes*).

Hobson's choice is not *the lesser of two evils*; it is *no choice at all.*

holistic properly refers to a theory developed by Jan Smuts, who argued that, through creative evolution, nature tended to form wholes greater than the sum of the parts. If this is not what you mean by *holistic*, you would probably be wise to avoid it.

homeland Although it is now used as a synonym for the United States' domestic territory, your homeland is your *native land*, your *motherland* or even your *fatherland*.

homogeneous, homogenous *Homogeneous* means of the same kind or nature. *Homogenous* means similar because of common descent.

homograph, homophone *Homographs* are words with the same spelling but different meanings and sometimes different pronunciations. If they are spelt and pronounced the same they are also *homonyms*: *bear* (animal), *bear* (carry); *like* (similar), *like* (be fond of); *stalk* (part of a plant), *stalk* (to follow someone or something). If they are spelt the same but pronounced differently they are also *heteronyms*: *content* (happy), *content* (subject matter); *entrance* (way in), *entrance* (charm); *rebel* (to resist or fight against authority), *rebel* (someone who rebels).

Homophones are words that are pronounced the same regardless of how they are spelt and their meaning: *baited* (food put on a hook or trap), *bated* (diminished, restrained); *birth* (the process of bearing children); *berth* (somewhere to sleep in a ship, train etc); *heroin* (a Class A drug), *heroine* (a courageous woman).

homonym *see above.*

homosexual Since this word comes from the Greek word *homos* (same), not the Latin word *homo* (man), it applies as much to women as to men. It is therefore as daft to write *homosexuals and lesbians* as to write *people and women*.

hopefully Some authorities say it is pedantic and outmoded to object to the use of *hopefully* to mean *it is hoped that*. The practice originated in America, where English has been much influenced by German immigrants, who found the language of their new country had only one adverb to serve for both *hoffnungsvoll*, meaning full of hope, and *hoffentlich*, which can mean let's hope so. In *The Economist*, however, by all means begin an article hopefully, but do not write: *Hopefully, it will be finished by Wednesday.* Try *with luck, if all goes well, it is hoped that...*

horrible words Words that are horrible to one writer may not be horrible to another, but if you are a writer for whom no words are horrible, you would do well to take up some other activity. No words or phrases should be banned outright from appearing in print, but if you use any of the following you should be aware that they may have an emetic effect on some of your readers.

carer – and most caring
  expressions
chattering classes
facilitate
famously
governance
grow the business
guesstimate
informed (as in *his love of language informed his memos*)
kids
likely (meaning *probably*, rather than *probable*)
looking to (meaning *intending to*)

materiel	rack up (profits, etc)
ongoing	savvy
poster child	segue
prestigious	showcase
proactive	source (meaning *obtain*)

See also **clichés**.

hyphens There is no firm rule to help you decide which words are run together, hyphenated or left separate. If in doubt, consult a dictionary. Do not overdo the literary device of hyphenating words that are not usually linked: the stringing-together-of-lots-and-lots-of-words-and-ideas tendency can be tiresome.

1 Words with common or short prefixes

In general, try to avoid putting hyphens into words formed of one word and a short prefix.

asexual	overeducated	repurchase
biplane	overemployment	subcommittee
declassify	precondition	subcontinent
disfranchise	predate	subcontract
geopolitical	preoccupied	subhuman
neoclassicism	preordained	submachinegun
neoconservative	prepay	suboptimal
but neo-cons	realign	subprime
neoliberal	rearm	tetravalent
neolithic	rearrange	underdog
neologism	reborn	underdone
neonatal	redirect	underinvest
overcapacity	reopen	underpaid
overdone	reorder	upended

2 Words beginning with re-

Some words that begin with *re* are hyphenated to avoid confusion:

re-cast	re-present (meaning present again)
re-create (meaning create again)	re-sort (meaning sort again)

3 Unfamiliar combinations

Long words making unfamiliar combinations, especially if they would involve running consonants together, may benefit from a hyphen, so:

cross-reference (a cross reference would be unpleasant)
demi-paradise
over-governed
sub-investment grade
under-secretary

Antidisestablishmentarianism would, however, lose its point if it were hyphenated.

See also 5 *below.*

4 Fractions

Whether nouns or adjectives, these take hyphens:

one-half	one-sixth
four-fifths	two-thirds

But note that it is *a half, a fifth, a sixth.*

5 Words that begin with

agri	infra	post
anti	inter	pre
counter	mid	semi
extra	multi	ultra
half	non	

The rules vary:

agri-business, agriculture
anti-aircraft, anti-fascist, anti-submarine (*but* antibiotic, anticlimax, antidote, antiseptic, antitrust)
counter-attack, counter-clockwise, counter-espionage, counter-intuitive (*but* counteract, countermand, counterpane)
extraordinary, extraterrestrial, extraterritorial (*but* extra-judicial)
half-baked, half-hearted, half-serious (*but* halfway)
infra-red
inter-agency, inter-county, inter-faith, inter-governmental inter-regional (*but* intermediate, international, interpose)
mid-August, mid-week
multibillion, multilingual, multiracial (*but* multi-occupancy, multi-storey, multi-user)
non-combatant, non-existent, non-payment, non-violent (*but* nonaligned, nonconformist, nonplussed, nonstop)
postdate, post-war, pre-war

semi-automatic, semi-conscious, semi-detached
ultra-violet

6 The word *worth*

A sum followed by the word *worth* needs a hyphen: *$25m-worth of
goods.*

7 Some titles

attorney-general	lieutenant-colonel	under-secretary
director-general	major-general	vice-president
field-marshal	secretary-general	

But:

deputy director	district attorney
deputy secretary	general secretary

8 Avoiding ambiguities

a little-used car	fine-tooth comb (most people	third-world war
a little used-car	do not comb their teeth)	third world war
cross complaint	high-school results	
cross-complaint	high school results	

9 Aircraft

DC-10	MiG-23
Mirage F-1E	Lockheed P-3 Orion

(If in doubt, consult Jane's "All the World's Aircraft".)
Note that Airbus A340, BAe RJ70 do not have hyphens.

10 Calibres

The style for calibres is 50mm or 105mm with no hyphen, but 5.5-
inch and 25-pounder.

11 Adjectives formed from two or more words

70-year-old judge
balance-of-payments difficulties
private-sector wages
public-sector borrowing requirement
right-wing groups (*but* the right wing of the party)

state-of-the-union message
value-added tax (VAT)

12 Adverbs

Adverbs do not need to be linked to participles or adjectives by hyphens in simple constructions:

The regiment was ill equipped for its task.
The principle is well established.
Though expensively educated, the journalist knew no grammar.

But if the adverb is one of two words together being used adjectivally, a hyphen may be needed:

The ill-equipped regiment was soon repulsed.
All well-established principles should be periodically challenged.

The hyphen is especially likely to be needed if the adverb is short and common, such as *ill*, *little*, *much* and *well*. Less common adverbs, including all those that end -ly, are less likely to need hyphens:

Never employ an expensively educated journalist.

13 Separating identical letters

book-keeping	re-emerge
coat-tails	re-entry
co-operate	side-effect
pre-eminent	trans-ship
pre-empt	unco-operative

Exceptions include:

overrate	overrun
overreach	skiing
override	underrate
overrule	withhold

14 Some nouns formed from prepositional verbs

bail-out	pay-off	shake-out
build-up	pull-out	shake-up
buy-out	rip-off	stand-off
call-up	round-up	start-up
get-together	run-up	
lay-off	set-up	

But:

fallout	lockout
handout	payout
knockout	turnout

15 The quarters of the compass

mid-west(ern)	south-east(ern)
north-east(ern)	south-west(ern)
north-west(ern)	

16 Hybrid ethnics

Greek-Cypriot, Irish-American, etc, whether noun or adjective.

17 Makers and making

A general, though not iron, rule for *makers* and *making*: if the prefix is of one or two syllables, attach it without a hyphen to form a single word, but if the prefix is of three or more syllables, introduce a hyphen.

antimacassar-maker	clockmaker	rule-maker
bookmaker	holiday-maker	steelmaker
candlestick-maker	lawmaker	tiramisu-maker
carmaker	marketmaker	troublemaker
chipmaker	peacemaker	

Policymaker and *profitmaking* are one word and an exception. But: note *foreign-policy maker (-ing)*.

18 Other words ending -er (-ing) that are similar to *maker* and making

The general rule should be to insert a hyphen:

arms-trader	gun-runner
copper-miner	home-owner
drug-dealer	hostage-taker
drug-trafficker	mill-owner
field-worker	truck-driver
front-runner	vegetable-grower

But some prefixes, especially those of one syllable, can be used to form single words.

coalminer   metalworker   shipowner
farmworker   muckraker   steeplechaser
foxhunter   nitpicker (-ing)   steelworker
gatekeeper   peacekeeper   taxpayer
householder   shipbroker
landowner   shipbuilder

Less common combinations are better written as two words:

currency trader   insurance broker
dog owner   crossword compiler
gun owner   tuba player

19 Quotes

Words gathered together in quotation marks to serve as adjectives do not usually need hyphens as well: the *"Live Free or Die"* state.

20 One word

airfield	cyberspace	kowtow
airspace	dotcom	lacklustre
airtime	downturn (noun)	landmine
bedfellow	faultline	laptop
bestseller	figleaf	logjam
(-ing)	fivefold	loophole
bilingual	foothold	lopsided
blackboard	forever (adv, when	lukewarm
blackout	preceding verb)	machinegun
blueprint	foxhunter (-ing)	marketplace
bookseller	frontline (adj, *but*	minefield
businessman	noun front line)	nationwide
bypass	goodwill	nevertheless
cashflow (*but*	grassroots (adj and	nonetheless
cash flow in	noun)	offline
accountancy)	groundsman	offshore
catchphrase	halfhearted	oilfield
ceasefire	halfway	oilrig
checklist	handpicked	online
coastguard	handwriting	onshore
codebreaker	hardline	peacetime
comeback	headache	petrochemical
commonsense (adj)	hijack	pickup truck
crossfire	hobnob	placename

rainforest
ringtone
roadblock
rustbelt
salesforce
seabed
shorthand
shortlist
shutdown
sidestep
soyabean
spillover

statewide
stockmarket
streetwalker
strongman
sunbelt
takeover
threefold
threshold
timetable
trademark
transatlantic
transpacific

twofold
videocassette
videodisc
wartime
watchdog
website
windfall
workforce
worldwide
worthwhile

21 Two words

ad hoc
air base
air force
air strike
all right
any time
arm's length
any more
ballot box
birth rate
call centre

child care (noun)
cluster bombs
common sense
  (noun)
dare say
errand boy
for ever (when
  used after a verb)
girl friend
hedge fund
health care (noun)

home page
joint venture
Land Rover
no one
photo opportunity
some day
some time
under way
vice versa
wild flowers (*but*
  adj. wildflower)

22 Two hyphenated words

aid-worker
aircraft-carrier
asylum-seekers
baby-boomer
balance-sheet
bell-ringer
come-uppance
court-martial (noun
  and verb)
cross-border
cross-dresser
cross-sell
death-squads
derring-do

down-payment
drawing-board
end-game
end-year
faint-hearted
fund-raiser (-ing)
hand-held
health-care (adj)
heir-apparent
home-made
hot-head
ice-cream
interest-group
kerb-crawler

know-how
laughing-stock
like-minded
long-standing
machine-tool
money-laundering
nation-building
nation-state
nest-egg
news-stand
number-plate
pot-hole
pressure-group
question-mark

rain-check	talking-shop	vote-winner
short-lived	task-force	well-being
starting-point	tear-gas	Wi-Fi
sticking-point	think-tank	Wi-Max
stumbling-block	time-bomb	window-dressing
suicide-bomb (-er, -ing)	turning-point	working-party
	voice-mail	write-down (noun)

23 Three words

ad hoc agreement (meeting, etc) in so far
armoured personnel carrier multiple rocket launcher
chief(s) of staff nuclear power station
half a dozen third world war (if things get bad)
in as much

24 Three hyphenated words

A-turned-B (unless this leads to something unwieldy, so jobbing churchwarden turned captain of industry)

brother-in-law	prisoners-of-war
chock-a-block	second-in-command
commander-in-chief	stock-in-trade
no-man's-land	

25 Numbers

Avoid *from 1947-50* (say *in 1947-50* or *from 1947 to 1950*) and *between 1961-65* (say *in 1961–65, between 1961 and 1965* or *from 1961 to 1965*). *See also* **figures**.

"If you take hyphens seriously, you will surely go mad." (Oxford University Press style manual)

hypothermia is what kills old folk in winter. If you say it is *hyperthermia*, that means they have been carried off by heat stroke.

Icelandic names *see* **names.**

iconoclasm Many good writers break the rules of English, and readers may occasionally forgive *The Economist* for doing so too. It is, however, possible to write well while showing respect for grammar and punctuation. An article may be improved by an original phrase or even an unusual word, but *The Economist* is not meant to be a work of literature. It is simply meant to be well written.

identical *with* not *to*.

ilk means *same*, so *of that ilk* means *of the place of the same name as the family*, not *of that kind*. Best avoided.

immolate means to *sacrifice*, not to *burn*.

important If something is *important*, say why and to whom. Use sparingly, and avoid such unexplained claims as *this important house, the most important painter of the 20th century. See also* **interesting**.

impractical, impracticable If something is *impractical*, it is *not worth trying to do it*. If it's *impracticable*, it *cannot be done. See also* **practical, practicable**.

inchoate means *not fully developed* or *at an early stage*, not *incoherent* or *chaotic*.

including When *including* is used as a preposition, as it often is, it must be followed by a noun, pronoun or noun clause, not by a preposition. So *Iran needs more investment, including for its tired oil industry* is ungrammatical. The sentence should be rephrased, perhaps, as *Iran, including its tired oil industry, needs more investment*.

individual (noun) used occasionally, can be a useful colloquial term for *chap* or *bloke* or *guy* ("*In a corner, Parker, a grave, lean individual, bent over the chafing-dish, in which he was preparing for his employer and his guest their simple lunch.*" P.G. Wodehouse). Used indiscriminately as a term for person or, in the plural, *people*, it becomes bureaucratic ("*Individuals desiring to function as operators using instruments listed under paragraph (A)(3) of rule 3701–53–02 of the Administrative Code shall apply to the director of health for permits on forms prescribed and provided by the director of health.*" Ohio Department of Health).

Indonesian names *see* **names**.

initially Prefer *first, at first*.

interesting Like **important** and *funny*, *interesting* makes assumptions about the word or words it describes that may not be shared by the reader. Facts and stories introduced as interesting often turn out to be something else. "Interestingly, my father-in-law was born in East Kilbride," for instance. If something really is interesting, you probably do not need to say so.

inverted commas (quotation marks) *see* **punctuation**.

investigations of not *into*.

Iranian names *see* **names**.

Islamic, Islamist *Islamic* means relating to Islam; it is a synonym of the adjective *Muslim*, but it is not used for a follower of Islam, who is always *Muslim*. But *Islamic art and architecture* is conventional usage. *Islamist* refers to those who see Islam as a political and social ideology as well as a religious one.

issues *The Economist* has issues – 51 a year – but if you think you have issues with *The Economist*, you probably mean you have *complaints, irritations* or *delivery problems*. If you disagree with *The Economist*, you may take issue with it. Be precise.

Italian names *see* **names**.

italics

foreign words and phrases should be set in italics:

cabinet (French type)	*loya jirga*
dalits	*Mitbestimmung*
de rigueur	*pace*
fatwa	*papabile*
jihad (jihadi, but *jihadist)*	*perestroika*
glasnost	*persona non grata*
Hindutva	*sarariman*
in camera	*Schadenfreude*
intifada	*ujamaa*

If they are so familiar that they have become anglicised, they should be in roman. For example:

ad hoc	grand prix
apartheid	in absentia
a priori	in situ
a propos	machismo
avant-garde	nom de guerre
bête noire	nouveau riche
bona fide	parvenu
bourgeois	pogrom
café	post mortem
chargé d'affaires	putsch
coup d'état (but *coup de*	raison d'être
foudre, coup de grâce)	realpolitik
de facto, de jure	status quo
dirigisme	tsunami
elite	vice versa
en masse, en route	vis-à-vis

Remember to put appropriate accents and diacritical signs on French, German, Spanish and Portuguese words in italics (and give initial capital letters to German nouns when in italics, but not if not). Make sure that the meaning of any foreign word you use is clear. *See also* **accents**.

For the Latin names of animals, plants, etc, *see* **spelling** and Part 3.

newspapers and periodicals Only *The Economist* has *The* italicised. Thus the *Daily Telegraph*, the *New York Times*, the

Financial Times, the *Spectator* (but *Le Monde, Die Welt, Die Zeit*).
The *Yomiuri Shimbun* should be italicised, but you can also
say the *Yomiuri*, or the *Yomiuri* newspaper, as *shimbun* simply
means newspaper in Japanese. The *Nikkei* is an abbreviation
(for *Nihon Keizai*) and so should not be written as *Nikkei
Shimbun* as that is not strictly this financial daily's name.

**books, pamphlets, plays, operas, ballets, radio and television
programmes** Titles are roman, not italic, with capital letters
for each main word, in quotation marks. Thus: "Pride and
Prejudice", "Much Ado about Nothing", "Any Questions",
"Crossfire", etc. But the Bible and its books (Genesis,
Ecclesiastes, John, etc), as well as the Koran, are written
without inverted commas. These rules apply to footnotes as
well as bodymatter.

Note that book publishers generally use italics for the
titles of books, pamphlets, plays, operas, ballets, radio and
television programmes, paintings and sculptures.

headings, captions, cross-heads, rubrics Do not use italics.

lawsuits

> *Brown v Board of Education*
> *Coatsworth v Johnson*
> *Jarndyce v Jarndyce*

If abbreviated, *versus* should always be shortened to *v*, with
no point after it. The v should not be italic if it is not a lawsuit.

names of ships, aircraft, spacecraft

> *HMS Illustrious*
> *Spirit of St Louis*
> *Challenger*

Japanese names *see* **names.**

jargon Avoid it. You may have to think harder if you are not to use jargon, but you can still be precise. Technical terms should be used in their proper context; do not use them out of it. In many instances simple words can do the job of *creative writing (fiction), exponential* (try *fast*), *interface (frontier* or *border*) and so on. If you find yourself tempted to write about *affirmative action* or *corporate governance*, you will have to explain what it is; with luck, you will then not have to use the actual expression.

Resist the kind of jargon that tries to dignify nonsense with seriousness:

The appointee ... should have a proven track record of operating at a senior level within a multi-site international business, preferably within a service- or brand-oriented environment

declared an advertisement for a financial controller for The Economist Group.

At a national level, the department engaged stakeholders positively ... This helped ... to improve stakeholder buy-in to agreed changes

avowed a British civil servant in a report.

The City Safe T3 Resilience Project is a cross-sector initiative bringing together experts ... to enable multi-tier practitioner-oriented collaboration on resilience and counter-terrorism challenges and opportunities

explained Chatham House.

Resist, too, jargon used to obscure the truth:

These grants will incentivise administrators and educators to apply relevant metrics to assess achievement in the competencies they seek to develop

said a memo cited by Tony Proscio in "Bad Words for Good" (The

Edna McConnell Clark Foundation). What it meant, as Mr Proscio points out, was that the grants would be used to pay teachers who agreed to test their students.

Almost as bad is jargon used simply to obfuscate:

A multi-agency project catering for holistic diversionary provision to young people for positive action linked to the community safety strategy and the pupil referral unit

was how Luton Education Authority described go-karting lessons.

Someone with good *interpersonal skills* probably just *gets on well with others*. Someone with poor *parenting skills* is probably a *bad father* or a *bad mother*. *Negative health outcomes* are probably *illness, mutilation* or *death*. *Intelligent media brands for the high-end audience that clients value* are presumably *good publications for rich people*.

See also **due process, holistic**.

jib, gibe, gybe

jib (noun)	sail or boom of a crane
jib (verb)	to balk or shy
gibe (verb)	to scoff or flout
gibe (noun)	taunt
gybe (verb)	to alter course

Don't *jibe*.

jihad is the Arabic word for *striving*. For modern Muslims, it may mean *military war* to propagate Islamism, that is, to spread Islam as a religious, political and social ideology (*jihad* of the sword). Or it may mean *spiritual struggle* for personal purification and moral betterment (*jihad* against one's self). Or it may merely mean *doing right, improving society* and *being virtuous* (*jihad* of the tongue or of the hand). A religious obligation for all Muslims, *jihad* is for most a non-violent duty, though for some a violent one. Do not therefore use it simply to mean *holy war*, which it never did in classical Arabic. Rather, make clear what sort of *jihad* is under discussion in the context.

Someone engaged in *jihad* is a *mujahid* (plural, *mujahideen*) or a *jihadist* (*jihadi*). Logically, *mujahideen* and jihadists might be considered to be engaged in a struggle that could be either violent or non-violent. In practice, the terms nowadays are always used of Muslims engaged in an armed struggle, though *mujahideen* may simply be Muslim militants fighting for a cause, whereas jihadists are always fighting to spread Islamism by force.

journalese and slang Do not be too free with slang like *He really hit the big time in 2001*. Slang, like metaphors, should be used only occasionally if it is to have effect. Avoid expressions used only by journalists, such as giving people *the thumbs up, the thumbs down* or *the green light*. Stay clear of *gravy trains* and *salami tactics*. Do not use *the likes of*, or *Big Pharma* (*big drug firms*).

And avoid words and expressions that are ugly or overused, such as:

the bottom line
crisis
guesstimate (use guess)
key
major (unless something else nearby is minor)
massive (as in massive inflation)
meaningful
perceptions
prestigious
schizophrenic (unless the context is medical)
significant

Politicians are often said to be highly *visible* or *high-profile*, when *conspicuous* or *prominent* would be more appropriate. Regulations are sometimes said to be designed to create *transparency*, which presumably means *openness*. *Governance* usually means *government*, but not when used with *corporate*. Elections described as *too close to call* are usually just *close*. *Ethics violations*, if they are not crimes, are likely to be *shenanigans*, *immorality*, *scandalous behaviour* or mere *misdemeanours*. *Traffic violations* are *traffic offences*.

Try not to be predictable, especially predictably jocular. Spare your readers any mention of *mandarins* when writing about the civil service, of *their lordships* when discussing the House of Lords, and of *comrades* when analysing communist parties. Must all stories about Central Asia include a reference to the *Great Game*? Must all lawns be *manicured*? Must all small towns in the old confederacy be called the *buckle on the Bible belt*? Are drug-traffickers inevitably *barons*? Must starlets and models always be *scantily clad*? Is there any other kind of *wonk* than a *policy wonk*?

Resist saying *This will be no panacea*. When you find something that is indeed a *panacea* (or a *magic* or *silver bullet*), that will indeed be news. Similarly, hold back from offering the reassurance *There is no need to panic*. Instead, ask yourself exactly when there is a need to panic.

In general, try to make your writing fresh. It will seem stale if it reads like hackneyed journalese. One weakness of journalists, who on daily newspapers may plead that they have little time to search for the apposite word, is a love of the ready-made, seventh-hand phrase. Lazy journalists are always at home in *oil-rich* country A, ruled by *ailing* President B, the *long-serving strongman*, who is, according to the *chattering classes*, not *squeaky clean* but a *wily political operator* – hence the present *uneasy peace* – but, after his recent *watershed* (or *ground-breaking* or *landmark* or *sea-change*) decision to arrest his prime minister (the *honeymoon is over*), will soon face a *bloody uprising* in the *breakaway* south. Similarly, lazy business journalists always enjoy describing the problems of *troubled* company C, a victim of the *revolution* in the widget industry (change is always revolutionary in such industries), which, *well-placed insiders* predict, will be riven by a *make-or-break* strike unless one of the *major players* makes an *11th-hour* (or *last-ditch*) intervention in a *marathon* negotiating session.

Prose such as this is often freighted with codewords (writers apply *respected* to someone they approve of, *militant* to someone they disapprove of, *prestigious* to something you won't have heard of). The story usually starts with *First the good news*, inevitably to be followed in due course by *Now the bad news*. An alternative is *Another week, another bomb* (giving rise to thoughts of *Another story, another hackneyed opening*). Or, *It was the best of times, it was the worst of times* – and certainly the feeblest of introductions. A quote will then be inserted, attributed to *one* (never *an*) *industry analyst*, and often the words *If, and it's a big if* ... Towards the end, after an admission that the author has no idea what is going on, there is always room for *One thing is certain*, before rounding off the article with *As one wag put it* ...

See also **clichés, headings and captions, metaphors**.

key A *key* may be *major* or *minor*, but not *low*. Few of the decisions, people, industries described as *key* are truly *indispensable*, and fewer still *open locks*.

This overused word is a noun and, like many nouns, may be used adjectivally (as in the *key ministries*). Do not, however, use it as a free-standing adjective, as in *The choice of running-mate is key*.

Do not use *key* to make the subject of your sentence more important than he, she or it really is. The words *key players* are a sure sign of a puffed-up story and a lazy mind.

Korean names *see* **names.**

Kyrgyzstan, Kirgiz *see* **placenames.**

lag If you *lag* transitively, you *lag a pipe* or *a loft*. Anything failing to keep up with a front-runner, rate of growth, fourth-quarter profit or whatever is *lagging behind it*.

last The *last* issue of *The Economist* implies its extinction; prefer *last week's* or the *latest* issue. *Last year*, in 2010, means 2009; if you mean the 12 months up to the time of writing, write the *past year*. The same goes for the *past* month, *past* week, *past* (not *last*) ten years. *Last week* is best avoided; anyone reading it several days after publication may be confused. *This week* is permissible.

Latin names When it is necessary to use a Latin name for animals, plants, etc, follow the standard practice. Thus for all creatures higher than viruses, write the binomial name in italics, giving an initial capital to the first word (the genus): *Turdus turdus*, the songthrush; *Metasequoia glyptostroboides*, the dawn redwood; *Culicoides clintoni*, a species of midge. This rule also applies to *Homo sapiens* and to such uses as *Homo economicus*. On second mention, the genus may be abbreviated (*T. turdus*). In some species, such as dinosaurs, the genus alone is used in lieu of a common name: *Diplodocus*, *Tyrannosaurus*. Also *Drosophila*, a fruitfly favoured by geneticists. But *Escherichia coli*, a bacterium also favoured by geneticists, is known universally as *E. coli*, even on first mention.

leverage If you really cannot find a way of avoiding the word *leverage*, you must explain what it means (unless it is simply *the use of a lever to gain a mechanical advantage*). In its technical sense, as a noun, it may mean *the ratio of long-term debt to total capital employed*. But note that *operating leverage* and *financial leverage* are different. The verb is even viler than the noun (try *lever*). *See also* **gearing**.

liberal in Europe, someone who believes above all in the freedom of the individual; in the United States, someone who believes in the progressive tradition of Franklin D. Roosevelt.

lifestyle Prefer *way of life*.

like, unlike govern nouns and pronouns, not verbs and clauses. So *as in America* not *like in America*, *as I was saying*, not *like I was saying*, *as Grandma used to make them*, not *like Grandma used to make them*. English has no word for the opposite of *as* that would be the equivalent of *unlike*, so you must rephrase the sentence if you are tempted to write *unlike in this context*, *unlike at Christmas*, or *unlike when I was a child*.

If you find yourself writing *She looked like she had had enough* or *It seemed like he was running out of puff*, you should replace *like* with *as if* or *as though*, and you probably need the subjunctive: *She looked as if she had had enough*, *It seemed as if he were running out of puff*.

Like the hart panteth for the water brooks I pant for a revival of Shakespeare's "Like You Like It".
I can see tense draftees relax and purr
When the sergeant barks, 'Like you were.'
– And don't try to tell me that our well has been defiled by immigration;
Like goes Madison Avenue, like so goes the nation.
(Ogden Nash)

But *authorities like Fowler and Gowers* is a perfectly acceptable alternative to *authorities such as Fowler and Gowers*.

likely Avoid such constructions as *He will likely announce the date on Monday* and *The price will likely fall when results are posted Friday*. Prefer *He is likely to announce ...* or *It is likely that the price will ...*

locate (in all its forms) can usually be replaced by something less ugly. *The missing scientist was located* means he was *found*. *The diplomats will meet at a secret location* means either that they will meet *in a secret place* or that they will meet *secretly*. *A company located in Texas* is simply *a company in Texas*.

lower case see **capitals**.

luxurious, luxuriant *Luxurious* means *indulgently pleasurable*; *luxuriant* means *exuberant* or *profuse*. A tramp may have a *luxuriant* beard but not a *luxurious* life.

masterful, masterly *Masterful* means *imperious*; *masterly* means *skilled*.

may and might are not always interchangeable, and you may want *may* more often than you think. If in doubt, try *may* first. *I might be wrong, but I think it will rain later* should be *I may be wrong, but I think it will rain later*.

Much of the trouble arises from the fact that *may* becomes *might* in both the subjunctive and in some constructions using past tenses. *Mr Blair admits that weapons of mass destruction may never be found* becomes, in the past, *Mr Blair admitted that weapons of mass destruction might never be found*.

Conditional sentences using the subjunctive also need *might*. Thus *If Sarah Palin were to write a novel, it might be called a thriller from Wasilla*. This could be rephrased by *If Sarah Palin writes a novel, it may be called a thriller from Wasilla*. Conditional sentences stating something contrary to fact, however, need *might*: *If pigs had wings, birds might raise their eyebrows*.

The facts are crucial. *New research shows Tutankhamun may have died of a broken leg* is fine, if indeed that is what the research shows. *New research shows Tutankhamun might have died of a broken leg* is not fine, unless it is followed by something like *if his mummy hadn't dressed the wound before it became infected*. This, though, is saying something quite different. In the first example, it is clear both that Tutankhamun died and that a broken leg may have been responsible. In the second, it is clear only that his wound was dressed; as a result, Tutankhamun seems to have survived.

Sometimes it is all right to use *might* if part of the sentence is understood though not explicitly stated: *Silvio Berlusconi would never tell a fib, but Jeffrey Archer might (if circumstances demanded or if he had forgotten the truth). That might be actionable (if a judge said it was)*.

Facts remain crucial: *I might have called him a liar (but I didn't have the guts). I may have called him a liar (I can't now remember).*

Do not write *He might call himself an ardent free-market banker, but he did not reject a government rescue.* It should be *He may call himself an ardent free-market banker, but he did not reject a government rescue.* Only if you are putting forward a hypothesis that may or may not be true are *may* and *might* interchangeable. Thus *If he is honest with himself, he may (or might) call himself something else in future.*

Could is sometimes useful as an alternative to *may* and *might*: *His coalition could (or may) collapse.* But take care. Does *He could call an election in May* mean *He may call an election in May* or *He would be allowed to call an election in May?*

Do not use *may* or *might* when the appropriate verb is *to be*. *His colleagues wonder how far the prime minister may go. The danger for them is that they may all lose their seats* should be *His colleagues wonder how far the prime minister will go. The danger for them is that they will all lose their seats.*

See also **grammar and syntax.**

measures *see* Part 3.

media Prefer *press and television* or, if the context allows it, just *press*. If you have to use the *media*, remember they are plural.

meta- is a prefix derived from the Greek word for *with, beyond* or *after*, has long been used before the name of a science to designate what the *Oxford English Dictionary* calls a higher science of the same nature but dealing with ulterior problems, such as metachemistry, metaphysiology. This, says the OED, is done in supposed analogy to metaphysics, which is misapprehended as meaning the science of that which transcends the physical. Philosophers have extended the usage to, for example, metalanguage, language about language, which is used to express metatheorems, and computer geeks have fallen on it with delight, coining meta-elements, metadata, metatags. The practice of meta-naming is now adopted by those who wish to add scientific gravitas to almost any subject, especially any that is intrinsically jejune.

metaphors "A newly invented metaphor assists thought by evoking a visual image," said Orwell, "while on the other hand a metaphor which is technically 'dead' (eg, iron resolution) has in effect reverted to being an ordinary word and can generally be used without loss of vividness. But in between these two classes there is a huge dump of worn-out metaphors which are merely used because they save people the trouble of inventing phrases for themselves."

Every issue of The Economist contains scores of metaphors:

gay soldiers booted back on to Civvy Street, asset-price bubbles pricked, house prices getting monetary medicine, gauntlets thrown down, ideas floated, tides turned, accounts embraced, barrages of criticism unleashed, retailing behemoths arriving with a splash, foundering chains, both floods and flocks of job-seekers, limelight hogged, inflation ignited, the ratio of chiefs to Indians, landmark patent challenges, drug giants taking steps towards the dark side, cash-strapped carmakers, football clubs teetering on the brink, prices inching up (or peaking, spiking or even going north), a leaden overhang of shares, giddying rises, rosy scenarios being painted, a fat lady not singing

Some of these are tired, and will therefore tire the reader. Most are so exhausted that they may be considered dead, and are therefore permissible. But use all metaphors, dead or alive, sparingly, otherwise you will make trouble for yourself.

An issue of The Economist chosen at random had:

a package cutting the budget deficit, the administration loath to sign on to higher targets, the lure of eastern Germany as a springboard to the struggling markets of eastern Europe, west Europeanness helping to dilute an image, someone finding a pretext to stall the process before looking for a few integrationist crumbs, a spring clean that became in the next sentence a stalking-horse for greater spending, and Michelin axing jobs in painful surgery

Within four consecutive sentences in another issue lay:

a chance to lance the Israel-Palestine boil, Americans and Europeans sitting on their hands while waiting for Israel to freeze settlement building, or for Palestinians to corral militants, the need to stop the two sides playing the "after you" game, a confidence-building and money-begging conference followed by a shot in the arm for the Americans

Another article included this:

During a long and improbable life Spiegel sloughed off more skins than a bed of snakes, and a biographer's first task is to keep their footing.

An attempt to "*defuse simmering tensions*" was taken out of another article before it was published, but this slipped through:

Like Japan's before it, America's stockmarket bubble was inflated on the back of a mountain of corporate debt. So onerous was this debt that many American companies were forced to the wall.

mete You may *mete out* punishment, but if it is to fit the crime it is *meet*.

metrics are the *theory of measurement*. Do not use the term as a pretentious word for *figures, dimensions* or *measurements* themselves, as in "*I can't take the metrics I'm privileged to and work my way to a number in [that] range*" (General George Metz, talking about the number of insurgents killed in Iraq).

migrate is intransitive. Do not *migrate people* or *things*.

millionaire The time has gone when young women would think that the term *millionaire* adequately described the man who broke the bank at Monte Carlo. If you wish to use it, make it plain that *millionaire* refers to income (in dollars or pounds), not to capital. Otherwise try *plutocrat* or *rich man*.

mitigate, militate *Mitigate* mollifies or makes better; *militate* tells against.

monopoly, monopsony A *monopolist* is the sole seller. A sole buyer is a *monopsonist. See* **oligopoly**.

moot in British English means *arguable, doubtful* or *open to debate*. Americans often use it to mean *hypothetical* or *academic*, ie *of no practical significance*. Prefer the British usage.

mortar If not a *vessel* in which herbs, etc, are pounded with a pestle, a *mortar* is a *piece of artillery* for throwing a shell, bomb or lifeline. Do not write *He was hit by a mortar* unless you mean he was struck by the artillery piece itself, which is improbable.

move Do not use *move* (noun) if you mean *decision, bid, deal* or something more precise. But *move* (verb) rather than *relocate*.

mujahid, mujahideen see **jihad**.

named after, not for.

names

For guidance on spelling people's names, see the list below. As with all names, spell them the way the person concerned has requested, if a preference has been expressed. Here are some names that cause spelling difficulties:

Issaias Afwerki (Mr Issaias)
Joaquín Almunia
Yasser Arafat
Bashar Assad
José María Aznar
José Manuel Barroso (no need to include his third name, Durão)
Traian Basescu
Deniz Baykal
Ritt Bjerregaard
Mangosuthu Buthelezi
Leopoldo Calvo-Sotelo
Cuauhtémoc Cardenas
Josep Lluis Carod-Rivera
Nicolae Ceausescu
Jean-Pierre Chevènement
Wlodzimierz Cimoszewicz
Carlo De Benedetti
Gianni De Michelis
Ciriaco De Mita
Yves-Thibault de Silguy
Carlo Ripa di Meana
Fyodor Dostoyevsky
Recep Tayyip Erdogan
Gandhi
Valéry Giscard d'Estaing
Felipe González
Mikhail Gorbachev
Habsburg
Juan José Ibarretxe
Radovan Karadzic
Costas Karamanlis
Bob Kerrey (Nebraska)
John Kerry (Massachusetts)
Nikita Khrushchev
Kim Dae-jung
Kim Jong Il
Vojislav Kostunica
Sergei Kozalev
Emile Lahoud
Alain Lamassoure
Alyaksandr Lukashenka
Luiz Inácio (Lula) da Silva
Milan Martic
Slobodan Milosevic
François Mitterrand
Ratko Mladic
Mahathir Mohamad (Dr)
King Mohammed of Morocco
Daniel arap Moi
Milan Mrsic
Muhammad (unless it is part of the name of someone who spells it differently)
Franz Müntefering

Nursultan Nazarbayev
Binyamin Netanyahu
Gaafar Numeiri
Andrej Olechowski
Mullah Mohammed Omar
Velupillai Prabhakaran
Viktor Pynzenyk
Muammar Qaddafi
Burhanuddin Rabbani
Yitzhak Rabin
Akbar Hashemi Rafsanjani
Cyril Ramaphosa
Prince Ranariddh
Rodrigo de Rato (Mr de Rato)
Reichmann brothers
Condoleezza Rice
Mikheil Saakashvili
Andrei Sakharov
Nicolas Sarkozy
Wolfgang Schäuble
Otto Schily
Gerhard Schröder
Robert Schumann (composer)
Arnold Schwarzenegger

Mohammed Zahir Shah
Yitzhak Shamir
Eduard Shevardnadze
Haris Silajdic
Banharn Silpa-archa
José Sócrates
Javier Solana
Alexander Solzhenitsyn
Aung San Suu Kyi (Miss Suu Kyi)
Jean Tiberi
Viktor Tymoshenko
Yulia Tymoshenko
Hans van den Broek (Mr Van
   den Broek)
Atal Behari Vajpayee
Tabaré Vázquez (Dr)
Grigory Yavlinsky
Viktor Yushchenko
José Luis Rodríguez Zapatero
   (Mr Zapatero)
Vladimir Zhirinovsky
Goodwill Zwelithini
Gennady Zyuganov

See also specific listings below.

Afghan

Gulbuddin Hikmatyar
Ahmad Shah Masoud
Mullah Mohammed Omar

Burhanuddin Rabbani
Mazar-i-Sharif

Arabic names and words

Al, al- Try to leave out the *Al*, *Al-*, *al* or *al-*. This is common practice with well-known figures like Bashar Assad (not al-Assad) and Muammar Qaddafi (not al-Qaddafi). Many names, however, would look peculiar without *al-*, so with less well-known people it should be included (lower case, usually followed by a hyphen). On subsequent mentions, it can be dropped. *Bin* (son of) must be repeated: *Osama bin Laden*, thereafter *Mr bin Laden*. But it is often ignored in alphabetisation.

The *Al-*, *Al-*, *al* or *al-* (or *Ad-*, *Ar-*, *As-*, etc) before most
Arab towns can be dropped (so *Baquba* not *al-Baquba*,
Ramadi not *ar-Ramadi*). But *al-Quds* because it is the Arab
name for Jerusalem and will be important in any context
in which it appears.

Some common Arabic names are:

Adel Abd al-Mahdi
Abdullah, King
Zine el-Abidine Ben Ali
Abu Alaa (aka Ahmed Qurei)
Abu Mazen (aka Mahmoud
  Abbas)
Abu Musab al-Zarqawi
Ahmad Jibril
Ahmed Chalabi
Ahmed Qurei
Ali Abdullah Saleh
Ali al-Sistani (Grand
  Ayatollah)
Iyad Allawi
al-Qaeda
Al Saud (*not* al-Saud, since
  the Al in this instance
  means house of)
Yasser Arafat
Bashar Assad
Hafez Assad
Abdel Aziz (founder of
  kingdom of Saudi Arabia)
Bahrain
Marwan Barghouti
Mustafa Barghouti
Masoud Barzani
Omar Al-Bashir
Boutros Boutros-Ghali
Chouf (the)
Muhammad Dahlan
Mohamed ElBaradei
King Fahd
Salam Fayyad
Suleiman Franjieh

Gaza Strip (and City)
Amin Gemayel
Rafik Hariri
Hassan, Crown Prince
Hizbullah
Hussein, King
Saddam Hussein
Ibn Khaldoun
Islamic Jihad
jamaat islamiya
Ibrahim al-Jaafari (Dr)
Jeddah
Walid Jumblatt
Abdel Halim Khaddam
Sadiq el-Mahdi
Mohammed al-Maktoum
Nuri al-Maliki
Maronite
Masjid Sulayman
Mosul
Hosni Mubarak
Muhammad the Prophet
Mukhabarat
Jaafar Numeiri
Qaboos, Sultan
Muammar Qaddafi
Farouq Qaddoumi
Ras Tanura
Riyadh
Sabah al-Ahmad, Sheikh
Anwar Sadat
Muqtada al-Sadr
Barham Saleh
Samarra
Sana'a

Saud al-Faisal, Prince
Saud ibn Abdel Aziz (king of
    Saudi Arabia who followed
    Abdel Aziz)
Sharjah
Sharm el-Sheikh
Shatt al-Arab

Strait of Hormuz
Jalal Talabani
Tal Afar
Tawheed
Umm al Aish
Wahhabi
Zayed, Sheikh

And some common Arabic words are:

burqa
Fatah
Hadith
haj
hijab

Hizbullah
hudna
intifada
niqab

See also **Arabic**.

Bangladeshi If the name includes the Islamic definite article, it should be lower case and without any hyphens: *Mujib ur Rahman*.

Belarusian If *Belarusians* (not *Belarussians*) wish to be known by the Belarusian form of their names (*Ihor*, *Vital* and *Life-President Alyaksandr Lukashenka*), so be it.

Cambodian On second reference, repeat both names, adding *Mr*: *Mr Hun Sen*, *Mr Sam Rainsy*.

Central Asian For those with Russified names, *see* **Russian**.

Askar Akayev
Heidar Aliyev

Nursultan Nazarbayev
Saparmurat Niyazov

Chinese In general, follow the pinyin spelling of Chinese names, which has replaced the old Wade-Giles system, except for people from the past, and people and places outside mainland China. *Peking* is therefore *Beijing* and *Mao* is *Zedong*, not *Tse-tung*.

There are no hyphens in pinyin spelling. So:

Deng Xiaoping
Guangdong (Kwangtung)
Guangzhou (Canton)
Hu Jintao
Jiang Qing (Mrs Mao)

Mao Zedong (Tse-tung)
Qingdao (Tsingtao)
Tianjin (Tientsin)
Xinjiang (Sinkiang)
Zhao Ziyang

But:

Chiang Kai-shek   Li Ka-shing
Hong Kong   Lee Teng-hui

The family name comes first, so *Hu Jintao* becomes *Mr Hu* on a later mention.

Note that *Peking University* and *Tsinghua University* have kept their pre-pinyin romanised names.

Dutch If using first name and surname together, *vans* and *dens* are lower case: *Dries van Agt* and *Joop den Uyl*. But without their first names they become *Mr Van Agt* and *Mr Den Uyl*; *Hans van den Broek* becomes *Mr Van den Broek*. These rules do not always apply to Dutch names in Belgium and South Africa: *Herman Van Rompuy* (thereafter *Mr Van Rompuy*); *Karel Van Miert* (*Mr Van Miert*).

Note that *Flemings* speak *Dutch*.

French Any *de* is likely to be lower case, unless it starts a sentence. *De Gaulle* goes up; *Charles de Gaulle* and plain *de Gaulle* go down. So does *Yves-Thibault de Silguy*.

German Any *von* is likely to be upper case only at the start of a sentence.

Icelandic Most Icelanders do not have family names. They take their last name from the first name of their father, so *Leifur Eiriksson*, say, is the son of *Eirikur*, and *Freyja Haraldsdottir* is the daughter of *Harald*. If she marries Leifur Eiriksson, she continues to be known as Freyja Haraldsdottir, their son has Leifsson as his last name (patronym) and their daughter Leifsdottir. Both names (or more, if someone has two first names) should be used on first and all subsequent references (when they should be preceded by Mr, Mrs or the appropriate title). A few Icelanders, such as the late *President Kristjan Eldjarn*, do have family names. These are the only people who can be referred to by one name only.

Indonesian Generally straightforward, but:

Abu Bakar Basyir   Muhammadiyah   Syafii Maarif
Jemaah Islamiah   Nahdlatul Ulama

Some Indonesians have only one name. On first mention give it to them unadorned: *Budiono*. Thereafter add the appropriate title: *Mr Budiono*. For those who have several names, be sure to get rid of the correct ones on second and subsequent mentions: *Susilo Bambang Yudhoyono*, for example, becomes *President* (or *Mr*) *Yudhoyono*.

Iranian *Farsi*, an Arabised version of *Parsi* (meaning *of Persia*), is the term Iranians use for their language. In English, the language is properly called *Persian*.

The language spoken in Iran (and Tajikistan) is *Persian*, not *Farsi*.

Here is a list of some words and proper names.

Abadan	Mahdavi-Kani, Ayatollah
Abu Musa	*maqnaeh*
Mahmoud Ahmadinejad	Hossein-Ali Montazeri,
Ahwaz	Ayatollah
Ali Akbar Velayati	Hossein Moussavi
Bahai	Qeshm
Bandar Abbas	Akbar Hashemi Rafsanjani
baseej	Massoud Rajavi
Bushehr	Rezaiyeh
Hojjatieh	Yusef Saanei, Ayatollah
Kermanshah	Abdolkarim Soroush
Keyhan	Strait of Hormuz
Ali Khamenei, Ayatollah	Jalaluddin Taheri, Ayatollah
Kharg island	Taqi Banki
Muhammad Khatami	Tehran
Bandar Khomeini	Tudeh
Khorramshahr	Tumbs
Khuzestan	*velayat-e faqih*
Lavan island	Yahyaoui

Italian Any *De* is likely to be upper case, but there are exceptions (especially among aristocrats such as *Carlo Ripa di Meana*), so check.

Japanese Although the Japanese put the family name first in their own language (*Koizumi Junichiro*), they generally reverse the order in western contexts. So: Junichiro Koizumi, Heizo Takenaka, Shintaro Ishihara, etc.

Korean South Koreans have changed their convention from *Kim Dae Jung* to *Kim Dae-jung*. But North Koreans, at least pending unification, have stuck to *Kim Jong Il*. Kim is the family name.

The South Korean party formed in 2003 is the Uri Party.

Pakistani If the name includes the Islamic definite article *ul*, it should be lower case and without any hyphens: *Zia ul Haq*, *Mahbub ul Haq* (but *Sadruddin*, *Mohieddin* and *Saladin* are single words).

The genitive *e* is hyphenated: *Jamaat-e-Islami*, *Muttahida Majlis-e-Amal*.

Russian Each approach to transliterating Russian has drawbacks. The following rules aim for phonetic accuracy, except when that conflicts with widely accepted usage.

No *y* before *e* after consonants: *Belarus*, *perestroika*, *Oleg*, *Lev*, *Medvedev*. (The actual pronunciation is somewhere between *e* and *ye*.)

1   Where pronunciation dictates, put a *y* before the *a* or *e* at the start of a word or after a vowel:

Aliyev *not* Aliev	Dostoyevsky
Baluyevsky	Yavlinsky
Dudayev	Yevgeny *not* Evgeny

2   Words spelled with *e* in Russian but pronounced *yo* should be spelled *yo*. Thus:

Fyodorov *not* Fedorov
Pyotr *not* Petr
Seleznyov *not* Seleznev

But stick to *Gorbachev*, *Khrushchev* and other famous ones that would otherwise look odd.

3   With words that could end *-i*, *-ii*, *-y* or *-iy*, use *-y* after consonants and *-i* after vowels. This respects both phonetics and common usage.

Georgy	Yury
Gennady	Zhirinovsky
Nizhny	

But:

Bolshoi	Rutskoi
Nikolai	Sergei

Exception (because conventional): *Tolstoy*.

4　Replace *dzh* with *j*.
　　Jokhar, Jugashvili (for Stalin; bowing to convention, give his first name as *Josef*, not Iosif).

5　Prefer *Aleksandr, Viktor, Eduard, Piotr* to Alexander, Victor, Edward, Peter, unless the person involved has clearly chosen an anglicised version. But keep the familiar spelling for historical figures such as *Alexander Nevsky, Alexander Solzhenitsyn* and *Peter the Great*.

Singaporean names have no hyphens and the family name comes first: *Lee Kuan Yew* (thereafter *Mr Lee*).

Spanish Spaniards sometimes have several names, including two surnames. On first mention, spell out in full all the names of such people, if they use both surnames. Thereafter the normal practice is to write the first surname only, so *Joaquín Almunia Amann* becomes *Mr Almunia* on second and subsequent mentions.

Often, though, the second surname is used only by people whose first surname is common, such as *Fernández, López* or *Rodríguez*. To avert confusion with others, they may choose to keep both their surnames when they are referred to as Mr This or Mr That, so *Miguel Ángel Fernández Ordóñez*, for instance, becomes *Mr Fernández Ordóñez*, just as *Andrés Manuel López Obrador* becomes *Mr López Obrador* and *Juan Fernando López Aguilar* becomes *Mr López Aguilar*. A few people, notably *José Luis Rodríguez Zapatero*, choose to have their names shortened to just the second of their surnames, so he becomes *Mr Zapatero*.

Although on marriage Spanish women sometimes informally add their husband's name (after a *de*) to their own, they do not usually change their legal name, merely adopting *Señora* in place of *Señorita*. Unless the woman you are writing about prefers some other title, you should likewise simply change from *Miss* to *Mrs*.

Swiss personal names follow the rules for the two languages mostly spoken in Switzerland: French and German.

Turk, Turkic, Turkmen, Turkoman, etc *see* **placenames.**

Ukrainian After an orgy of retransliteration from their Russian versions, a convention has emerged. Its main rules are these.

1   Since Ukrainian has no g, use *h*: *Hryhory, Heorhy, Ihor* (not *Grigory, Georgy, Igor*). Exception: *Georgy Gongadze.*

2   Render the Ukrainian i as an i, and the И as a y. So *Vital, Kharkiv, Chernivtsi*; but *Volodymyr, Yanukovych, Tymoshenko, Borys, Zhytomyr.* Change words ending *-iy* to *-y* (*Hryhory*).

However, respect the wishes of those Ukrainians who wish to be known by their Russian names, or by an anglicised transliteration of them: *Alexander Morozov.*

Vietnamese names have no hyphens and the family name comes first:

Ho Chi Minh
Tran Duc Luong (thereafter Mr Tran)

See also **placenames.**

neither ... nor *see* **none.**

new words and new uses for old words Part of the strength and vitality of English is its readiness to welcome new words and expressions, and to accept new meanings for old words. Yet such meanings and uses often depart as quickly as they arrived, and early adopters risk looking like super-trendies if they bring them into service too soon. Moreover, to anyone of sensibility some new words are more welcome than others, even if no two people of sensibility would agree on which words should be ushered in and which kept firmly on the doorstep.

Before grabbing the latest usage, ask yourself a few questions. Is it likely to pass the test of time? If not, are you using it to show just how cool you are? Has it already become a cliché? Does it do a job no other word or expression does just as well? Does it rob the language of a useful or well-liked meaning? Is it being adopted to make the writer's prose sharper, crisper, more euphonious, easier to understand – in other words, better? Or to make it seem more with it (yes, that was cool once, just as cool is cool now), more pompous, more bureaucratic or more politically correct – in other words, worse? *See also* **clichés, horrible words, jargon, journalese and slang**.

none usually takes a singular verb. So does *neither* (or *either*) *A nor* (or) *B*, unless B is plural, as in *Neither the Dutchman nor the Danes have done it*, where the verb agrees with the element closest to it. Similarly,

"Come live with me and be my love,
And we will all the pleasures prove
That hills and valleys, dales and fields,
Or woods or steepy mountain yields."
(Christopher Marlowe)

nor means *and not*, so should not be preceded by *and*.

oblivious If you are *oblivious* of something, you are not simply *unaware* of it. You have *forgotten* it or are *absent-mindedly unaware* of it.

offensive In Britain, *offensive* (as an adjective) means *rude*; in America, it often means *attacking*. Similarly, to the British an *offence* is usually a *crime* or *transgression*; to Americans it is often an *offensive*, or the counterpart to a *defence*.

oligopoly Limited competition between a small number of producers or sellers. *See also* **monopoly, monopsony**.

only Put *only* as close as you can to the words it qualifies. Thus *These animals mate only in June*. To say *They only mate in June* implies that in June they do nothing else.

one Try to avoid *one* as a personal pronoun. *You* will often do instead.

onto *On* and *to* should be run together when they are closely linked as in *He pranced onto the stage*. If, however, the sense of the sentence makes the *on* closer to the preceding word, or the *to* closer to the succeeding word, than they are to each other, keep them separate: *He pranced on to the next town* or *He pranced on to wild applause*.

overwhelm means *submerge utterly, crush, bring to sudden ruin*. Majority votes, for example, seldom do any of these things. As for the ethnic Albanians in Kosovo, although 90% of the population, they turned out to be an *overwhelmed majority*, not an *overwhelming* one, until NATO stepped in.

oxymoron An *oxymoron* is not an unintentional contradiction in terms but *a figure of speech in which contradictory terms are deliberately combined*, as in: *bitter-sweet, cruel kindness, friendly fire, jolie laide, open secret, sweet sorrow*, etc.

Pakistani names *see* **names.**

palate, pallet, palette Your *palate*, the roof of your mouth (or your capacity to appreciate food and drink), is best not confused with a *pallet*, a mattress on which you may sleep or a wooden frame for use with fork-lift trucks, still less with a *palette*, on which you may mix paints.

panacea Universal remedy. Beware of cliché usage. *See also* **journalese and slang**.

parliaments Do not confuse one part of a parliament with the whole thing. The Dail is only the lower house of Ireland's parliament, as the Duma is of Russia's and the Lok Sabha is of India's.

partner is useful for those who value gender-neutrality above all else, but others may prefer *boyfriend* or *girlfriend* or even *lover*. And remember that, if you take a *partner for the Gay Gordons*, you may not end up in bed together – just as lawyers and accountants and others *in partnerships* are not necessarily fornicating, even if they are *sleeping partners*.

passive *see* **grammar and syntax** (active, not passive).

peer (noun) is one of those words beloved of sociologists and eagerly co-opted by journalists who want to make their prose seem more authoritative. A *peer* is not a *contemporary, colleague* or *counterpart* but an *equal*.

per caput is the Latin for per head. *Per capita* is the Latin for by heads; it is a term used by lawyers when distributing an inheritance among individuals, rather than among families (*per stirpes*). Unless the context demands this technical expression, never use either *per capita* or *per caput* but *per head* or *per person. See also* **figures**.

per cent is not the same as a *percentage point*. Nothing can fall, or be devalued, by more than 100%. If something trebles, it increases by 200%. If a growth rate increases from 4% to 6%, the rate is two percentage points or 50% faster, not 2%. *See also* **figures**.

percolate means to pass *through*, not *up* or *down*.

phone (noun) is permissible, especially when preceded by *mobile*. But use sparingly, and generally prefer *telephone*.

photo Prefer *photograph*.

placenames In most contexts favour simplicity over precision and use Britain rather than Great Britain or the United Kingdom, and America rather than the United States. ("In all pointed sentences, some degree of accuracy must be sacrificed to conciseness." Dr Johnson)

    Sometimes, however, it may be important to be precise. Remember therefore that *Great Britain* consists of *England*, *Scotland* and *Wales*, which together with *Northern Ireland* (which we generally call *Ulster*, though Ulster strictly includes three counties in *Ireland*) make up the *United Kingdom*.

    Americans: Remember too that, although it is usually all right to talk about the inhabitants of the United States as *Americans*, the term also applies to everyone from Canada to Cape Horn. In a context where other North, Central or South American countries are mentioned, you should write *United States* rather than *America* or *American*, and it may even be necessary to write *United States citizens*.

    EU should not be used without first spelling out the *European Union*. *Europe* and *Europeans* may sometimes be used as shorthand for citizens of countries of the European Union, but be careful: there are plenty of other Europeans too.

    Europe: Note that although the place is *western* (or *eastern*) *Europe*, euphony dictates that the people are *west* (or *east*) *Europeans*.

    Holland, though a nice, short, familiar name, is strictly only two of the 11 provinces that make up *the Netherlands*, and the *Dutch* do not like the misuse of the shorter name. So use *the Netherlands*.

    Ireland is simply *Ireland*. Although it is a republic, it is not the Republic of Ireland. Neither is it, in English, Eire.

Madagascar: *Malagasy* is its adjective and the name of the inhabitants.

Scandinavia is primarily Norway and Sweden, but the term is often used to include Denmark, Iceland, Norway and Sweden, which, with Finland, make up the *Nordic countries*.

USA and *US* are not to be used (if they were they would spatter the paper), except in charts and as part of an official name (eg, *US Steel*).

Do not use the names of capital cities as synonyms for their governments. *Britain will send a gunboat* is fine, but *London will send a gunboat* suggests that this will be the action of the people of London alone. To write *Washington and Moscow now differ only in their approach to Havana* is absurd.

Note that a country is *it*, not *she*.

changes of name Where countries have made it clear that they wish to be called by a new (or an old) name, respect their requests. Thus:

Burkina Faso	Sri Lanka
Côte d'Ivoire	Thailand
Myanmar	Zimbabwe

Zaire has now reverted to *Congo*. In contexts where there can be no confusion with the ex-French country of the same name, plain *Congo* will do. But if there is a risk of misunderstanding, call it the *Democratic Republic of Congo* (never *DRC*). The other Congo can be *Congo-Brazzaville* if necssary. The river is now also the *Congo*. The people of either country are also *Congolese*.

Former Soviet republics that are now independent countries include:

Belarus (*not* Belorus or Belorussia), Belarusian (adjective)
Kazakhstan
Moldova (*not* Moldavia)
Tajikistan
Turkmenistan (*see* **Turk, Turkic, Turkmen, Turkoman**, page 114)

Kyrgyzstan is the name of the country. Its adjective is *Kyrgyzstani*, which is also the name of one of its inhabitants. But *Kirgiz* is the noun and adjective of the language, and the adjective of Kirgiz people outside Kyrgyzstan.

Follow local practice when a country changes the names of rivers, towns, etc, within it. Thus:

Almaty *not* Alma Ata
Chemnitz *not* Karl-Marx-Stadt
Chennai *not* Madras
Chernihiv *not* Chernigov
Chur *not* Coire
Kyiv *not* Kiev
Kolkata *not* Calcutta
Lviv *not* Lvov
Mumbai *not* Bombay
Nizhny Novgorod *not* Gorky
Papua *not* Irian Jaya
Polokwane *not* Pietersburg
Yangon *not* Rangoon
St Petersburg *not* Leningrad
Timor-Leste (*not* East Timor)
Tshwane is the new name for the area round Pretoria but not yet for the city itself.

definite article Do not use the definite article before:

Krajina	Sudan
Lebanon	Transkei
Piedmont	Ukraine
Punjab	

But:

Los Angeles	Le Havre
the Caucasus	the Maghreb
the Gambia	the Netherlands
The Hague	La Paz

English forms are preferred when they are in common use:

Andalusia	Corunna	Genoa
Archangel (*not* Archangelsk *or* Arkhangelsk)	Cracow	Hanover
	Dagestan	Leghorn
	Dnieper	Majorca
Cassel (*not* Kassel)	Dniester (*but* Transdniestria)	Milan
Castile		Minorca
Catalonia (Catalan)	Dusseldorf (*not* Düsseldorf)	Minsk
Cologne		Munich
Cordoba	Florence	Naples
Corinth	Geneva	Nuremberg

Odessa
Pomerania
Salonika (*not*
   Thessaloniki)
Saragossa

Saxony (*and*
   Lower Saxony,
   Saxony-Anhalt)
Sebastopol
Seville

Turin
Zurich (*not*
   Zürich)

Use British English rather than American – *Rockefeller Centre, Pearl Harbour* – unless the placename is part of a company's name, such as *Rockefeller Center Properties Inc.*

The final *s* sometimes added by English-speakers to *Lyon, Marseille* and *Tangier* now seems precious, so use the *s*-less form.

some spellings

Abkhazia
Ajaria (*not* Adjaria)
Argentina (adj and people
   Argentine, *not*
   Argentinian)
Ashgabat
Azerbaijan
Baden-Württemberg
Baghdad
Bahamas (Bahamian)
Bahrain
Basel
Bengalooru
Beqaa
Bermuda, Bermudian
Bern
Bophuthatswana
Bosporus (not Bosphorus)
British Columbia
Brittany, Breton
Cameroon
Cape Town
Caribbean
Catalan
Chechnya
Cincinnati
Colombia (South America)
Columbia (university, District
   of)

the Comoros
Côte d'Ivoire, Ivorian
Czech Republic; Czech Lands
Dar es Salaam
Dhaka
Djibouti
Dominica (Caribbean island)
Dominican Republic (part of
   another island)
El Salvador, Salvadorean
Falluja
Gaza Strip (and City)
Gettysburg
Gothenburg
Grozny
Guantánamo
Gujarat, Gujarati
Guyana (*but* French Guiana)
Gweru (*not* Gwelo)
Hercegovina
Hong Kong
Ingushetia
Issyk-Kul
Jeddah
KaNgwane
Kathmandu
Kinmen (*not* Quemoy)
KwaNdebele
KwaZulu-Natal

Kwekwe (*not* Que Que)
Laos, Lao (*not* Laotian)
Ljubljana
Londonderry (Derry also permissible)
Luhansk
Luxembourg
Macau
Mafikeng
Mauritania
Middlesbrough
Mpumalanga (formerly Eastern Transvaal)
Nagorno-Karabakh
Nepal, Nepali (*not* Nepalese)
North Rhine-Westphalia
Ouagadougou
Philippines (the people are Filipinos and Filipinas)
Phnom Penh
Pittsburgh
Putumayo
Pyrenees, Pyrenean
Quebec, Quebecker (*but* Parti Québécois)

Reykjavik
Rheims
Romania
Rwanda, Rwandan (*not* Rwandese)
Sana'a
St Petersburg
Salzburg
São Paulo
Sindh
Srebrenica
Strasbourg
Suriname
Taipei
Tehran
Teesside
Tigray, Tigrayan
Uffizi
Uzbekistan
Valletta
Yangzi
Zepa
Zepce

See also **capitals** (places).

Turk, Turkic, Turkmen, Turkoman, etc

Turk, Turkish: noun and adjective of Turkey.

Turkoman, Turkomans: member, members, of a branch of the Turkish race mostly living in the region east of the Caspian sea once known as Turkestan and parts of Iran and Afghanistan; *Turkoman* may also be the language of the Turkmen and an adjective.

Turkic: adjective applied to one of the branches of the Ural-Altaic family of languages – Uighur, Kazan Tatar, Kirgiz.

Turkmen: Turkoman or Turkomans living in Turkmenistan; adjective pertaining to them.

Turkmenistani: adjective of Turkmenistan; also a native of that country.

plants For the spelling of the Latin names of animals, plants, etc, *see* **Latin names**.

plurals *see* **spelling**. For plural nouns, *see* **grammar and syntax**.

political correctness Avoid, if you can, giving gratuitous offence (*see* **euphemisms**): you risk losing your readers, or at least their goodwill, and therefore your arguments. But pandering to every plea for politically correct terminology may make your prose unreadable, and therefore also unread.

So strike a balance. If you judge that a group wishes to be known by a particular term, that the term is widely understood and that using any other would seem odd, old-fashioned or offensive, then use it. Context may be important: *Coloured* is a common term in South Africa for people of mixed race; it is not considered derogatory. Elsewhere it may be. Remember that both times and terms change: expressions that were in common use a few decades ago are now odious. Nothing is to be gained by casually insulting your readers.

But do not labour to avoid imaginary insults, especially if the effort does violence to the language. So avoid terms like *the non-disabled person* used (on BBC Radio 3) to mean *normal person*. Some people, such as the members of the Task-force on Bias-Free Language of the Association of American University Presses, believe that *ghetto-blaster* is "offensive as a stereotype of African-American culture", that it is invidious to speak of a *normal* child, that *massacre* should not be used "to refer to a successful American Indian raid or battle victory against white colonisers and invaders", and that the use of the term *cretin* is distressing. They want, they say, to avoid "victimisation" and to get "the person before the disability". The intent may be admirable, but they are unduly sensitive, often inventing slights where none exists. The term *cretin* came into use as a way of acknowledging the essential humanity of a physically deformed or intellectually subnormal person. It is now used for a definable medical condition. The aversion to *cretin* may arise from its slight similarity to *cripple*, a plain word now almost universally discarded in favour of the euphemistic *physically handicapped* or *disabled*.

Thomas Bowdler provides a cautionary example. His version of Shakespeare, produced in 1818 using "judicious" paraphrase and expurgation, was designed to be read by men to their families so that no one would be offended or embarrassed. In doing so, he gave his name to an insidious form of censorship (bowdlerism).

Some people believe the possibility of giving offence, causing embarrassment, lowering self-esteem, reinforcing stereotypes, perpetuating prejudice, victimising, marginalising or discriminating to be more important than stating the truth, never mind the chance of doing so with any verve or panache. They are wrong. Do not self-bowdlerise your prose. You may be neither Galileo nor Salman Rushdie, but you too may sometimes be right to cause offence. Your first duty is to the truth.

he, she, they You also have a duty to grammar. The struggle to be gender-neutral rests on a misconception about gender, a grammatical convention to make words masculine, feminine or neuter. Since English is unusual in assigning few genders to nouns other than those relating to people (ships are exceptions), feminists have come to argue that language should be gender-neutral.

This would be a forlorn undertaking in most tongues, and even in English it presents difficulties. It may be no tragedy that *policemen* are now almost always *police officers* and *firemen firefighters*, but to call *chairmen chairs* serves chiefly to remind everyone that the world of committees and those who make it go round are largely devoid of humour. Avoid also *chairpersons* (*chairwoman* is permissible), *humankind* and the *person in the street* – ugly expressions all.

It is no more demeaning to women to use the words *actress*, *ballerina* or *seamstress* than *goddess*, *princess* or *queen*. (Similarly, you should feel as free to separate *Siamese twins* or *welsh* on debts – at your own risk – as you would to go on a *Dutch treat*, pass through *french windows*, or play *Russian roulette*. Note, though, that you risk being *dogged* by *catty* language police.)

If you believe it is "exclusionary" or insulting to women to use *he* in a general sense, you can rephrase some sentences in the plural. Thus *Instruct the reader without lecturing him* may be put as *Instruct readers without lecturing them*. But some sentences resist this treatment: *Find a good teacher and take his advice* is not easily rendered gender-neutral. So do not be ashamed of sometimes using *man* to include *women*, or making *he* do for *she*.

And, so long as you are not insensitive in other ways, few

women will be offended if you restrain yourself from putting *or she* after every *he*.

He or she which hath no stomach to this fight,
Let him or her depart; his or her passport shall be made,
And crowns for convoy put into his or her purse:
We would not die in that person's company
That fears his or her fellowship to die with us.

In some contexts, though, *she* can be a substitute for *he*:

That ever was thrall, now is he free;
That ever was small, now great is she;
Now shall God deem both thee and me
Unto His bliss if we do well.
(15th-century carol)

Avoid, above all, the sort of scrambled syntax that people adopt because they cannot bring themselves to use a singular pronoun:

We can't afford to squander anyone's talents, whatever colour their skin is.

When someone takes their own life, they leave their loved ones with an agonising legacy of guilt.

There's a child somewhere in Birmingham and all across the country and needs somebody to put their arm around them and to say: "I love you; you're a part of America." (George Bush)

See also **ethnic groups, gender, tribe.**

populace is a term for the *common people*, not a synonym for the *population*.

positive means *definitely laid down, beyond possibility of doubt, absolute, fully convinced* or *greater than zero*. It does not mean *good*. *It was a positive meeting* probably means *It was a good,* or *fruitful, meeting.*

practical, practicable *Practical* means *useful; practicable* means *feasible.*

pre- is often unnecessary as a prefix, as in *pre-announced, precondition, pre-prepared, pre-cooked.* If it seems to be serving a function, try making use of a word such as *already* or *earlier*: *Here's one I cooked earlier.*

Pre-owned is *second-hand.*

premier (as a noun) should be confined to the first ministers of Canadian provinces, German *Länder* and other subnational states. Do not use it as a synonym for the prime minister of a country.

presently means *soon*, not *at present.* ("Presently Kep opened the door of the shed, and let out Jemima Puddle-Duck." Beatrix Potter)

press, pressure, pressurise *Pressurise* is what you want in an aircraft, but not in an argument or encounter where persuasion is being employed – the verb you want there is *press.* Use *pressure* only as a noun.

prevaricate, procrastinate *Prevaricate* means evade the truth; *procrastinate* means delay. ("Procrastination – or punctuality, if you are Oscar Wilde – is the thief of time.")

pristine means *original* or *former*; it does not mean *clean.*

proactive Not a pretty word: try *active* or *energetic.*

process Some writers see their prose in industrial terms: *education* becomes an *education process*, elections an *electoral process*, development a *development process*, writing a *writing process.* If you follow this fashion, do not be surprised if readers switch off.

prodigal If you are *prodigal*, that does not mean you are *welcomed home* or *taken back without recrimination.* It means you have *squandered your patrimony.*

proofreading *see* Part 3.

propaganda (which is singular) means a *systematic effort to spread doctrine or opinions.* It is not a synonym for *lies.*

protagonist means the *chief actor* or *combatant.* If you are referring to several people, they cannot all be protagonists.

protest By all means *protest your innocence*, or *your intention to write* *good English*, if you are making a declaration. But if you are making a complaint or objection, you must *protest at* or *against* it.

pry Unless you mean *peer* or *peep*, the word you probably should be using is *prise*.

public schools in Britain, the places where fee-paying parents send their children; in the United States, the places where they don't.

punctuation Some guidelines on common problems.

apostrophes

1   With singular words and names that end in s use the normal possessive ending *'s*:

boss's	St James's
caucus's	Jones's
Delors's	Shanks's

2   After plurals that do not end in s also use *'s*: *children's, Frenchmen's, media's*.

3   Use the ending s' on plurals that end in s: *Danes', bosses', Joneses'*.

And on plural names that take a singular verb:

Barclays'	Goldman Sachs'
Cisco Systems'	Reuters'

5   Some plural nouns, although singular in other respects, such as the United States, the United Nations, the Philippines, have a plural possessive apostrophe:

Who will be the United States' next president?

6   *Lloyd's* (the insurance market): try to avoid using as a possessive; like Christie's and Sotheby's it poses an insoluble problem.

7   *Achilles heel*: the vulnerable part of the hero of the Trojan war.

8   Decades do not have apostrophes: *the 1990s*.

9   Phrases like *two weeks' time, four days' march, six months' leave* need apostrophes. So do those involving *worth*,

when it follows a quantity or other measurement: *three months' worth of imports, a manifesto's worth of insincerity* (*see also* **hyphens**, page 77).

10   People:

people's = of (the) people
peoples' = of peoples

See also **grammar and syntax** (false possessive).

brackets If a whole sentence is within brackets, put the full stop inside. Square brackets should be used for interpolations in direct quotations: "*Let them [the poor] eat cake.*" To use ordinary brackets implies that the words inside them were part of the original text from which you are quoting.

colons Use a colon "to deliver the goods that have been invoiced in the preceding words" (Fowler).

They brought presents: gold, frankincense and oil at $100 a barrel.

Use a colon before a whole quoted sentence, but not before a quotation that begins in mid-sentence.

She said: "It will never work." He retorted that it had "always worked before".

commas Use commas as an aid to understanding. Too many in one sentence can be confusing.

1   It is not always necessary to put a comma after a short phrase at the start of a sentence if no natural pause exists:

That night she took a tumble.

2   But a breath, and so a comma, is needed after longer passages:

When day broke and she was able at last to see what had happened, she realised she had fallen through the roof and into the Big Brother house.

3   Use two commas, or none at all, when inserting a clause in the middle of a sentence. Thus, do not write:

Use two commas, or none at all when inserting … or

Use two commas or none at all, when inserting …

Similarly, two commas or none at all are needed with constructions like:

And, though he denies it, he couldn't tell a corncrake from a cornflake ...

But, when Bush came to Shuv, he found it wasn't a town, just a Hebrew word for Return.

4 American states: commas are essential (and often left out) after the names of American states when these are written as though they were part of an address: *Kansas City, Kansas, proves that even Kansas City needn't always be Missourible* (Ogden Nash). If the clause ends with a bracket, but is not the end of a sentence, which is not uncommon (this one does), the bracket should be followed by a comma.

5 For sense: commas can alter the sense of a sentence. To write *Mozart's 40th symphony, in G minor,* with commas indicates that this symphony was written in G minor. Without commas, *Mozart's 40th symphony in G minor* suggests he wrote 39 other symphonies in G minor.

6 Lists: do not put a comma before *and* at the end of a sequence of items unless one of the items includes another *and*. Thus:

The doctor suggested an aspirin, half a grapefruit and a cup of broth. But he ordered scrambled eggs, whisky and soda, and a selection from the trolley.

7 Question-marks: do not put commas after question-marks, even when they would be separated by inverted commas:

"May I have a second helping?" he asked.

8 Quotations: within a sentence a quotation needs to be preceded by a comma, or a colon, or a word such as *that* (or *if, because, whether* etc), if it is an entire sentence. The first quoted word should also have an initial capital. Thus *The doctor responded, "You'll probably be better in the morning, or dead," before sampling a crème caramel.* If the words quoted are not an entire sentence, neither comma nor capital is needed: *The doctor responded that he would "probably be better in the morning, or dead," before sampling a crème caramel.* In this example, it is known that the final

quoted word was followed by a punctuation mark – a full stop, converted in the quotation into a comma – so the final comma is placed within the inverted commas. If, however, it is not known whether the quoted words constituted a full sentence, assume that the quotation is unpunctuated and put the appropriate punctuation mark outside the inverted commas: *Having impaled himself with a handle-bar in the back of the cab, he was heard to say he "now realised what was meant by fatal attraction"*.

If you want to quote a full sentence and precede it with the word *that* (etc), no comma is needed before the inverted commas, but the first quoted word still needs an initial capital: *On learning that he was only scratched, her comment was that "Next time I hope Cupid's dart will be tipped with curare."*

See also **inverted commas** *below.*

dashes You can use dashes in pairs for parenthesis, but not more than one pair per sentence, ideally not more than one pair per paragraph.

"Use a dash to introduce an explanation, amplification, paraphrase, particularisation or correction of what immediately precedes it. Use it to gather up the subject of a long sentence. Use it to introduce a paradoxical or whimsical ending to a sentence. Do not use it as a punctuation maid-of-all-work." (Gowers)

Do not use a parenthetical dash as a catch-all punctuation device when a comma, colon, etc could be used.

full stops Use plenty. They keep sentences short. This helps the reader. Do not use full stops in abbreviations or at the end of headings and subheadings.

inverted commas (quotation marks) Use single ones only for quotations within quotations. Thus:

"When I say 'immediately', I mean some time before April," said the builder.

For the relative placing of quotation marks and punctuation, follow Oxford rules. Thus, if an extract ends with a full stop or question-mark, put the punctuation before the closing inverted commas.

His maxim was that "love follows laughter." In this spirit came his opening gambit: "What's the difference between a buffalo and a bison?"

If a complete sentence in quotes comes at the end of a larger sentence, the final stop should be inside the inverted commas. Thus:

The answer was, "You can't wash your hands in a buffalo." She replied, "Your jokes are execrable."

If the quotation does not include any punctuation, the closing inverted commas should precede any punctuation marks that the sentence requires. Thus:

She had already noticed that the "young man" looked about as young as the New Testament is new. Although he had been described as "fawnlike in his energy and playfulness", "a stripling with all the vigour and freshness of youth", and even as "every woman's dream toyboy", he struck his companion-to-be as the kind of old man warned of by her mother as "not safe in taxis". Where, now that she needed him, was "Mr Right"?

When a quotation is broken off and resumed after such words as *he said*, ask yourself whether it would naturally have had any punctuation at the point where it is broken off. If the answer is yes, a comma is placed within the quotation marks to represent this. Thus:

"If you'll let me see you home," he said, "I think I know where we can find a cab."

The comma after home belongs to the quotation and so comes within the inverted commas, as does the final full stop.

But if the words to be quoted are continuous, without punctuation at the point where they are broken, the comma should be outside the inverted commas. Thus:

"My bicycle", she assured him, "awaits me."

Do not use quotation marks unnecessarily:

Her admirer described his face as a "finely chiselled work of art"; she wrote in her diary that it looked more like a "collapsed lung".

Note that the Bible contains no quotation marks, with no consequent confusions.

question-marks Except in sentences that include a question in inverted commas, question-marks always come at the end of the sentence. Thus:

Where could he get a drink, he wondered?

Had Zimri peace, who slew his master?

semi-colons Use them to mark a pause longer than a comma and shorter than a full stop. Don't overdo them.

Use them to distinguish phrases listed after a colon if commas will not do the job clearly. Thus:

They agreed on only three points: the ceasefire should be immediate; it should be internationally supervised, preferably by the AU; and a peace conference should be held, either in Geneva or in Ouagadougou.

question-marks *see* **punctuation**.

quite In America, *quite* is usually an intensifying adverb similar to *altogether, entirely* or *very*; in Britain, depending on the emphasis, the tone of voice and the adjective that follows, it usually means *fairly, moderately* or *reasonably*, and often damns with faint praise.

quotes Be sparing with quotes. Direct quotes should be used when either the speaker or what was said is surprising, or when the words used are particularly pithy or graphic. Otherwise you can probably paraphrase more concisely. The most pointless quote is the inconsequential remark attributed to a nameless source: *"Everyone wants to be in on the act,"* says one high-ranking civil servant.

For *quotation marks* (inverted commas), *see* **punctuation**.

real Is it really necessary? When used to mean *after taking inflation into account*, it is legitimate. In other contexts (*Investors are showing real interest in the country, but Colombians wonder if real prosperity will ever arrive*) it is often better left out.

rebut, refute *Rebut* means *repel* or *meet in argument*. *Refute*, which is stronger, means *disprove*. Neither should be used as a synonym for *deny*. "Shakespeare never has six lines together without a fault. Perhaps you may find seven: but this does not refute my general assertion." (Samuel Johnson)

red and blue In Britain, colours that are associated with socialism and conservatism respectively; in the United States, colours that are associated with Republicans and Democrats respectively.

redact in Latin means *bring back*. Do not use it, as is now fashionable, to mean the opposite: *obscure, blot out, obliterate*. In fact, do not use it at all.

reduce, diminish, lessen, shrink are not interchangeable. *Reduce* is transitive, so must be followed by a noun. *Diminish* and *shrink* can be transitive or intransitive. So can *lessen*, though it is usually used before a noun.

reductive is a technical term in chemistry and philosophy, now often dropped into general conversation by pretentious people anxious to impress. It is seldom clear what they mean. Avoid.

references *see* **footnotes, sources, references** in Part 3.

regrettably means *to be regretted*. Do not confuse with *regretfully*, used of someone showing regret.

relationship is a long word often better replaced by *relations*. *The two* *countries hope for a better relationship* means *The two countries hope for better relations.* But *relationship* is an appropriate word for two people in a close friendship.

report on not *into.*

reshuffle, resupply *Shuffle* and *supply* will do, except for British Cabinets, which are *reshuffled* from time to time.

resources, resourceful *Resourceful* is a useful word; the term *natural resources*, less satisfactory, also has its merits. Most other uses of *resource* tend to be vile. The word is entirely at home in the following sentence, taken from an advertisement placed by Skill for Business (2005): "Sector Skills Councils ... assess what resource is already out there, and then create comprehensive deals with supply-side partners to fill skills gaps and shortages." Beware.

revert means *return to* or *go back to*, as in *The garden has reverted to wilderness.* It does not mean *come back to* or *get back to*, as in *I'll give you an answer as soon as I can.*

Richter scale Beloved of journalists, the Richter scale is unknown to seismologists. The strength of an earthquake is its *magnitude*, so say *an earthquake of magnitude 8.9*. See **earthquakes** in Part 3.

ring, wring (verbs) bells are rung; hands are wrung. Both may be seen at weddings.

Roma is the name of the people. Their language is *Romany*. Remember that *Sinti* are also gypsies.

run In countries with a presidential system you may *run* for office. In those with a parliamentary one, you *stand*.

Russian names *see* **names.**

S

same is often superfluous. If your sentence contains *on the same day that*, try *on the day that*.

scotch To *scotch* means to *disable*, not to *destroy*. ("*We have scotched the snake, not killed it.*") The people may also be *Scotch*, *Scots* or *Scottish*; choose as you like. *Scot-free* means free from payment of a fine (or punishment), not *free from Scotsmen*.

second-biggest (third-oldest, fourth-wisest, fifth-commonest, etc) Think before you write.

> *Apart from New York, a Bramley is the second-biggest apple in the world. Other than home-making and parenting, prostitution is the third-oldest profession. After Tom, Dick and Harriet, Henry I was the fourth-wisest fool in Christendom. Besides justice, prudence, temperance and fortitude, the fifth-commonest virtue of the Goths was punctuality.*

None of these sentences should contain the ordinal (*second-* , *third-* , *fourth-* , *fifth-* , etc).

sector Try *industry* instead or, for example, *banks* instead of *banking sector*.

semi-colons *see* **punctuation.**

sensual, sensuous *Sensual* means *carnal* or *voluptuous*. *Sensuous* means *pertaining to aesthetic appreciation*, without any implication of lasciviousness.

sequestered, sequestrated *Sequestered* means *secluded*. *Sequestrated* means *confiscated* or *made bankrupt*.

ship A ship is feminine.

short words Use them. They are often Anglo-Saxon rather than Latin in origin. They are easy to spell and easy to understand. Thus prefer:

about *to* approximately	plant *to* facility
after *to* following	set up *to* establish
but *to* however	show *to* demonstrate
enough *to* sufficient	spending *to* expenditure
let *to* permit	take part *to* participate
make *to* manufacture	use *to* utilise

Underdeveloped countries are often better described as *poor*. *Substantive* often means *real* or *big*. "Short words are best and the old words when short are best of all." (Winston Churchill)

simplistic Prefer *simple-minded, naive*.

Singaporean names *see* **names**.

singular or plural? *see* **grammar and syntax**.

skills are turning up all over the place – in learning skills, thinking skills, teaching skills – instead of *the ability to*. *He has the skills* probably means *He can*.

skyrocketed *Rocketed*, not *skyrocketed*.

slither, sliver As a noun, *slither* is scree. As a verb, it means *slide*. If you mean a *slice*, the word you want is *sliver*.

sloppy writing Use words with care.

If *This door is alarmed*, does its hair stand on end? If this envelope says *Urgent: dated material*, is it really too old-fashioned to be worth reading? Is a *handicapped toilet* really *faultily designed* or *carrying extra weight*? Is *offensive marketing* just rude salesmanship?

More serious difficulties may arise with *indicted war criminals*. As their lawyers could one day remind you, these may turn out to be *innocent people accused of war crimes*.

Some familiar words may cause trouble. When Gordon Brown wrote in the *Guardian*, "No one can *underestimate* the scale of the challenge climate change represents," he presumably meant just the opposite. The man who said, "Now that we're all part of a global world," merely conjured up images of a flat earth.

A *heart condition* is usually a *bad heart*. A *near miss* is probably a *near hit*. *Positive thoughts* (held by long-suffering creditors, according to *The Economist*) presumably means *optimism*, just as a *negative* report is probably a *critical* report. *Industrial action* is usually *industrial inaction*, *industrial disruption* or a *strike*. A *courtesy call* is generally a *sales offer* or an *uninvited visit*. A *substantially finished* bridge is an *unfinished* bridge. Someone with *high name-recognition* is *well known*. Something with *reliability problems* probably *does not work*. If yours is a *live audience*, what would a dead one be like?

And what is an *ethics violation*? An error of judgment? A crime? A moral lapse?

See also **unnecessary words**.

small capitals   *see* **abbreviations** (small caps usage).

smart   generally means *well dressed*, but *smart cards*, *smart sanctions* and *smart weapons*, etc may be allowed as terms of art.

social security   in America, *Social Security* means *pensions* and should be capitalised. Elsewhere it usually means *state benefits* more generally, which are called *welfare* in the United States.

soft   is an adverb as well as an adjective and a noun. *Softly* is also an adverb. You can speak softly and carry a big stick, but if you have a quiet voice you are *soft* – not *softly* – *spoken*.

soi-disant   means *self-styled*, not *so-called*.

sources   *see* **footnotes, sources, references** in Part 3.

Spanish names   *see* **names**.

specific   A *specific* is a *medicine*, not a *detail*.

spelling   Use British English rather than American English or any other kind. Sometimes, however, this injunction will clash with the rule that people and companies should be called what they want to be called, short of festooning themselves with titles. If it does, adopt American (or Canadian or other local) spelling when it is used in the name of an American (etc) company or private organisation (*Alcan Aluminum, Carter Center, Pulverizing Services Inc, Travelers Insurance*), but not when it is used for a place or government institution (*Pearl Harbour, Department of Defence, Department* *of Labour*). The principle behind this ruling is that placenames are habitually changed from foreign languages into English: *Deutschland* becomes *Germany*, *München* Munich, *Torino* Turin, etc. And to respect the local spelling of government institutions would present difficulties: a sentence containing both the *Department of Labor* and the *secretary of labour*, or the *Defense Department* and the *need for a strong defence*, would look unduly odd. That oddity will arise nonetheless if you have to explain that *Rockefeller Center Properties is in charge of Rockefeller Centre*, but with luck that will not happen too often. *See* **placenames**.

The Australian *Labor Party* should be spelt without a *u* not only because it is not a government institution but also because the Australians spell it that way, even though they spell *labour* as the British do.

s spelling Use *-ise, -isation* (*realise, organisation*) throughout. But please do not *hospitalise*.

common problems

abattoir
abut, abutted, abutting
accommodate
acknowledgment
acquittal, acquitted,
  acquitting
adrenalin
adviser, advisory
aeon
aeroplane
aesthetic
aficionado
Afrikaans (the language),
  Afrikaner (the person)
ageing (*but* caging, paging,
  raging, waging)
agri-business (*not* agro-
  business)
aircraft, airliner
algorithm
al-Qaeda
amiable
amid (*not* amidst)

amok (*not* amuck)
among (*not* amongst)
annex (verb), annexe (noun)
antecedent
appal, appals, appalling,
  appalled
aqueduct
aquifer
arbitrager
artefact
asinine
balk (*not* baulk)
balloted, balloting
bandanna
bandwagon
battalion
bellwether
benefiting, benefited
biased
bicentenary (noun, *not*
  bicentennial)
billeting, billeted
blanketing, blanketed

block (*never* bloc)
blowzy (*not* blousy)
bogey (bogie is on a
 locomotive)
borsch
braggadocio
brethren
bumf
bused, busing (keep bussing
 for kissing)
by-election, bylaw, bypass,
 by-product, byword
bye (in sport)
caddie (golf), caddy (tea)
caesium
cannon (gun), canon
 (standard, criterion,
 clergyman)
cappuccino
carcass
caviar
chancy
channelling, channelled
checking account (spell it
 thus when explaining
 to Americans a current
 account, which is to be
 preferred)
choosy
cipher
clubable (coined, and spelled
 thus, by Dr Johnson)
colour, colouring, colourist
combating, combated
commemorate
connection
consensus
cooled, cooler, coolly
coral (stuff found in sea),
 corral (cattle pen)
coruscate
cosseted, cosseting

defendant
dependant (person),
 dependent (adj)
depository (unless referring
 to American depositary
 receipts)
desiccate, desiccation
detente (*not* détente)
dexterous (*not* dextrous)
dignitary
dilapidate
disk (in a computer context),
 otherwise disc (including
 compact disc)
dispatch (*not* despatch)
dispel, dispelling
distil, distiller
divergences
doppelganger(s)
doveish
dryer, dryly
dullness
dwelt
dyeing (colour)
dyke
ecstasy
embarrass (*but* harass)
encyclopedia
enroll, enrolment
ensure (make certain), insure
 (against risks)
enthrall
extrovert
farther (distance), further
 (additional)
favour, favourable
ferreted
fetus (*not* foetus, misformed
 from the Latin fetus)
field-marshal (soldier),
 Marshall Field's (Chicago
 department store)

Filipino, Filipina (person), Philippine (adj of the Philippines)

filleting, filleted

flotation

flyer, frequent flyer, high-flyer

focused, focusing

forbear (abstain), forebear (ancestor)

forbid, forbade

foreboding

foreclose

forefather

forestall

forewarn

forgather

forgo (do without), forego (precede)

forsake

forswear, forsworn

fuelled

-ful, not -full (thus armful, bathful, handful, etc)

fulfil, fulfilling

fullness

fulsome

funnelling, funnelled

furore

gallivant

gelatine

glamour, glamorise, glamorous

graffito, graffiti

gram (not gramme)

grey

guerrilla

gulag

Gurkha

gypsy

haj

hallo (not hello)

harass (*but* embarrass)

hiccup (*not* hiccough)

high-tech

Hizbullah

honour, honourable

hotch-potch

humour, humorist, humorous

hurrah (*not* hooray)

idiosyncrasy

impostor

impresario

inadvertent

incur, incurring

innocuous

inoculate

inquire, inquiry (*not* enquire, enquiry)

install, instalment, installation

instil, instilling

intransigent

jail (not gaol)

Janjaweed

jewellery (*not* jewelry)

judgment

kilogram or kilo (*not* kilogramme)

labelling, labelled

laissez-faire

lama (priest), llama (beast)

lambast (*not* lambaste)

launderette

leukaemia

levelled

libelling, libelled

licence (noun), license (verb), licensee (person with a licence)

limited

linchpin, lynch law

liquefy

literal
littoral (shore)
logarithm
loth (reluctant), loathe (hate),
  loathsome
low-tech
madrassa
manilla envelope, *but*
  Manila, capital of the
  Philippines
manoeuvre, manoeuvring
marshal (noun and verb),
  marshalled
mayonnaise
medieval
mêlée
meter (a measuring tool),
  metre (metric measure,
  meter in American)
mileage
millennium, but
  millenarian
minuscule
moccasin
modelling, modelled
mould
Muslim (*not* Moslem)
naivety
'Ndrangheta
nonplussed
nought (for numerals),
  otherwise naught
obbligato
occur, occurring
oesophagus
oestrus (oestrogen, etc)
optics (optician,
  etc) ophthalmic
  (ophthalmology, etc)
paediatric, paediatrician
palaeontology,
  palaeontologist

panel, panelled
paraffin
parallel, paralleled
pastime
pavilion
phoney (*not* phony)
piggyback (*not* pickaback)
plummeted, plummeting
poky
practice (noun), practise
  (verb)
praesidium (*not* presidium)
predilection
preferred (preferring, *but*
  proffered)
preventive (*not* preventative)
pricey
primeval
principal (head, loan; or adj),
  principle (abstract noun)
proffered (proffering, *but*
  preferred)
profited
program (only in a computer
  context), otherwise
  programme
prophecy (noun), prophesy
  (verb)
protester
Pushtu (language), Pushtun
  (people)
pygmy
pzazz
queuing
rack, racked, racking (as in
  racked with pain, nerve-
  racking)
racket
rankle
rarefy
razzmatazz
recur, recurrent, recurring

regretted, regretting
restaurateur
resuscitate
rhythm
rivet (riveted, riveter, riveting)
rococo
ropy
rottweiler
rumoured
sacrilegious
sanatorium
savannah
seize
shaky
sharia
shenanigans
sheriff
Shia (noun and adj), Shias, Shiism
shibboleth
Sibylline
siege
sieve
siphon (*not* syphon)
skulduggery
smelt
smidgen (*not* smidgeon)
smoky
smooth (both noun and verb)
snigger (*not* snicker)
sobriquet
somersault
soothe
souped up
soyabean
specialty (only in context of medicine, steel and chemicals), otherwise speciality
sphinx
spoilt

squirrelled
stanch (verb)
staunch (adj)
storey (floor)
straitjacket and strait-laced *but* straight-faced
stratagem
strategy
supersede
Sunni, Sunnis
swap (not swop)
swathe
synonym
Taliban (plural)
tariff
Tatar (*not* Tartar)
taoiseach (*but* prefer prime minister, or leader)
threshold
titbits
titillate
tonton-macoutes
tormentor
trade union, trade unions (*but* Trades Union Congress)
transatlantic, transpacific
transferred, transferring
travelled
tricolor
trouper (as in old trouper)
tsar
tyre
unnecessary
unparalleled
untrammelled
vaccinate
vacillate
vermilion
wacky
wagon (*not* waggon)
weasel, weaselly

while *not* whilst
wiggle (*not* wriggle) room
wilful
wisteria

withhold
yarmulke (prefer to *kippah*)
yogurt

-able

debatable	indictable	tradable
dispensable	indispensable	unmissable
disputable	indistinguishable	unmistakable
forgivable	lovable	unshakable
imaginable	movable	unusable
implacable	ratable	usable
indescribable	salable (but prefer sellable)	

-eable

bridgeable	manageable	traceable
changeable	noticeable	unenforceable
knowledgeable	serviceable	unpronounceable
likeable	sizeable	

-ible

accessible	inadmissible	irresistible
convertible	indestructible	permissible
digestible	investible	submersible
dismissible		

plurals No rules here. The spelling of the following plurals may have been decided by either practice or derivation.

-a

consortia	memoranda	sanatoria
corrigenda	millennia	spectra
data	phenomena	strata
media	quanta	

-ae

amoebae	formulae
antennae	lacunae

-eaus

bureaus   plateaus

-eaux

chateaux   tableaux

-fs, -efs

dwarfs   still-lifes
oafs   turfs
roofs

-i

alumni   nuclei   termini
bacilli   stimuli

-oes

archipelagoes   haloes   potatoes
buffaloes   heroes   salvoes
cargoes   innuendoes   tomatoes
desperadoes   mangoes   tornadoes
dominoes   mementoes   torpedoes
echoes   mosquitoes   vetoes
embargoes   mottoes   volcanoes
frescoes   noes

-os

albinos   Eskimos   manifestos
armadillos   falsettos   memos
calicos   fandangos   mulattos
casinos   fiascos   neutrinos
commandos   flamingos   oratorios
demos   folios   peccadillos
dynamos   ghettos   pianos
egos   impresarios   placebos
embryos   librettos   provisos
quangos   sopranos   virtuosos
radios   stilettos   weirdos
silos   studios   zeros
solos

-s

agendas

-ums

conundrums	moratoriums	stadiums
crematoriums	nostrums	symposiums
curriculums	quorums	ultimatums
forums	referendums	vacuums

-uses

buses	focuses
caucuses	geniuses
circuses	prospectuses
fetuses	

-ves

calves	hooves	scarves
halves	loaves	wharves

Note: *indexes* (of books), but *indices* (indicators, index numbers); *appendices* (supplements), but *appendixes* (anatomical organs).

split infinitives see **grammar and syntax**.

stanch, staunch *Stanch* the flow, though the man be *staunch* (*stout*). The distinction is useful, if bogus (since both words derive from the same old-French *estancher*).

stationary, stationery *Stationary* is still; *stationery* is writing paper, envelopes, etc.

stentorian, stertorous *Stentorian* means loud (like the voice of Stentor, a warrior in the Trojan war). *Stertorous* means *characterised by a snoring sound* (from *sterto*, snore).

straight, strait *Straight* means *direct* or *uncurved*; *strait* means *narrow* or *tight*. The *strait-laced* tend to be *straight-faced*. *Straits* are narrow bodies of water between bits of land.

strategy, strategic *Strategy* may sometimes have some merit, especially in military contexts, as a contrast to *tactics*. But *strategic* is usually meaningless except to tell you that the writer is pompous and is trying to invest something with a seriousness it does not deserve.

-style Avoid *German-style supervisory boards, an* EU-*style rotating presidency*, etc. Explain what you mean.

subcontract If you engage someone to do something, you are *contracting* the job to that person (or company); only if that person (or company) then asks someone else to do it is the job *subcontracted*.

surreal Surrealism was a revolutionary movement of philosophers, writers and artists who in the 1920s wanted to change the world by drawing on the subconscious, escaping the control of reason and bringing about "the state where the distinction between the subjective and the objective loses its necessity and value" (André Breton). Occasionally *surreal* is used in reference to this movement. More often it is used freely to describe anything bizarre or peculiar, as in the paintings of Salvador Dali or René Magritte. Avoid casually debasing the word.

swear words Avoid them, unless they convey something genuinely helpful or interesting to the reader (eg, you are quoting someone). Usually, they will annoy rather than shock. But if you do use them, spell them out in full, without asterisks.

Swiss names *see* **names**.

syntax *see* **grammar and syntax**.

systemic, systematic *Systemic* means *relating to a system or body as a whole. Systematic* means *according to system, methodical* or *intentional.*

table Avoid *table* as a transitive verb. In Britain to *table* means to bring something forward for action, and should be kept to committees. In America it sometimes means exactly the opposite.

target Not so long ago *target* was almost unknown as a verb, except when used to mean *provide with a shield*. Now it turns up everywhere, even though *aim* or *direct* would often serve as well.

terrorist Use with care, preferably only to mean *someone who uses terror as an organised system of intimidation.*
    Prefer *suspected terrorists* to *terrorist suspects.*

testament, testimony A *testament* is a will; *testimony* is evidence. It is *testimony to the poor teaching of English that journalists habitually write testament instead.*

the Occasionally, the use of the definite article may be optional: *Maximilien Robespierre, the leader of the Committee of Public Safety,* is preferable to *Maximilien Robespierre, leader of the Committee of Public Safety,* but in this context the *the* after *Robespierre* is not essential. However, *Given that leaders of mainstream left and right parties* means something different from *Given that the leaders of both mainstream left and right parties.* Likewise, *If polls are right* means something different from *If the polls are right. They include freedom to set low flat taxes* is similarly, if subtly, different from *They include the freedom to set low flat taxes.* In each of these examples the crucial *the* was left out. *See also* **grammar and syntax.**

there is, there are Often unnecessary. *There are three problems facing the prime minister* is better as *Three problems face the prime minister.*

throe, throw *Throe* is a *spasm* or *pang* (and is usually in the plural). *Throw* is to *cast* or *hurl through the air. Last throws* may be all right on the cricket pitch, but *last throes* are more likely on the battlefield.

ticket, platform, manifesto The *ticket* lists the names of the candidates for a particular party (so if you *split your ticket* you vote for, eg, a Republican for president and a Democrat for Congress). The *platform* is the statement of basic principles (*planks*) put forward by an American party, usually at its pre-election convention. It is thus akin to a British party's *manifesto*, which sets out the party's policies.

time If you have to give an exact time, you should write *6.25am, 11.15pm,* etc. But it is permissible to write *two o'clock, 11 o'clock, half past ten, quarter past four,* if you wish to be less precise.

times Take care. *Three times more than X is four times as much as X.*

titles The overriding principle is to treat people with respect. That usually means giving them the title they themselves adopt. But some titles are ugly (Ms), some misleading (all Italian graduates are Dr) and some tiresomely long (Mr Dr Dr Federal Sanitary-Inspector Schmidt). Do not therefore indulge people's self-importance unless it would seem insulting not to.

Do not use Mr, Mrs, Miss, Ms or Dr on first mention. Plain *Barack Obama, David Beckham* or other appropriate combination of first name and surname will do. But thereafter the names of all living people should be preceded by Mr, Mrs, Miss or some other title. Serving soldiers, sailors, airmen, etc should be given their title on first and subsequent mentions. Those (such as Colin Powell, but not Pervez Musharraf) who cast aside their uniforms for civvy street become plain Mr (or whatever). Governor X, President Y, the Rev John Z may be Mr, Mrs or Miss on second mention.

On first mention use forename and surname; then drop the forename (unless there are two people with the same surname mentioned):

Nicolas Sarkozy, then *Mr Sarkozy*

1   Avoid nicknames and diminutives unless the person is always known (or prefers to be known) by one:

Joe Biden Tony Blair Bill Emmott Maggie Smith Tiger Woods

2   Avoid the habit of joining office and name: *Prime Minister Brown, Enlargement Commissioner Olli Rehn.* But *Chancellor Merkel* is permissible.

3   Knights, dames, princes, kings, etc should have their titles on first and subsequent mentions.

   Many peers are, however, better known by their former names. Those like Paddy Ashdown, Richard Rogers and Helena Kennedy can be given their familiar names on first mention. After that, they should be called by their titles. Life peeresses may be called *Lady*, not *Baroness*, just as barons are called *Lord*. Note that some people choose not to use their titles. So *Sir Donald Tsang*, for instance, prefers to be just *Mr Tsang*. (*See* **British titles** *below*.)

4   If you use a title, get it right. *Rear-Admiral* Jones should not, at least on first mention, be called *Admiral* Jones.

5   Titles are not necessary in headings or captions, although surnames are: no *Baracks, Davids, Gordons, Hillarys*, etc. Sometimes they can also be dispensed with for athletes and pop stars, if titles would make them seem more ridiculous than dignified.

6   The dead: no titles, except those whom you are writing about because they have just died. *Dr Johnson* and *Mr Gladstone* are also permissible.

7   *Ms* is permissible, though avoid it if you can. To call a woman *Miss* is not to imply that she is unmarried, merely that she goes by her maiden name. Married women who are known by their maiden names – eg, Aung San Suu Kyi, Jane Fonda – are therefore Miss, unless they have made it clear that they want to be called something else.

8   Foreign titles: take care. Malaysian titles are so confusing that it may be wise to dispense with them altogether. Do not call *Tunku Razaleigh Hamzah Mr Razaleigh Hamzah*; if you are not giving him his Tunku, refer to him, on each mention, as *Razaleigh Hamzah*. Avoid *Mr Tunku Razaleigh Hamza*.

9   Dr: use *Dr* only for qualified medical people, unless the correct alternative is not known or it would seem perverse to use *Mr*. And try to keep *Professor* for those who hold chairs, not just a university job or an inflated ego.

10 Middle initials: omit. You may have to distinguish between *George Bush junior* and *George Bush senior*, but nobody will imagine that the *Lyndon Johnson* you are writing about is *Lyndon A. Johnson* or *Lyndon C. Johnson*.

11 Some titles serve as names, and therefore have initial capitals, though are also descriptions: *the Archbishop of Canterbury, the Emir of Kuwait.* If you want to describe the office rather than the individual, use lower case: *The next archbishop of Canterbury will be a woman.* Use lower case in references simply to the *archbishop, the emir: The Duchess of Scunthorpe was in her finery, but the duke wore jeans.*

British titles Long incomprehensible to all foreigners and most Britons, British titles and forms of address now seem just as confusing to those who hold them. Snobbery, embarrassment and obscurity make it difficult to know whether to write Mrs Thatcher, Mrs Margaret Thatcher, Lady Thatcher, Baroness Thatcher, Lady Margaret Thatcher or Baroness Margaret Thatcher. Properly, she is Margaret, Baroness Thatcher, but on first mention the following are preferable: *Margaret Thatcher* or *Lady Thatcher.* On subsequent mentions, *Lady Thatcher* is fine. If the context is historical, *Margaret Thatcher* and thereafter *Mrs (now Lady) Thatcher.*

On first mention all *viscounts, earls, marquesses, dukes* should be given their titles (shorn of all Right Honourables, etc). Thereafter they can be plain *Lord* (except for dukes). *Barons*, a category that includes all *life peers*, can always be called *Lord.* The full names of *knights* should be spelled out on first mention. Thereafter they become *Sir Firstnameonly.*

clerical titles Ordained clerics should be given their proper titles on first and subsequent mentions, though not their full honorifics (no need for His Holiness, His Eminence, the Right Reverend, etc). But:

the Rev Michael Wall (thereafter Mr Wall)
Father Ted (Father Ted)
Bishop Cuthbert Auckland (Bishop Auckland)
Archbishop Desmond Tutu (Archbishop Tutu)

Imams, muftis, ayatollahs, rabbis, gurus, etc should be given an appropriate title if they use one, and it should be repeated on second and subsequent mentions, so:

Ayatollah Hossein-Ali Montazeri (Ayatollah Montazeri)
Rabbi Lionel Bloom (Rabbi Bloom)
Sri Sri Ravi Shankar (Sri Sri Ravi Shankar)

to or and? *To try and end the killing* does not mean the same as *to try to end the killing.*

tortuous, torturous *Tortuous* means *causing torture. Torturous* means *winding* or *twisting.*

total is all right as a noun, but as a verb prefer *amount to* or *add up to.*

transpire means *exhale,* not *happen, occur* or *turn out.*

transportation in America, a means of getting from A to B; in Britain, a means of getting rid of convicts.

tribe Regarded as politically incorrect in some circles, *tribe* is widely used in Africa and other places. It should not be regarded as derogatory and is often preferable to *ethnic group. See also* **ethnic groups, political correctness.**

trillion A thousand billion (*see* **figures**).

trooper, trouper An old trooper is an old *cavalry soldier* (supposedly good at swearing), old *private soldier* in a tank regiment, or old *mounted policeman.* An old trouper is an old *member of a theatrical company,* or perhaps a *good sort.*

Turk, Turkic, Turkmen, Turkoman, etc *see* **placenames.**

twinkle, twinkling *In the twinkling of an eye* means *in a very short time. Before he was even a twinkle in his father's eye* means *Before* (perhaps *just before*) *he was conceived.* So, more loosely, *Before the Model T was even a twinkle in Henry Ford's eye* could mean *Before Henry Ford was even thinking about a mass-produced car. Before the internet was even a twinkle in Al Gore's eyes,* however, suggests Al Gore invented the internet.

Ukrainian names *see* **names**.

underprivileged Since a privilege is a special favour or advantage, it is by definition not something to which everyone is entitled. So *underprivileged*, by implying the right to privileges for all, is not just ugly jargon but also nonsense.

unique do not use it unless it is true. Unique means, literally, of which there is only one.

unlike should not be followed by *in*. Like *like*, *unlike* governs nouns and pronouns, not verbs and clauses.

unnecessary words Some words add nothing but length to your prose. Use adjectives to make your meaning more precise and be cautious of those you find yourself using to make it more emphatic. The word *very* is a case in point. If it occurs in a sentence you have written, try leaving it out and see whether the meaning is changed. *The omens were good* may have more force than *The omens were very good*.
Avoid:

strike action (strike will do)
cutbacks (cuts)
track record (record)
wilderness area (usually either a wilderness or a wild area)
large-scale (big)
the policymaking process (policymaking)
sale events (sales)
weather conditions (weather)

This time around means *This time*, just as *any time soon* means *soon*. And *at this moment in time* means *now* or *at present*. *Currently*, *actually* and *really* often serve no purpose.
Shoot off, or rather shoot, as many prepositions after verbs as possible. Thus:

Companies can be *bought* and *sold* rather than *bought up* and *sold off*.

Budgets may be *cut* rather than *cut back*.

Plots can be *hatched* but not *hatched up*.

Markets should be *freed*, rather than *freed up*.

Organisations should be *headed by* rather than *headed up by* chairmen.

People can *meet* rather than *meet with* each other.

Children can be *sent* to bed rather than *sent off* to bed – though if they are to *sit up* they must first *sit down*.

Pre-prepared just means *prepared*.

This advice you are given *free*, or *for nothing*, but not *for free*.

Certain words are often redundant:

The leader of the *so-called* Front for a Free Freedonia is the leader of the Front for a Free Freedonia.

A *top politician* or *top priority* is usually just a *politician* or a *priority*.

A *major speech* is usually just a *speech*, an *executive summary* a *summary* and a *role model* a *model*.

A *safe haven* is a *haven*, a *free gift* a *gift* and a *whole raft* a *raft* (who has ever had *half a raft*?).

Most probably and *most especially* are *probably* and *especially*.

the fact that can often be shortened to *that* (*That I did not do so was a self-indulgence*).

Loans to the *industrial and agricultural sectors* are just *loans to industry and farming*.

Member states or *member countries* of the EU may simply be referred to as *members*.

In general, be concise. Try to be economical in your account or argument ("*The best way to be boring is to leave nothing out*" – Voltaire). Similarly, try to be economical with words – but not with the truth. "*As a general rule, run your pen through every other word you have written; you have no idea what vigour it will give to your style*" (Sydney Smith). Raymond Mortimer put it even more crisply when commenting about Susan Sontag: "*Her journalism, like a diamond, will sparkle more if it is cut.*"

See also **community, jargon, sloppy writing**.

use and abuse are much used and abused. You *take* drugs, not *use* them (*Does he use sugar?*). And *drug abuse* is just *drug taking*, as is *substance abuse*, unless it is *glue sniffing* or *bun throwing*.

venerable means *worthy of reverence*. It is not a synonym for *old*.

venues Avoid them. Try *places*.

verbal Every agreement, except the nod-and-wink variety, is *verbal*. If you mean one that was not written down, describe it as *oral*.

viable means *capable of living*. Do not apply it to things like railway lines. *Economically viable* means *profitable*.

Vietnamese names *see* **names**.

warn is transitive, so you must either *give warning* or *warn somebody*.

wars Prefer lower case for the names of wars:

American civil war
cold war
Gulf war
war of the Spanish succession
the war of Jenkins' ear

But these are exceptions:

the Thirty Years War
the War of Independence
the Wars of the Roses

Write:

the first world war or *the 1914-18 war*, not *world war one*, *I* or *1*
the second world war or *the 1939-45 war*, not *world war two*, *II* or *2*

Post-war and *pre-war* are hyphenated.

which and that *Which* informs, *that* defines. *This is the house that Jack built.* But *This house, which Jack built, is now falling down.* Americans tend to be fussy about making a distinction between *which* and *that*. Good writers of British English are less fastidious. ("*We have left undone those things which we ought to have done.*")

while is best used temporally. Do not use it in place of *although* or *whereas*.

who, whom *Who* is one of the few words in English that differs in the accusative (objective) case, when it becomes *whom*, often throwing native English-speakers into a fizzle.
In the sentence *This is the man who can win the support of most Tory MPs*, the word you want is *who*, since *who* is the subject of

the relative clause. It remains the subject, and therefore also *who*, in the sentence *This is the man who she believes (or says or insists, etc)* can win the support of most Tory MPs. That becomes clearer if the sentence is punctuated thus: *This is the man who, she believes (or says or insists, etc), can win the support of most Tory MPs.*

However, in the sentence *This is the man whom most Tory MPs can support,* the word in question is *whom* because the subject of the relative clause has become *most Tory MPs. Whom* is also necessary in the sentence *This is the man whom she believes to be able to win the support of most Tory MPs.* This is because the verb *believe* is here being used as a transitive verb, when it must be followed by an infinitive. If, however, the word *insists* were used instead of *believes*, the sentence could not be similarly changed, because the verb *insist* cannot be used transitively.

wrack is an old word meaning *vengeance, punishment* or *wreckage* (as in *wrack and ruin*). It can also be *seaweed*. And as a verb it can mean to *wreck, devastate* or *ruin*. It has nothing to do with *wreak*, and it is not an instrument of torture or a receptacle for toast: that is *rack*. Hence *racked with pain, by war, drought*, etc. *Rack* your brains – unless they be *wracked*.

part 2

American and British English

The differences between English as written and spoken in America and English as used in Britain are considerable, as is the potential for misunderstanding, even offence, when using words or phrases that are unfamiliar or that mean something else on the other side of the Atlantic. This section highlights the important differences between American and British English syntax and punctuation, spelling and usage. (There are also differences between American and Canadian English, but these are not covered here.)

A number of subjects call for detailed, specialised guidance beyond the scope of this book, though some of the vocabulary is dealt with here. These include food and cookery (different names for ingredients and equipment, different systems of measurement); medicine and health care (different professional titles, drug names, therapies); human anatomy; and gardening (different seasons and plants). Many crafts and hobbies also use different terms for equipment, materials and techniques. *See also* **Americanisms** in Part 1.

Grammar and syntax

Written American English tends to be more declarative than its British counterpart, and adverbs and some modifying phrases are frequently positioned differently. For example, British English may say: "*As well as going shopping, we went to the park.*" American English would turn the opening phrase around: "*We went to the park as well as going shopping*", or would begin the sentence with "*In addition to*". British English also tends to use more modifying phrases, while American English prefers to go with simpler sentence structure.

In British English, doctors and lawyers are to be found *in* Harley Street or Wall Street, not *on* it. And they rest from their labours *at* weekends, not *on* them. During the week their children are *at* school, not *in* it.

Words may also be inserted or omitted in some standard phrases. British English goes *to hospital*, American English *to the hospital*. British English chooses *one or other thing*; American English chooses *one thing or the other*.

Punctuation

commas in lists The use of a comma before the final *and* in a list is called the serial or Oxford comma: *eggs, bacon, potatoes, and cheese.* Most American writers and publishers use the serial comma; most

British writers and publishers use the serial comma only when necessary to avoid ambiguity: *eggs, bacon, potatoes and cheese* but *The musicals were by Rodgers and Hammerstein, Sondheim, and Lerner and Loewe.*

full stops (periods) The American convention is to use full stops (periods) at the end of almost all abbreviations and contractions; specifically, full stops with abbreviations in lower case, *a.m., p.m.,* and no full stops with abbreviations in capitals or small capitals, *US, UN, CEO.* The British convention is to use full stops after abbreviations – eg, *abbr., adj., co.* – but not after contractions – eg, *Dr, Mr, Mrs, St.*

hyphens American English is far readier than British English to accept compound words. In particular, many nouns made of two separate nouns are spelt as one word in American English, while in British English they either remain separate or are joined by a hyphen: eg, *applesauce, highborn* (hyphenated in British English).

British English also tends, more than American English, to use hyphens as pronunciation aids, to separate repeated vowels in words such as *pre-empt* and *re-examine,* and to join some prefixes to nouns – eg, *pseudo-science.* Americans tend to get rid of hyphens more rapidly than the British, as new editions of dictionaries reflect.

In British English, hyphens are more frequently used in compound adjectives or adjectival phrases than in American English. *See also* **hyphens** in Part 1.

American English determines word breaks at the ends of justified lines of type phonetically. Traditional British English generally breaks words first according to etymology, and then phonetically where there is no clear etymological guide. For example, *know-ledge, phys-ical* and *triumph-ant* in British English, and *knowl-edge, physi-cal* and *trium-phant* in American English. Unfortunately, in practice word-processing software often dictates where words break, but for those who care about such things, word-division dictionaries exist for both forms of English.

quotation marks In American publications and those of some Commonwealth countries, and also international publications like *The Economist,* the convention is to use double quotation marks, reserving single quotation marks for quotes within quotes. In many British publications (excluding *The Economist*), the convention is the reverse: single quotation marks are used first, then double.

With other punctuation the relative position of quotation marks and other punctuation also differs. The British convention is to place such punctuation according to sense. The American convention is simpler but less logical: all commas and full stops precede the final quotation mark (or, if there is a quote within a quote, the first final quotation mark). Other punctuation – colons, semi-colons, question and exclamation marks – is placed according to sense. The following examples illustrate these differences.

British

The words on the magazine's cover, '*The link between coffee and cholesterol*', caught his eye.

'*You're eating too much,*' she told him. '*You'll soon look like your father.*'

'*Have you seen this article, "The link between coffee and cholesterol"?*' he asked.

'*It was as if*', he explained, '*I had swallowed a toad, and it kept croaking "ribbut, ribbut", from deep in my belly.*'

She particularly enjoyed the article '*Looking for the "New Man"*'.

American

The words on the magazine's cover, "*The link between coffee and cholesterol,*" caught his eye.

"*You're eating too much,*" she told him. "*You'll soon look like your father.*"

"*Have you seen this article, 'The link between coffee and cholesterol'?*" he asked.

"*It was as if,*" he explained, "*I had swallowed a toad, and it kept croaking 'Ribbut, ribbut,' from deep in my stomach.*"

She particularly enjoyed the article "*Looking for the 'New Man.'*"

Spelling

Some words are spelt differently in American English and British English. The spellings are sufficiently similar to identify the word, but the unfamiliar form may still disturb the reader. If writing for an international audience, it may be better to use a synonym than to take this risk, although sometimes it cannot be avoided.

American English is more obviously phonetic than British English. The word *cosy* becomes *cozy*, *aesthetic* becomes *esthetic*, *sizeable* becomes *sizable*, *arbour* becomes *arbor*, *theatre* becomes *theater*.

Main spelling differences

-ae/-oe Although it is now common in British English to write *medieval* rather than *mediaeval*, other words – often scientific terms such as *aeon*, *diarrhoea*, *anaesthetic*, *gynaecology*, *homoeopathy* – retain their classical composite vowel. In American English, the composite vowel is replaced by a single *e*; thus, *eon*, *diarrhea*, *anesthetic*, *gynecology*, *homeopathy*. There are exceptions to this in scientific publications. *Fetus* is the preferred spelling on both sides of the Atlantic (not *foetus*), and *oestrogen* generally becomes *estrogen*, if only to ensure that the hormone appears in the same place in alphabetical lists in both countries.

-ce/-se In British English, the verb that relates to a noun ending in -*ce* is sometimes given the ending -*se*; thus, *advice* (noun), *advise* (verb), *device/devise*, *licence/license*, *practice/practise*. In the first two instances, the spelling change is accompanied by a slight change in the sound of the word; but in the other two instances, noun and verb are pronounced the same way, and American English spelling reflects this, by using the same spelling for both noun and verb: thus, *license* and *practice*. It also extends the use of -*se* to other nouns that in British English are spelt -*ce*: thus, *defense*, *offense*, *pretense*.

-e/-ue The final silent *e* or *ue* of several words is omitted in American English but retained in British English: thus, *analog/ analogue*, *ax/axe*, *catalog/catalogue*.

-eable/-able The silent *e*, created when forming some adjectives with this suffix, is more often omitted in American English; thus, *likeable* is spelt *likable*, *unshakeable* is spelt *unshakable*. But the *e* is sometimes retained in American English where it affects the sound of the preceding consonant; thus, *traceable* and *manageable*.

-ize/-ise The American convention is to spell with *z* many words that some British people and publishers (including *The Economist*) spell with *s*. The *z* spelling is, of course, also a correct British form. Remember, though, that some words must end in -*ise*, whichever spelling convention is being followed. These include:

advertise	despise	incise
advise	devise	merchandise
apprise	disguise	premise
arise	emprise	prise
chastise	enfranchise	revise
circumcise	excise	supervise
comprise	exercise	surmise
compromise	franchise	surprise
demise	improvise	televise

Words with the ending -*lyse* in British English, such as *analyse* and *paralyse*, are spelt -*lyze* in American English.

-ll/-l In British English, when words ending in the consonant *l* are given a suffix beginning with a vowel (eg, the suffixes -*able*, -*ed*, -*ing*, -*ous*, -*y*), the *l* is doubled; thus, *annul/annulled*, *model/modelling*, *quarrel/quarrelling*, *rebel/rebellious*, *wool/ woolly*. This is inconsistent with the general rule in British English that the final consonant is doubled before the suffix only when the preceding vowel carries the main stress: thus, the word *regret* becomes *regretted*, or *regrettable*; but the word *billet* becomes *billeted*. American English mostly does not have this inconsistency. So if the stress does not fall on the preceding vowel, the *l* is not doubled: thus, *model/modeling*, *travel/traveler*; but *annul/annulled*.

Several words that end in a single *l* in British English – eg, *appal*, *fulfil* – take a double *ll* in American English. In British English the *l* stays single when the word takes a suffix beginning with a consonant (eg, the suffixes -*ful*, -*fully*, -*ment*): thus, *fulfil/ fulfilment*. Words ending in -*ll* usually lose one *l* when taking one of these suffixes: thus, *skill/skilful*, *will/wilfully*. In American English, words ending in -*ll* usually remain intact, whatever the suffix: thus, *skill/skillful*, *will/willfully*.

-m/-mme American English tends to use the shorter form of ending, thus *gram* and *program*, and British English tends to use the longer: *gramme* and *programme* (but *program* when referring to a computer program).

-our/-or Most British English words ending in -*our* – *ardour*, *behaviour*, *candour*, *demeanour*, *favour*, *valour* and the like – lose the *u* in American English: thus, *ardor*, *candor*, etc. The major exception is *glamour*, which retains its u (but loses it in both types of English for the adjective *glamorous*). Note, however, that *squalor* is spelt the same on both sides of the Atlantic.

-re/-er Most British English words ending in *-re* – such as *centre*, *fibre*, *metre*, *theatre* – end in *-er* in American English: thus, *center*, *fiber*, etc. Exceptions include: *acre*, *cadre*, *lucre*, *massacre*, *mediocre*, *ogre*.

-t/-ed Although this seems to be a mere difference in spelling the past tense of some verbs, it is really a different form; *see* 'Verbs: past tenses' below.

Other common spelling differences

British	American
aluminium	aluminum
apophthegm	apothegm
behove	behoove
chequered	checkered (pattern)
cosy	cozy
draught	draft
dyke	dike
eyrie	aerie
furore	furor
grey	gray
kerb/kerbside	curb/curbside
liquorice	licorice
manoeuvre/manoeuvrable	maneuver/maneuverable
mould/moulder/moult	mold/molder/molt
moustache	mustache
plough	plow
podgy	pudgy
polythene	polyethylene
rumbustious	rambunctious
specialist shop	specialty shop
speciality (but specialty for medicine, steel and chemicals)	specialty
sulphur(ous) (but sulfur(ous) in scientific publications)	sulfur(ous)
titbit	tidbit
towards	toward
tyre	tire
vice (tool)	vise

Usage

dates Americans are at odds with the rest of the world in the way
they express dates in numerical form. In Britain and elsewhere, the
order is always: day, month, year – eg, 7/9/2008 for 7 September
2008. In the United States, it is: month, day, year – eg, 9/7/2008.
This can lead to misunderstanding – not least with the common
term "9/11" to refer to the destruction of the World Trade Center on
11 September 2001, which the rest of the world will automatically
translate as 9 November.

exclusivity What is familiar in one culture may be entirely alien in
another. British English exploits terms and phrases borrowed
from the game of cricket; American English uses baseball terms.
Those writing for readers in both markets use either set of terms
at their peril. Do not make references or assumptions that are
geographically exclusive, for example by specifying months or
seasons when referring to seasonal patterns, by using north or
south to imply a type of climate, or by making geographical
references that give a state's name followed by USA, as in
Wyoming, USA. You can help to avoid confusion: *Cambridge,
England*; *Cambridge, MA*.

race and sex The difficulties that arise in Europe as a result
of references to race and sex (*see* **ethnic groups, political
correctness**) are even greater in America. When referring to
Americans whose ancestors came from Africa, most people use
the adjective *African-American* rather than *black*. It is also generally
unacceptable to use *black* to mean all "people of colour"; instead,
different groups are referred to by their specific ethnicity – for
instance, *Latinos/Latinas*.

    American Indians are often called *native Americans*; it is
unacceptable to refer to them as *red*. It can also cause offence
to describe the original inhabitants of the lands stretching from
Greenland to Alaska as *Eskimos*; this was a corruption of a
Cree word meaning *raw-flesh eater*. The people themselves are
distributed among at least three major tribal groupings. Alaska
natives are usually called *native Americans* in Alaska. *Inuit* should
be used only to refer to people of that tribe.

    It is unwise to describe an adult African-American female as a
girl, and offensive to address or refer to an adult African-American
man as a *boy*.

units of measurement In British publications measurements are now largely expressed in SI units (the modern form of metric units), although imperial measures are still used in certain contexts. In American publications measurements may be expressed in SI units but imperial units are still more common.

Although the British imperial and American standard measures are usually identical, there are some important exceptions, eg, the number of fluid ounces in a pint: 16 in the American system and 20 in the British. This difference has a knock-on effect in the volumes of gallons, which are smaller in America than in Britain. Americans also use the measure *quart* (one-quarter of a gallon), which is now considered archaic in Britain.

Some measures are peculiar to one or other national system, particularly units of mass relating to agriculture. *See also* **measures** in Part 3.

verbs: past tenses *-t/-ed* Both forms of ending are acceptable in British English, but the *-t* form is dominant – *burnt, learnt, spelt* – whereas American English uses *-ed*: *burned, learned, spelled.* Contrarily, British English uses *–ed* for the past tense and past participle of certain verbs – *quitted, sweated* – while American English uses the infinitive spelling – *quit, sweat.* Some verbs have a different form of past tense and past participle, eg, the past tense of *dive* is *dived* in British English but *dove* in American English. Although *loaned* is still sometimes used as the past tense of *lend* in American English, it is not standard.

Vocabulary

Sometimes the same word has gradually taken on different meanings on the two sides of the Atlantic, creating an opportunity for misunderstanding. The word *homely*, for example, means *simple* or *informal* in British English, but *plain* or *unattractive* in American English.

This also applies to figures of speech. *It went like a bomb* in British English means it was a great success; *it bombed* in American English means it was a disaster. *To table* something in British English means to bring it forward for action; but in American English it means the opposite, i.e. *to shelve.*

One writer's slang is another's lively use of words; formal language to one is pomposity to another. This is the trickiest area to negotiate when writing for both British and American readers.

At its best, distinctively American English is more direct and vivid than its British English equivalent. Many American words and expressions have passed into British English because they are shorter or more to the point: eg, *lay off* is preferable to *make redundant*, and *fire* is preferable to *dismiss*. But American English also has a contrary tendency to lengthen words, creating a (to British readers) pompous tone: for instance, *transportation* (in British English, *transport*).

British English is slower than American English to accept new words and suspicious of short cuts, and sometimes it resists the use of nouns as verbs (*see* **grammar and syntax** in Part 1).

Below is a list of words that are acceptable in both American and British English, for use when you want to produce a single version of written material for both categories of reader.

ambience *not* ambiance
annex *not* annexe
among *not* amongst
artifact *not* artefact
backward *not* backwards
baptistry *not* baptistery
Bible, *not* bible (for *Scriptures*)
bus *not* coach
burned *not* burnt
canvases *not* canvasses
car rental *not* car hire
cater to *not* cater for (for needs)
custom-made *not* bespoke
development *not* estate (for housing)
diesel fuel *not* derv
disc *not* disk (except in computing)
dispatch *not* despatch
encyclopedia *not* encyclopaedia
except for *not* save
farther *not* further (for distance)
first name *not* Christian name
flip *not* toss (for coins, etc)
focusing, focused, etc
fuel *not* petrol (UK) or gasoline (US)

forward *not* forwards
(eye)glasses *not* spectacles
gypsy *not* gipsy
hairdryer *not* hairdrier
horse-racing *not just* racing
insurance coverage *not* insurance cover
intermission *not* interval
jail *not* gaol
learned *not* learnt
line *not* queue
location *not* situation
maid *not* chambermaid
mathematics *not* maths (UK) *or* math (US)
motorcycle *not* motorbike
neat *not* spruce or tidy
news-stand *not* kiosk
nightgown *not* nightdress
orangeade/lemonade *not* orange/lemon squash
package *not* parcel
parking spaces/garage *not* car park (UK) or parking lot (US)
phoney *not* phony
refrigerator *not* fridge
railway *not* railroad

raincoat *not* mac, mackintosh
rent *not* hire (except for people)
reservation, reserve (seats, etc)
  not booking, book
retired person *not* old-age
  pensioner (UK) *or* retiree (US)
slowdown *not* go-slow (in
  production)
soccer *not* football (except for
  American football)
spelled *not* spelt
spoiled *not* spoilt
street musician *not* busker
swap *not* swop
swimming *not* bathing
team *not* side (in sport)

tearoom *not* teashop
thread *not* cotton
toilet *not* lavatory
toll-free *not* free of charge (for
  telephone numbers)
tuna *not* tunny
underwear *not* pants or
  knickers (or use lingerie for
  women's underwear)
unmistakable *not*
  unmistakeable
unspoiled *not* unspoilt
while *not* whilst
yogurt *not* yoghourt *or* yoghurt
zero *not* nought

The following lists draw attention to commonly used words and
idioms that are spelt differently or have different meanings in
American English and British English. When you do not want to
produce a single version, follow one or other convention and, if
this means using a word that will mystify or mislead one group
of readers, provide a translation. The lists do not cover slang or
colloquialisms.

Accounting, banking and finance

British	*American*
acquisition accounting	purchase accounting
articles of association	bylaws
balance sheet	statement of financial position
banknote	bill
bonus or scrip issue	stock dividend or stock split
building society	savings and loan association
Chartered Accountant (CA)	Certified Public Accountant (CPA)
cheque (bank)	check
clerk (bank)	teller
closing rate method	current rate method
creditors	payables
current account	checking account
debtors	receivables
deferred tax	deferred income tax

British	American
depreciation	amortisation
exceptional items	unusual items
finance leases	capital leases
HM Revenue and Customs (HMRC)	Internal Revenue
land and buildings	real estate
merger accounting	pooling of interests
nominal value	par value
non-pension post-employment benefits	OPEBS (other post-employment benefits)
old-age pension, state pension	Social Security
ordinary shares	common stock
pay rise	raise
preference shares	preferred stock
price rise	price hike
profit for the financial year	net income
provisions	allowances
share premium	additional paid-in capital
shareholders' funds	stockholders' equity
stock	inventory
Treasury share	Treasury stock
turnover	revenues
undistributable reserves	restricted surplus or deficiency
unit trust	mutual fund
value-added tax (VAT)	sales tax

Baby items

British	American
baby's dummy	pacifier
cot	crib
nappy	diaper
pram, push-chair	baby carriage, stroller

Clothes

British	American
bag, handbag	purse, pocketbook
braces	suspenders
clothes cupboard/wardrobe	closet
dressing gown	bathrobe/housecoat/robe
jumper	sweater
ladder (in stocking)	run

British	American
pants	underpants
pinafore dress	jumper
press studs	snaps
purse	wallet
pyjamas	pajamas
sports jacket	sport jacket
tartan	plaid
tights	pantyhose, (opaque) tights
trousers	pants, slacks, trousers
vest	undershirt
waistcoat	vest
zip (noun)	zipper

Food, cooking and eating

British	American
aubergine	eggplant
bill (restaurant)	check
biscuit (sweet)	cookie
biscuit (savoury)	cracker
black treacle	molasses
chilli/chillies	chile/chiles, chili powder, chili con carne
chips	French fries
cling film	plastic wrap
cooker	stove
coriander	cilantro
cornflour	cornstarch
courgette	zucchini
crayfish	crawfish
crisps	potato chips
crystallised	candied
digestive biscuit	graham cracker
double cream	heavy cream
essence (eg, vanilla)	extract or flavoring
flour, plain	flour, all-purpose
flour, self-raising	flour, self-rising
flour, wholemeal	flour, whole-wheat
golden syrup	corn syrup
greengrocer's	fruit and vegetable store
grill (verb and noun)	broil (verb), broiler (noun)

British	American
icing sugar	powdered or confectioners' sugar
main course	entrée
maize/sweetcorn	corn
mince	hamburger meat
minced meat	ground meat
pastry case	pie crust
pepper (red, green, etc)	sweet pepper, bell pepper, capsicum
pips	seeds (in fruit)
rocket (salad)	arugula
shortcrust pastry	short pastry/basic pie dough
single cream	light cream
soya	soy
spring onion	scallion, green onion
starter	appetizer
stoned (cherries, etc)	pitted
sultana	golden raisin
sweet shop	candy store
water biscuit	cracker

Homes and other buildings

British	American
camp bed	cot
cinema	movie theater
council estate	public housing or project
flat	apartment, flat (ie, apartment on only one floor)
ground floor	first floor
home from home	home away from home
homely	homey (homely = plain, unattractive)
housing estate	housing development
lavatory, toilet	bathroom, restroom, washroom
lift	elevator
power point	electrical outlet, socket
property (land)	real estate
storey	story, floor
terraced house	row house

People, professions and politics

British	American
adopt a candidate	nominate a candidate
barrister	trial lawyer

British	American
doctor	physician
estate agent	realtor/real estate agent
ex-serviceman	veteran
headmistress/headmaster	principal
jeweller/jewellery	jeweler/jewelry
lawyer	attorney
manifesto (political)	platform
old-age pensioner, OAP	senior citizen, senior
sceptic	skeptic
senior (politician)	ranking
solicitor	attorney, lawyer
stand for office	run for office

Travel, transport and pedestrians

British	American
accelerator	gas pedal
bonnet, car	hood
boot, car	trunk
bumper	fender
car park	parking lot
caravan	trailer, motorhome, RV
coach	bus
crossroads/junction	intersection
cul-de-sac	dead end, cul-de-sac
demister	defogger
driving licence	driver's license
dual carriageway	divided highway
estate car	station wagon
exhaust, car	muffler
flyover	overpass
gearbox	transmission
give way	yield
high street	main street
hire (a car)	rent or hire
indicator	turn signal
jump leads	jumper cables
lorry	truck
motor-racing	auto-racing
motorway	highway, freeway, expressway, thruway

British	American
number plate	license plate
passenger	rider
pavement	sidewalk
pedestrian crossing	crosswalk
petrol	gasoline, gas
petrol station	gas/service station
puncture	flat tire
railway station	train station
rambler	hiker
return ticket	round-trip ticket
riding (horses)	horseback riding
ring road	beltway
road surface	pavement
rowing boat	rowboat
single ticket	one-way ticket
slip road	ramp
subway	pedestrian underpass
transport	transportation
turning (road)	turnoff
underground (or tube train)	subway
walk	hike (only if more energetic than a walk)
windscreen	windshield

Other words and phrases

British	American
aerial (TV)	antenna
ageing	aging
anti-clockwise	counterclockwise
at weekends	on weekends
autumn	fall
bank holiday	public holiday
British Summer Time (BST)	Daylight Saving Time (DST)
chemist	drugstore, pharmacy
clever	smart
diary (appointments)	calendar
diary (record)	journal
dustbin	garbage can
earthed (wire)	ground
ex-serviceman, woman	veteran

British	American
film	movie
flannel	washcloth
fortnight	two weeks
from ... to ...	through
got (past participle)	gotten
grey	gray
holiday	vacation
in (Fifth Avenue, etc)	on
lease of life	lease on life
mean (parsimonious)	stingy, tight (mean = nasty)
mobile phone	cell phone
oblige	obligate
ordinary	regular, normal
outside	outside of
over	overly
paddling pool	wading pool
plait	braid
post, post box	mail, mailbox
post code	zip code
postponement	rain-check
public school	private school
queue (noun and verb)	line (noun), line up
quite	somewhat (quite = very)
reverse charges	call collect
ring up, phone	call, phone
spanner	wrench
state school	public school
stupid	dumb
torch	flashlight
upmarket	upscale
work out (problem)	figure out
Zimmer frame	walker
zed (the letter z)	zee

part 3

useful reference

Abbreviations

Here is a list of some common business abbreviations.
See *also* **abbreviations** in Part 1, **internet**, pages 194–6.

ABC	activity-based costing
ACH	automated clearing house
ADR	American depositary receipt
AG	Aktiengesellschaft (Austrian, German or Swiss public limited company)
AGM	annual general meeting
AIBD	Association of International Bond Dealers
AIM	Alternative Investment Market (UK)
AMEX	American Stock Exchange
APR	annualised percentage rate (of interest)
APT	arbitrage pricing theory
ARPU	average revenue per user/unit
ARR	accounting rate of return
ASB	Accounting Standards Board (UK)
B2B	business-to-business
B2C	business-to-consumer
BACS	bankers' automated clearing services
BPO	business process outsourcing
BPR	business process re-engineering
CAPM	capital asset pricing model
CCA	current cost accounting
CD	certificate of deposit
CDO	Collateralised debt obligation
CEO	chief executive officer
CFO	chief financial officer
CHAPS	Clearing House Automated Payments Service
CIF	cost, insurance, freight
CIO	chief information officer

COB	Commission des Opérations de Bourse (Stock Exchange Commission, France)
Consob	Commissione Nazionale per le Società e la Borsa (Stock Exchange Commission, Italy)
COO	chief operating officer
COLA	cost of living adjustment
COSA	cost of sales adjustment
CPA	certified public accountant (US); critical path analysis
CPP	current purchasing power (accounting)
CRC	current replacement cost
CRM	customer (or client) relationship management
CSR	corporate social responsibility
CTO	chief technology officer; configure to order
CVP	cost-volume-profit analysis
DCF	discounted cash flow
EBIT	earnings before interest and tax
EBITDA	earnings before interest, tax, depreciation and amortisation
ECN	electronic communication network
EDI	electronic data interchange
EDLP	every day low price
EDP	electronic data processing
EFT	electronic funds transfer
EFTPOS	electronic funds transfer at point of sale
EOQ	economic order quantity
EPS	earnings per share
ERM	enterprise resource management
ESOP	employee stock or share ownership plan
ETF	exchange traded fund
Euribor	European Interbank Offered Rate
EV	economic value
EVA	economic value added
FAS	financial accounting standard (US)
FASB	Financial Accounting Standards Board (US)
FDI	foreign direct investment
FIFO	first in, first out (used for valuing stock/inventory)
FMCG	fast-moving consumer goods
FMS	flexible manufacturing systems
fob	free on board
FRN	floating-rate note
FTE	full-time equivalent

GAAP	generally accepted accounting principles (US)
GAAS	generally accepted audited standards
GDP	gross domestic product
GmbH	Gesellschaft mit beschränkter Haftung (Austrian, German or Swiss private limited company)
GNI	gross national income
GNP	gross national product
GPS	global positioning system
IAASB	International Auditing and Assurance Standards Board
IAS	international accounting standard
IASB	International Accounting Standards Board
IBF	international banking facility
ICGN	International Corporate Governance Network
IFA	independent financial adviser
IFRS	International Financial Reporting Standards
ILO	International Labour Organisation
IOSCO	International Organisation of Securities Commissions
IPO	initial public offering
IRR	internal rate of return
IRS	Internal Revenue Service (US)
ISA	individual savings account; International Standards on Auditing
ISMA	International Securities Market Association
ISO	International Organisation for Standardisation
JIT	just-in-time
KPI	key performance indicator
LBO	leveraged buy-out
Libor	London Interbank Offered Rate
LIFO	last in, first out (used for valuing stock/inventory value, popular in US)
LLP	limited liability partnership
LNG	liquefied natural gas
LPG	liquefied petroleum gas
LSE	London Stock Exchange
M&A	mergers and acquisitions
MBI	management buy-in
MBO	management buy-out
MLR	minimum lending rate
MOU	memorandum of understanding

NASDAQ	National Association of Securities Dealers Automated Quotations System (US)
NAV	net asset value
NBV	net book value
NGO	non-governmental organisation
NPV	net present value; no par value
NRV	net realisable value
NYMEX	New York Mercantile Exchange
NYSE	New York Stock Exchange
OBU	offshore banking unit
OCR	optical character recognition
OEIC	open-ended investment company
OEM	original equipment manufacturer
OFR	operating and financial review
OTC	over the counter
PCAOB	Public Company Accounting Oversight Board
P/E	Price/earnings (ratio)
PLC	public limited company (UK)
PPP	purchasing power parity; public–private partnership
PSBR	public-sector borrowing rate
R&D	research and development
REIT	real estate investment fund
RFID	radio frequency identification device
ROA	return on assets
ROCE	return on capital employed
ROE	return on equity
ROI	return on investment
RONA	return on net assets
RONOA	return on net operating assets
ROTA	return on total assets
RPI	retail price index
RPIX	retail price index excluding mortgage interest payments
RTM	route to market
S&L	Savings and Loan Association (US)
SA	société anonyme (French, Belgian, Luxembourg or Swiss public limited company)
Sarl	société à responsabilité limitée (French, etc private limited company)
SBU	strategic business unit
SCM	supply chain management

SDR	special drawing right (at the IMF)
SEAQ	Stock Exchange Automated Quotations (UK)
SEC	Securities and Exchange Commission (US)
SET	secure electronic transaction
SFO	Serious Fraud Office (UK)
SIB	Securities and Investments Board (UK)
SITC	standard international trade classification
SMART	specific, measurable, achievable, realistic, time bound
SME	small and medium-sized enterprises
SOE	state owned enterprise
SOHO	small office, home office
SOX	Sarbanes-Oxley Act (US)
SPA	societa per azioni (Italian public company)
SPV	special purpose vehicle
SRO	self-regulating organisation
SSAP	Statement of Standard Accounting Practice (UK)
STRGL	statement of total recognised gains and losses
SWIFT	Society for Worldwide Interbank Financial Telecommunications
SWOT	strengths, weaknesses, opportunities, threats
T-bill	Treasury bill
TSR	total shareholder return
UCITS	Undertakings for Collective Investments in Transferable Securities
USP	unique selling proposition
VAT	value-added tax
VCT	venture capital trust
WACC	weighted average cost of capital
WDV	written down value
WIP	work-in-progress
XBRL	extensible business reporting language
ZBB	zero base budgeting

For international bodies and their abbreviations, *see* **organisations**, pages 217–28.

Beaufort Scale

For devotees of the shipping forecast, here is the World Meteorological Organisation's classification of wind forces and effects.

	Conditions (abbreviated)			Equivalent speed at 10m height		
Force	Description	On land	At sea	knots	miles per hour	metres per second
0	Calm	Smoke rises vertically	Sea like a mirror	less than 1	less than 1	0.0–0.2
1	Light air	Smoke drifts	Ripples	1–3	1–3	0.3–1.5
2	Light breeze	Leaves rustle	Small wavelets	4–6	4–7	1.6–3.3
3	Gentle breeze	Wind extends light flag	Large wavelets, crests break	7–10	8–12	3.4–5.4
4	Moderate breeze	Raises paper and dust	Small waves, fairly frequent white horses	11–16	13–18	5.5–7.9
5	Fresh breeze	Small trees in leaf sway	Moderate waves, many white horses	17–21	19–24	8.0–10.7
6	Strong breeze	Large branches in motion	Large waves form, some spray	22–27	25–31	10.8–13.8
7	Near gale	Whole trees in motion	Sea heaps up, white foam streaks	28–33	32–38	13.9–17.1
8	Gale	Breaks twigs off trees	Moderately high waves, well-marked foam streaks	34–40	39–46	17.2–20.7
9	Strong gale	Slight structural damage	High waves, crests start to tumble over	41–47	47–54	20.8–24.4
10	Storm	Trees uprooted, considerable structural damage	Very high waves, white sea tumbles	48–55	55–63	24.5–28.4
11	Violent storm	Very rarely experienced, widespread damage	Exceptionally high waves, edges of wave crests blown to froth	56–63	64–72	28.5–32.6

| Conditions (abbreviated) | | | | Equivalent speed at 10m height | | |
Force	Description	On land	At sea	knots	miles per hour	metres per second
12–17	Hurricane	Devastation with driving spray	Sea completely white	64–over	72–over	32.7–over

Business ratios

These are ratios commonly used in corporate financial analysis.

Working capital

Working capital ratio = current assets/current liabilities, where current assets = inventory + receivables + cash at bank and in hand + quoted investments, etc, and current liabilities = payables + short-term bank borrowing + taxes payable + dividends, etc. The ratio varies according to type of trade and conditions; a ratio from 1 to 3 is usual with a ratio above 2 taken to be safe.

Liquidity ratio = liquid ("quick") assets/current liabilities, where liquid assets = receivables + cash at bank and in hand + quoted investments (that is, assets that can be realised within a month or so, which may not apply to all investments); current liabilities are those that may need to be repaid within the same short period, which may not necessarily include a bank overdraft where it is likely to be renewed. The liquidity ratio is sometimes referred to as the "acid test"; a ratio under 1 suggests a possibly difficult situation, and too high a ratio may mean that assets are not being usefully employed.

Turnover of working capital = sales/average working capital. The ratio varies according to type of trade; generally a low ratio can mean poor use of resources, and too high a ratio can mean overtrading. Average working capital or average inventory is found by taking the opening and closing working capital or inventory and dividing by 2.

Turnover of inventory = sales/average inventory, or (where cost of sales is known) cost of sales/average inventory. The cost of sales turnover figure is to be preferred, as both figures are then on the same valuation basis. This ratio can be expressed as number of times per year, or time taken for inventory to be turned over once = (52/number of times) weeks. A low inventory turnover can be a sign of inventory items that are difficult to move, and usually indicates adverse conditions.

Turnover of receivables = sales/average receivables. This indicates efficiency in collecting accounts. An average credit period of about one month is usual, but this varies according to credit stringency conditions in the economy.

Turnover of payables = purchases/average payables. Average payment period is best maintained in line with turnover of receivables.

Sales

Export ratio = exports as a percentage of sales.

Sales per employee = sales/average number of employees.

Assets

Ratios of assets can vary according to the measure of assets used:

Total assets = current assets + non-current assets + other assets, where non-current assets = property + plant and equipment + motor vehicles, etc, and other assets = long-term investment + goodwill, etc.

Net assets ("net worth") = total assets − total liabilities = share capital + reserves = equity.

Turnover of net assets = sales/average net assets. As for turnover of working capital, a low ratio can mean poor use of resources.

Assets per employee = assets/average number of employees. This indicates the amount of investment backing for employees.

Profits

Profit margin = (profit/sales) × 100 = profits as a percentage of sales; usually profits before tax.

Profitability = (profit/total assets) × 100 = profits as a percentage of total assets = return on total assets (ROTA).

Return on capital = (profit/net assets) × 100 = profits as a percentage of net assets ("net worth", "equity" or "capital employed") = return on net assets (RONA), return on equity (ROE) or return on capital employed (ROCE).

Profit per employee = profit/average number of employees.

Earnings per share (EPS) = after-tax profit − minorities/average number of shares in issue.

Calendars

There are five important solar calendars and the Jewish calendar, which is a combined solar/lunar calendar, like the Chinese.

Gregorian	Iranian[b]	Hindu[c]
January (31)[a]		
February (28 or 29)		
March (31)	Farvardin (31)	Chaitra (30/31)
April (30)	Ordibehesht (31)	Vaisakha (31)
May (31)	Khordad (31)	Jyaistha (31)
June (30)	Tir (31)	Asadha (31)
July (31)	Mordad (31)	Sravana (31)
August (31)	Shahrivar (31)	Bhadrapada (31)
September (30)	Mehr (30)	Asvina (30)
October (31)	Aban (30)	Karttika (30)
November (30)	Azar (30)	Margasirsa (30)
December (31)	Dey (30)	Pausa (30)
January	Bahman (30)	Magha (30)
February	Esfand (29 or 30)	Phalguna (30)

Gregorian	Ethiopian[d]	Jewish[e]
September	Meskerem (30)	Tishri (30)
October	Tikemet (30)	Heshvan (29 or 30)
November	Hidar (30)	Kislev (29 or 30)
December	Tahesas (30)	Tebet (29)
January	Tir (30)	Shebat (30)
February	Yekatit (30)	Adar (29)
March	Megabit (30)	Nisan (30)
April	Miyaza (30)	Iyar (29)
May	Ginbot (30)	Sivan (30)
June	Sene (30)	Tammuz (29)
July	Hamle (30)	Ab (30)
August	Nehase (30)	Elul (29)
	Paguma (5 or 6)	

a Figures in brackets denote the number of days in that month.

b Months begin about the 21st of the corresponding Gregorian month.

c Months begin about the 22nd of the corresponding Gregorian month.

d Months begin about the 11th of the corresponding Gregorian month. Ethiopia follows the Julian calendar.

e The date of the new year varies, but normally falls in the second half of September in the Gregorian calendar; the position is maintained by sometimes adding an extra period of 29 days, Adar Sheni, following the month of Adar.

Muslim calendar

Muslims use a lunar calendar which begins 10 or 11 days earlier each year in terms of the Gregorian. The months, whose names follow, do not have a fixed number of days. In each 30 years, 19 years have 354 days (are "common") and 11 have 355 days (are "intercalary").

Muharram	Rabi' II	Rajab	Shawwal
Safar	Jumada I	Sha'ban	Dhu al-Qidah
Rabi' I	Jumada II	Ramadan	Dhu al-Hijjah

The Muslim years in the columns below begin on the dates of the Gregorian calendar as shown.

1416	May 31st 1995	1425	February 22nd 2004
1417	May 19th 1996	1426	February 10th 2005
1418	May 9th 1997	1428	January 20th 2007
1419	April 28th 1998	1429	December 29th 2008
1427	January 31st 2006	1430	December 18th 2009
1420	April 17th 1999	1431	December 7th 2010
1421	April 6th 2000	1432	November 26th 2011
1422	March 26th 2001	1433	November 15th 2012
1423	March 15th 2002	1434	November 4th 2013
1424	March 5th 2003	1435	October 25th 2014

Currencies

See also **currencies** in Part 1 for *The Economist* newspaper usage.

Country	Currency	Symbol
Afghanistan	afghani	Af
Albania	lek	Lk
Algeria	Algerian dinar	AD
Angola	kwanza	Kz
Argentina	Argentinian peso	Ps

Country	Currency	Symbol
Armenia	dram	Dram
Aruba	Aruban florin	Afl
Australia	Australian dollar	A$
Austria	euro	€
Azerbaijan	manat	Manat
Bahamas	Bahamas dollar	B$
Bahrain	Bahraini dinar	BD
Bangladesh	taka	Tk
Barbados	Barbados dollar	Bd$
Belarus	rubel	BRb
Belgium	euro	€
Belize	Belize dollar	Bz$
Benin	CFA franc	CFAfr[a]
Bermuda	Bermuda dollar	Bda$
Bhutan	ngultrum	Nu
Bolivia	boliviano	Bs
Bosnia & Hercegovina	convertible marka	KM
Botswana	pula	P
Brazil	Brazilian real	R
Brunei	Brunei dollar/ringgit	Br$
Bulgaria	lev	Lv
Burkina Faso	CFA franc	CFAfr[a]
Burundi	Burundi franc	Bufr
Cambodia	riel	CR
Cameroon	CFA franc	CFAfr[a]
Canada	Canadian dollar	C$
Cape Verde	Cape Verde escudo	CVEsc
Central African Republic	CFA franc	CFAfr[a]
Chad	CFA franc	CFAfr[a]
Chile	Chilean peso	Ps
China	renminbi or yuan	Rmb
Colombia	Colombian peso	Ps
Comoros	Comorian franc	Cfr

Country	Currency	Symbol
Congo (Brazzaville)	CFA franc	CFAfr[a]
Congo (Dem. Rep. of)	Congolese franc	FC
Costa Rica	Costa Rican colón	C
Côte d'Ivoire	CFA franc	CFAfr[a]
Croatia	kuna	HRK
Cuba	Cuban peso	Ps
Cyprus	euro	€
Czech Republic	koruna	Kc
Denmark	Danish krone	Dkr
Djibouti	Djibouti franc	Dfr
Dominican Republic	Dominican Republic peso	Ps
Ecuador	US dollar	US$
Egypt	Egyptian pound	E£
El Salvador	US dollar	US$
Equatorial Guinea	CFA franc	CFAfr[a]
Eritrea	nakfa	Nfa
Estonia	kroon	EEK
Ethiopia	birr	Birr
Fiji	Fiji dollar	F$
Finland	euro	€
France	euro	€
Gabon	CFA franc	CFAfr[a]
The Gambia	dalasi	D
Georgia	lari	Lari
Germany	euro	€
Ghana	cedi	GH¢
Greece	euro	€
Grenada	East Caribbean dollar	EC$
Guatemala	quetzal	Q
Guinea	Guinean franc	Gnf
Guinea-Bissau	CFA franc	CFAfr[a]
Guyana	Guyana dollar	G$
Haiti	gourde	G

Country	Currency	Symbol
Honduras	lempira	La
Hong Kong	Hong Kong dollar	HK$
Hungary	forint	Ft
Iceland	krona	Ikr
India	Indian rupee	Rs
Indonesia	rupiah	Rp
Iran	Iranian rial	IR
Iraq	New Iraqi dinar	ID
Ireland	euro	€
Israel	New Israeli shekel	NIS
Italy	euro	€
Jamaica	Jamaican dollar	J$
Japan	yen	¥
Jordan	Jordanian dinar	JD
Kazakhstan	tenge	Tenge
Kenya	Kenya shilling	KSh
Kyrgyzstan	som	Som
North Korea	won or N Korean won	Won
South Korea	won or S Korean won	W
Kuwait	Kuwaiti dinar	KD
Laos	kip	K
Latvia	lat	LVL
Lebanon	Lebanese pound	L£
Lesotho	loti (pl. maloti)	M
Liberia	Liberian dollar	L$
Libya	Libyan dinar	LD
Lithuania	litas	LTL
Luxembourg	euro	€
Macau	pataca	MPtc
Macedonia	denar	Den
Madagascar	Madagascar ariary	AR
Malawi	kwacha	MK
Malaysia	Malaysian dollar/ringgit	M$
Mali	CFA franc	CFAfr[a]

Country	Currency	Symbol
Malta	euro	€
Mauritania	ouguiya	UM
Mauritius	Mauritius rupee	MRs
Mexico	Mexican peso	Ps
Moldova	Moldavian leu (pl. lei)	Lei
Mongolia	togrog	Tg
Montenegro	euro	€
Morocco	dirham	Dh
Mozambique	metical	MT
Myanmar	Kyat	Kt
Namibia	Namibia dollar	N$
Nepal	Nepali rupee	NRs
Netherlands	euro	€
Netherlands Antilles	Netherlands Antilles guilder	NAf
New Caledonia	French Pacific franc	CFPfr
New Zealand	New Zealand dollar	NZ$
Nicaragua	Córdoba	C
Niger	CFA franc	CFAfr[a]
Nigeria	Naira	N
Norway	Norwegian krone	Nkr
Oman	Omani riyal	OR
Pakistan	Pakistan rupee	PRs
Palestinian Territories	Jordanian dinar, New Israeli shekel	JD, NIS
Panama	Balboa	B
Papua New Guinea	Kina	Kina
Paraguay	guaraní	G
Peru	nuevo sol	Ns
Philippines	Philippine peso	P
Poland	zloty (pl. zlotys)	Zl
Portugal	euro	€
Puerto Rico	US dollar	US$
Qatar	Qatari riyal	QR
Romania	leu (pl. lei)	Lei

Country	Currency	Symbol
Russia	Rouble	Rb
Rwanda	Rwandan franc	Rwfr
Samoa	tala or Samoan dollar	Tala
São Tomé & Príncipe	Dobra	Db
Saudi Arabia	Saudi riyal	SR
Senegal	CFA franc	CFAfr[a]
Serbia	Serbian dinar	RSD
Seychelles	Seychelles rupee	SRs
Sierra Leone	Leone	Le
Singapore	Singapore dollar	S$
Slovakia	euro	€
Slovenia	euro	€
Solomon Islands	Solomon Islands dollar	SI$
Somalia	Somali shilling	SoSh
South Africa	rand	R
Spain	euro	€
Sri Lanka	Sri Lanka rupee	SLRs
Sudan	Sudanese pound	SP
Suriname	Suriname dollar	Sr$
Swaziland	lilangeni (pl. emalangeni)	E
Sweden	Swedish krona	Skr
Switzerland	Swiss franc	Swfr
Syria	Syrian pound	S£
Taiwan	New Taiwan dollar	NT$
Tajikistan	Somoni	S
Tanzania	Tanzanian shilling	TSh
Thailand	Baht	Bt
Timor-Leste	US dollar	US$
Togo	CFA franc	CFAfr[a]
Tonga	pa'anga or Tonga dollar	T$
Trinidad & Tobago	Trinidad & Tobago dollar	TT$
Tunisia	Tunisian dinar	TD
Turkey	Turkish lira	TL

Country	Currency	Symbol
Turkmenistan	manat	Manat
Turks & Caicos Islands	US dollar	US$
Uganda	Uganda shilling	USh
Ukraine	hryvnya	HRN
United Arab Emirates	UAE dirham	Dh
United Kingdom	pound/pound sterling	£
United States	dollar	US$
Uruguay	Uruguayan peso	Ps
Uzbekistan	som	Som
Vanuatu	vatu	Vt
Venezuela	bolívar	BsF
Vietnam	dong	D
Western Samoa	tala	Tala
Windward & Leeward Islands[b]	East Caribbean dollar	EC$
Yemen	Yemeni riyal	YR
Zambia	kwacha	ZK
Zimbabwe	Zimbabwe dollar	Z$

a CFA = Communauté financière africaine in West African area and Coopération financière en Afrique centrale in Central African area. Used in monetary areas of West and Central Africa. The CFA franc is pegged to the euro at a rate of CFAfr655.96:€1. Countries with this currency are members of the Comité monétaire de la Zone Franc, or Franc Zone.
b Antigua and Barbuda, Dominica, Grenada, Monserrat, St Kitts-Nevis, St Lucia, St Vincent & Grenadines, the British Virgin islands.

Earthquakes

An earthquake is measured in terms of its magnitude.

Magnitude		Explosion equivalent	
	Joules	TNT terms	Nuclear terms
0[a]	7.9×10^2	175mg	
1	6.0×10^4	13g	
2	4.0×10^6	0.89kg	
3	2.4×10^8	53kg	
4	1.3×10^{10}	3 tons	
5[b]	6.3×10^{11}	140 tons	
6[c]	2.7×10^{13}	6 kilotons	$\frac{1}{3}$ atomic bomb
7	1.1×10^{15}	240 kilotons	12 atomic bombs
8	3.7×10^{16}	8.25 megatons	$\frac{1}{3}$ hydrogen bomb
9	1.1×10^{18}	250 megatons	13 hydrogen bombs
10	3.2×10^{19}	7,000 megatons	350 hydrogen bombs

a About equal to the shock caused by an average man jumping from a table.
b Potentially damaging to structures.
c Potentially capable of general destruction; widespread damage is usually caused above magnitude 6.5.

Here are some examples.

	Magnitude		Magnitude
Samoa Islands, 2009	8.0	Rat Islands, Alaska	8.7
Solomon Islands, 2007	8.1	Northern Sumatra, 2005	8.7
Banda Sea, Indonesia, 1938	8.5	Ecuador, 1906	8.8
Chile, 1906	8.5	Kamchatka, 1952	9.0
Kamchatka, 1923	8.5	Northern Sumatra, 2004 (called the tsunami)	9.0
Kuril Islands, 1963	8.5	Andreanof Islands, Alaska, 1957	9.1
Ningxia-Gansu, China, 1920	8.6	Prince William Sound, Alaska, 1964	9.2
Sanriku, Japan, 1933	8.6	Chile, 1960	9.5
India/Assam/Tibet, 1950	8.7	Krakatoa, 1883 (estimate)	9.9

Elements

These are the natural and artificially created chemical elements.

Name	Symbol	Atomic number	Name	Symbol	Atomic number
Actinium	Ac	89	Fermium	Fm	100
Aluminium	Al	13	Fluorine	F	9
Americium	Am	95	Francium	Fr	87
Antimony (Stibium)	Sb	51			
Argon	Ar	18	Gadolinium	Gd	64
Arsenic	As	33	Gallium	Ga	31
Astatine	At	85	Germanium	Ge	32
			Gold (Aurum)	Au	79
Barium	Ba	56	Hafnium	Hf	72
Berkelium	Bk	97	Hassium	Hs	108
Beryllium	Be	4	Helium	He	2
Bismuth	Bi	83	Holmium	Ho	67
Bohrium	Bh	107	Hydrogen	H	1
Boron	B	5			
Bromine	Br	35	Indium	In	49
			Iodine	I	53
Cadmium	Cd	48	Iridium	Ir	77
Caesium	Cs	55	Iron (Ferrum)	Fe	26
Calcium	Ca	20			
Californium	Cf	98	Krypton	Kr	36
Carbon	C	6			
Cerium	Ce	58	Lanthanum	La	57
Chlorine	Cl	17	Lawrencium	Lr	103
Chromium	Cr	24	Lead (Plumbum)	Pb	82
Cobalt	Co	27			
Copper (Cuprum)	Cu	29	Lithium	Li	3
			Lutetium	Lu	71
Curium	Cm	96			
			Magnesium	Mg	12
Darmstadtium	Ds	110	Manganese	Mn	25
Dubnium	Db	105	Meitnerium	Mt	109
Dysprosium	Dy	66	Mendelevium	Md	101
			Mercury (Hydrargyrum)	Hg	80
Einsteinium	Es	99			
Erbium	Er	68	Molybdenum	Mo	42
Europium	Eu	63			

Name	Symbol	Atomic number	Name	Symbol	Atomic number
Neodymium	Nd	60	Sodium (Natrium)	Na	11
Neon	Ne	10			
Neptunium	Np	93	Strontium	Sr	38
Nickel	Ni	28	Sulphur	S	16
Niobium (Columbium)	Nb	41			
			Tantalum	Ta	73
Nitrogen	N	7	Technetium	Tc	43
Nobelium	No	102	Tellurium	Te	52
			Terbium	Tb	65
Osmium	Os	76	Thallium	Tl	81
Oxygen	O	8	Thorium	Th	90
			Thulium	Tm	69
Palladium	Pd	46	Tin (Stannum)	Sn	50
Phosphorus	P	15	Titanium	Ti	22
Platinum	Pt	78	Tungsten (Wolfram)	W	74
Plutonium	Pu	94			
Polonium	Po	84			
Potassium (Kalium)	K	19	Ununbium	Uub	112
			Ununhexium	UUh	116
Praseodymium	Pr	59	Ununoctium	Uuo	118
Promethium	Pm	61	Ununpentium	Uup	115
Protactinium	Pa	91	Ununquadium	Uuq	114
			Ununseptium	Uus	117
Radium	Ra	88	Ununtrium	Uut	113
Radon	Rn	86	Unununium	Uuu	111
Rhenium	Re	75	Uranium	U	92
Rhodium	Rh	45			
Rubidium	Rb	37	Vanadium	V	23
Ruthenium	Ru	44			
Rutherfordium	Rf	104	Xenon	Xe	54
Samarium	Sm	62	Ytterbium	Yb	70
Scandium	Sc	21	Yttrium	Y	39
Seaborgium	Sg	106			
Selenium	Se	34	Zinc	Zn	30
Silicon	Si	14	Zirconium	Zr	40
Silver (Argentum)	Ag	47			

Footnotes, sources, references

Footnotes appear at the foot of the page (or column) on which they occur; endnotes are listed at the end of a chapter or in one batch at the end of the work. The method depends on the publisher's conventions, the type of work and the readership. The author may have little say in the matter. Footnotes may also contain additional snippets of material or comment that the author feels is not appropriate to the main text.

1. Charts, tables and figures: place source underneath.
2. Page numbers: "page" is usually abbreviated to p., plural pp., except, for example, in *The Economist*, where these are written in full.
3. Footnote numbers, which are conventionally superscript, go after the punctuation in English works, before in American. If there are not many footnotes, some publishers prefer to use asterisks, daggers, etc.

The main methods (other than *The Economist*'s) of referring to sources are: the author–date (Harvard) system; the number-only (Vancouver) system; and the author–title system.

The Economist Books should be in quotation marks, periodicals in italics, authors, publishers, addresses (optional) and prices in roman. Commas should follow the title and the publisher (if an address is given). The other elements should each be followed by a full stop.

> "A Child's Guide to the Dismal Science", by Rupert Penandwig. Haphazard House, 1234 Madison Avenue, New York, NY 10019. $28.

In charts and tables, no final stop is necessary.

Harvard system The most commonly used system in physical and social sciences publications. The author's name and year of publication appear in parentheses in the text with the full details at the end of the publication in a list of references. For example:

> The variety of wildlife in our gardens (Murphy 2003) is amazing ...
> In his research, Murphy (2003) finds that ...

If you wish to include the page numbers, write Murphy 2003: 165 or Murphy 2003, p. 165 or pp. 165–6.
The reference section contains the full details:

> Murphy, P.L. (2003), *Birds, Bees and Butterflies* (Garden Press, London).

Vancouver system Most commonly used in scientific journals. Each publication is numbered and the text reference is a superscript number. For example:

> The variety of wildlife in our gardens[15] is amazing ...

The reference section contains the full details:

> 15. Murphy, P.L., *Birds, Bees and Butterflies* (London: Garden Press, 2003).

Note that any addition or subtraction from the list means that all subsequent items and the references will have to be renumbered.

author–title system Also known as the short-title system. A full reference is given only on the first mention in the chapter (or book if there is a bibliography).
    This is mostly for academic works. The whole title is cited in the first footnote, for example P.H. Clarke, *Visions of Utopia*, at which point you put, "hereafter Clarke, *Utopia*". Then on subsequent references you simply write "Clarke, *Utopia*", with page numbers if you wish.

mixed system Another system is common in academic publications. A superscript number is inserted in the text that corresponds with the number of a footnote (located at the bottom of the page) or endnote (located at the end of the chapter or the book). Footnotes and endnotes may be numbered per chapter or per book. The footnote or endnote consists of the bibliographical reference in full if there is no reference section or bibliography, or an abbreviated reference if there is. Sometimes the bibliographical reference appears in full at the first occurrence and is abbreviated subsequently even if there is a reference section or bibliography.

Notes

- ibid. (abbreviation of *ibidem*, in the same place), not italic, is used to mean that the quote comes from the same source.
- op. cit. (abbreviation of *opere citato*, in the work quoted), not italic, is used to mean that the source has already been given.

Fractions

Do not mingle fractions with decimals. If you need to convert one to the other, use this table. *See also* **figures** in Part 1.

Fraction	Decimal equivalent
$\frac{1}{2}$	0.5
$\frac{1}{3}$	0.333
$\frac{1}{4}$	0.25
$\frac{1}{5}$	0.2
$\frac{1}{6}$	0.167
$\frac{1}{7}$	0.143
$\frac{1}{8}$	0.125
$\frac{1}{9}$	0.111
$\frac{1}{10}$	0.1
$\frac{1}{11}$	0.091
$\frac{1}{12}$	0.083
$\frac{1}{13}$	0.077
$\frac{1}{14}$	0.071
$\frac{1}{15}$	0.067
$\frac{1}{16}$	0.063
$\frac{1}{17}$	0.059
$\frac{1}{18}$	0.056
$\frac{1}{19}$	0.053
$\frac{1}{20}$	0.05

Geological eras

Astronomers and geologists give this broad outline of the ages of the universe and the earth.

Era, period and epoch		Years ago (m)	Characteristics
Origin of the universe (estimates vary markedly)		20,000– 10,000	
Origin of the sun		5,000	
Origin of the earth		4,600	
Pre-Cambrian			
Archean		4,000	First signs of fossilised microbes
Proterozoic		2,500	
Palaeozoic			
Cambrian		570	First appearance of abundant fossils
Ordovician (obsolete)		500	Vertebrates emerge
Silurian		440	Fishes emerge
Devonian		400	Primitive plants emerge; age of fishes
Carboniferous		350	Amphibians emerge; first winged insects
Permian		270	Reptiles emerge
Mesozoic			
Triassic		250	Seed plants emerge
Jurassic		210	Age of dinosaurs
Cretaceous		145	Flowering plants emerge; dinosaurs extinct at end of this period
Cenozoic			
Palaeocene		65	
Tertiary:	Eocene	55	Mammals emerge
	Oligocene	40	
	Miocene	25	
	Pliocene	5	
Quaternary:	Pleistocene	2	Ice ages; stone age man emerges
	Holocene or Recent	c. 11,000[a]	Modern man emerges

a 10,000 years, not 10,000m years.

Greek alphabet

These are the letters of the Greek alphabet and their names. The first column gives the upper-case symbol and the second column the lower-case symbol in each case.

A	α	alpha	N	ν	nu
B	β	beta	Ξ	ξ	xi
Γ	γ	gamma	O	o	omicron
Δ	δ	delta	Π	π	pi
E	ε	epsilon	P	ρ	rho
Z	ζ	zeta	Σ	ς or σ	sigma
H	η	eta	T	τ	tau
Θ	θ	theta	Υ	υ	upsilon
I	ι	iota	Φ	φ	phi
K	κ	kappa	X	χ	chi
Λ	λ	lambda	Ψ	ψ	psi
M	μ	mu	Ω	ω	omega

Internet

Here is a list of commonly used internet abbreviations.

ADSL	asynchronous digital subscriber line
AOL	America Online
ASCII	American standard code for information interchange
ASP	application service provider (or active server pages)
BCC	blind carbon copy
BPS	bits per second
CAD	computer aided design
CC	carbon copy
CDMA	code-division multiple access
CSS	cascading style sheet (or client security software)
CGI	common gateway interface
COM	component object model
DES	data encryption standard
DHCP	dynamic host configuration protocol
DHTML	dynamic hypertext mark-up language
DNS	domain name system
DRM	digital rights management
DSL	digital subscriber line (or loop)
EDI	electronic data interchange
EFF	electronic frontier foundation
FAQ	frequently asked questions
FDM	frequency-division multiplexing
FSF	free software foundation
FTP	file transfer protocol
GIF	graphics interchange format
GPRS	general packet radio service
GSM	global system for mobile communications
GUI	graphical user interface
HTML	hypertext mark-up language
HTTP	hypertext transfer protocol
IAB	internet architecture board
IANA	internet assigned names authority

ICANN	internet corporation for assigned names and numbers
ICQ	I seek you
IDS	intrusion-detection system
IETF	internet engineering task force
IM	instant messaging
IMAP	internet message access protocol
IP	internet protocol
IPTV	internet protocol television
IRC	internet relay chat
IRL	in real life
ISDN	integrated services digital network
ISP	internet service provider
JANET	joint academic network
JPEG	joint picture experts group (or JPG)
KBPS	kilobits per second
LAN	local area network
LDAP	lightweight directory access protocol
LINX	London internet exchange
LTE	Long term evolution
MBPS	millions of bits per second
MIME	multipurpose internet mail extensions
MMS	multimedia message service
MOO	MUD Object Oriented
MPEG	motion picture experts group
NAP	network access point
NCSA	National Centre for Supercomputing Applications
NNTP	network news transport protocol
OFDM	orthogonal frequency-division multiplexing
OSI	open source initiative
PCS	personal communications service
PDA	personal digital assistant
PDF	portable document format
PGP	pretty good privacy
PHP	hypertext preprocessor
PKI	public key infrastructure
POP	point of presence
POP3	post office protocol (latest version)
POTS	plain old telephone service
PPP	point-to-point protocol
QOS	quality of service
RDF	resource description framework
RFC	request for comments

RSS	really simple syndication (or rich site summary)
SMS	short message service
SMTP	simple mail transport protocol
SOAP	simple access object protocol
SQL	structured query language
SSL	secure sockets layer
TCP	transmission control protocol
TCP/IP	transmission control protocol/internet protocol
TD-SCDMA	time division synchronous code division multiple access
TDM	time-division multiplexing
TLA	three-letter acronym
TLD	top-level domain
TTP	trusted third party
UC	unified communications
UDDI	universal description, discovery and integration
UDRP	uniform dispute resolution policy
UMTS	universal mobile telecommunications system
URI	uniform resource identifier
URL	uniform resource locator
UUCP	unix-to-unix copy protocol
UWB	ultra-wideband
VM	virtual machine
VOD	video-on-demand
VOIP	voice over IP
VPN	virtual private network
VRML	virtual reality modelling language
W3C	world wide web consortium
WAP	wireless application protocol
WASP	wireless application service provider
W-CDMA	wideband code-division multiple access
WDM	wavelength-division multiplexing
WEP	wired equivalent privacy
WI-FI	wireless fidelity
WIMAX	worldwide interoperability for microwave access
WMA	windows media audio
WML	wireless mark-up language
WSDL	web services description language
WWW	world wide web
XHTML	extensible hypertext mark-up language
XML	extensible mark-up language
XRBL	extensible business reporting language
XSL	extensible stylesheet language

Latin

Here are some common Latin words and phrases, together with their translations.

ab initio	from the beginning
ad hoc	for this object or purpose (implied and "this one only"); therefore, without a system, spontaneously
ad hominem	to an individual's interests or passions; used of an argument that takes advantage of the character of the person on the other side
ad infinitum	to infinity, that is, endlessly
ad lib., ad libitum	at pleasure. Used adverbially or even as a verb when it means to invent or extemporise
ad nauseam	to a sickening extent
ad valorem	according to value (as opposed to volume)
a fortiori	with stronger reason
annus mirabilis	wonderful year, used to describe a special year, one in which more than one memorable thing has happened; for instance 1666, the year of the Great Fire of London and the English defeats of the Dutch
a priori	from cause to effect, that is, deductively or from prior principle
bona fide	in good faith
casus belli	the cause of war
carpe diem	literally pluck the day, but seize the day is more common; enjoy the moment; make the most of life
cave!	"Watch out!" (imperative); once used at boys' private schools in Britain
caveat emptor	let the buyer beware
ceteris paribus	other things being equal
cf	short for confer, meaning compare
circa	around or about: used for dates and large quantities; can be abbreviated to c or c.
de facto	in point of fact

de jure	from the law; by right
de minimis	abbreviation of *de minimis non curat lex*, meaning the law is not concerned with trivial matters; too small to be taken seriously
de profundis	from the depths
deus ex machina	God from a machine; first used of a Greek theatrical convention, where a god would swing on to the stage, high up in a machine, solving humanly insoluble problems and thus resolving the action of a play. Now used to describe a wholly outside person who puts matters right
eg, exempli gratia	for example
et al., et alii	and others, used as an abbreviation in bibliographies when citing multiple editorship or authorship to save the writer the bother of writing out all the names. Thus, A. Bloggs *et al.*, *The Occurrence of Endangered Species in the Genus Orthodoptera*
ex ante	before the event
ex cathedra	from the chair of office, authoritatively
ex officio	by virtue of one's office, not unofficially
ex gratia	as a favour, not under any compulsion
ex parte	from or for one side only
ex post facto, ex post	after the fact, retrospectively
ex tempore	off the cuff, without preparation (extempore)
habeas corpus	that you have a body; a writ to bring a person before a court, in most cases to ensure that the person's imprisonment is not illegal
horror vacui	literally, "fear of empty space"; the compulsion to make marks in every space. *Horror vacui* is indicated by a crowded design
ibid., ibidem	in the same place; used in footnotes in academic works to mean that the quote comes from the same source
idem	the same, as mentioned before; like ibidem
ie, id est	that is, explains the material immediately in front of it
in absentia	in the absence of, used as "absent"
in camera	in a (private) room, that is, not in public

in flagrante delicto	in the act of committing a crime; caught red-handed; an expression that seems to have developed a sexual connotation
in loco	in the place of; eg, in loco parentis, in the place of a parent
in re	in the matter of
in situ	in (its) original place
inter alia/inter alios	among other things or people
intra vires	within the permitted powers (contrast with ultra vires)
ipso facto	by that very fact, in the fact itself
lapsus linguae	a slip of the tongue
lingua franca	a common tongue
loc. cit., loco citato	in the place cited; used in footnotes to mean that the source of the reference or quote has already been given
mea culpa	my fault
memento mori	remember you have to die; a reminder of death, such as a skull
mirabile dictum	literally, wonderful to relate
mutatis mutandis	after making the necessary changes
nem. con., nemine contradicente	no one against; unanimously
non sequitur	it does not follow; an inference or conclusion that does not follow from its premises
op. cit., opere citato	in the work quoted; similar to loc. cit. (see above)
pace	with due respect to
pari passu	on the same terms, at an equal pace or rate of progress
passim	adverb, here and there or scattered. Used in indexes to indicate that the item is scattered throughout the work and there are too many instances to enumerate them all
per se	by itself, for its own sake
persona non grata	person not in favour
per stirpes	among families; a lawyer's term used when distributing an inheritance
petitio elenchis	the sin of assuming a conclusion
post eventum	after the event

post hoc, ergo propter hoc	after this, therefore because of this. Used fallaciously in argument to show that because something comes after something it can be inferred that the first thing caused the second thing
post mortem	after death, used as an adjective and also as a noun, a clinical examination of a dead body
prima facie	from a first impression, apparently at first sight – no connection with love
primus inter pares	first among equals
pro rata	for the rate; divided in proportion
pro tem., pro tempore	for the moment
PS, post scriptum	written afterwards
quid pro quo	something for something (or one thing for another), something in return, an equivalent
q.v., quod vide	which see; means that the reader should look for the word just mentioned (eg in glossary)
re	with regard to, in the matter of
sic	thus; used in brackets in quotes to show writer has made a mistake. "Mrs Thacher (sic) resigned today."
sine die	without (setting) a date
sine qua non	without which, not. Anything indispensable, and without which another cannot exist
status quo ante	the same state as before; usually shortened to status quo. A common usage is "maintaining the status quo"
stet	let it stand or do not delete; cancels an alteration in proofreading; dots are placed under what is to remain
sub judice	under judgment or consideration; not yet decided
sub rosa	under the rose, privately or furtively; not the same as under the gooseberry bush
ultra vires	beyond (one's) legal power
vade mecum	a little book or something carried about on the person; literally "Go with me"
vae victis	Woe to the conquered! A Roman phrase
versus, v or v.	against; used in legal cases and games
viz, videlicet	that is to say; to wit; namely

Laws

Scientific, economic, facetious and fatalistic laws in common use are listed here.

Benford's law In lists of numbers from many sources of data the leading digit 1 occurs much more often than the others (about 30% of the time). The law was discovered by Simon Newcomb, an American astronomer, in 1881. He noted that the first pages of books of logarithms were much more thumbed than others. Furthermore, the higher the digit, the less likely it is to occur. This applies to mathematical constants as much as utility bills, addresses, share prices, birth and death statistics, the height of mountains, and so on.

Boyle's law The pressure of a gas varies inversely with its volume at constant temperature.

Brooks's law "Adding manpower to a late software project makes it later," said Fred Brooks, in his book *The Mythical Man-Month.*

Goodhart's law "Any observed statistical regularity will tend to collapse once pressure is placed upon it for control purposes" was the law stated by Charles Goodhart, a chief adviser to the Bank of England during the 1980s. It has been recast more succinctly as "When a measure becomes a target, it ceases to be a good measure."

Gresham's law When money of a high intrinsic value is in circulation with money of lesser value, it is the inferior currency which tends to remain in circulation, while the other is either hoarded or exported. In other words: "Bad money drives out good".

Grimm's law Concerns mutations of the consonants in the various Germanic languages. Proto-Indo-European voiced aspirated stops, voiced unaspirated stops and voiceless stops become respectively voiced unaspirated stops, voiceless stops and voiceless fricatives.

Heisenberg's uncertainty principle Energy and time or position and momentum cannot both be accurately measured simultaneously. The product of their uncertainties is h (Planck's constant).

Hooke's law The stress imposed on a solid is directly proportional to the strain produced within the elastic limit.

Laws of thermodynamics

1   The change in the internal energy of a system equals the sum of the heat added to the system and the work done on it.

2   Heat cannot be transferred from a colder to a hotter body within a system without net changes occurring in other bodies in the system.
3   It is impossible to reduce the temperature of a system to absolute zero in a finite number of steps.

Mendel's principles The law of segregation is that every somatic cell of an individual carries a pair of hereditary units for each character: the pairs separate during meiosis so that each gamete carries one unit only of each pair.

The law of independent assortment is that the separation of units of each pair is not influenced by that of any other pair.

Moore's law "The number of transistors on a chip doubles every 18–24 months." An observation by Gordon Moore, a founder of Intel, regarding the pace of semiconductor technology development in 1961.

Murphy's law Anything that can go wrong will go wrong. Also known as sod's law.

Ohm's law Electric current is directly proportional to electromotive force and inversely proportional to resistance.

Pareto principle Also known as the 80/20 rule, named after Vilfredo Pareto (1848–1923), an Italian economist, who determined that 80% of activity comes from 20% of the people. The principle was extended (or simply misunderstood) by Joseph Juran, an American management guru, who suggested that for many phenomena 80% of consequences stem from 20% of the causes. That is, in many instances a large number of results stem from a small number of causes, eg, 80% of problems come from 20% of the equipment or workforce.

Parkinson's law "Work expands so as to fill the time available for its completion." Formulated by C. Northcote Parkinson and first published in *The Economist*, November 19th 1955.

Parkinson's law of data Data expand to fill the space available for storage, so acquiring more memory will encourage the adoption of techniques that require more memory.

The Peter principle All members of a hierarchy rise to their own level of incompetence, according to Laurence Peter and Raymond Hull in their book of the same name published in 1969.

Reilly's law This law of retail gravitation suggests that people are generally attracted to the largest shopping centre in the area. William

Reilly, an American academic, proposed the law in a book published in 1931.

Say's law of markets Aggregate supply creates its own aggregate demand. Attributed to Jean-Baptiste Say (1767–1832), a French economist. If output increases in a free-market economy, the sales would give the producers of the goods the same amount of income which would re-enter the economy and create demand for those goods. Keynes's law, attributed to John Maynard Keynes (1883–1946), a British economist, says that the opposite is true and that "demand creates its own supply" as businesses produce more to satisfy demand up to the limit of full employment.

sod's law See **Murphy's law**.

Utz's laws of computer programming Any given program, when running, is obsolete. If a program is useful, it will have to be changed. Any given program will expand to fill all available memory.

Wolfe's law of journalism
You cannot hope
to bribe or twist,
thank God! the
British journalist.
But seeing what
the man will do
unbribed, there's
no occasion to.

Mathematical symbols

+	plus or positive	≫	much greater than
−	minus or negative	≪	much less than
±	plus or minus, positive or negative	∝	is proportional to or varies with
×	multiplied by	√	square root
÷ or /	divided by	$^r\!\sqrt{\;}$	rth root
=	equal to	r^n	r to the power of n
≡	identically equal to	$r!$ or ⌊r	factorial r
≠	not equal to	∞	infinity
≢	not identically equal to	%	per cent
≈ or ≅	approximately equal to, of the order of or similar to	‰	per mile (thousand)
~		Σ	sum of
>	greater than	Π	product of
<	less than	Λ	difference
≯	not greater than	∴	therefore
≮	not less than		
≥	equal to or greater than		
≤	equal to or less than		

Measures

UK imperial units

A change to the metric system has taken place in the UK, but dual labelling in imperial and metric was permitted by EU rules until the end of 2009.

The following imperial units may still be used in the UK after general conversion to the metric system: mile, yard, foot, inch for road traffic signs, distance and speed measurement; pint for draught beer and cider and for milk in returnable containers; acre for land registration; troy ounce for transactions in precious metals.

Conversions

Acceleration

Standard gravity	=	10 metres (m) per second squared
	=	32 feet (ft) per second squared

Volume and capacity

5 millilitres	=	1 teaspoonful
26 UK fluid oz	=	25 US liquid oz
1¾ UK pints	=	1 litre (l)
5 UK pints	=	6 US liquid pints
9 US liquid pints	=	9l
5 UK gallons	=	6 US gallons
1 US gallon	=	3¾l
3 cubic (cu.) ft	=	85 cu. decimetres
	=	85l
27½ UK bushels	=	1 cu. m
28⅓ US bushels	=	1 cu. m
11 UK bushels	=	4 hectolitres
14 US bushels	=	5 hectolitres
1 US bushel (heaped)	=	1¼ US bushels (struck)
1 US dry barrel	=	3¼ US bushels
1 US cranberry barrel	=	2¾ bushels
1 barrel (petroleum)	=	42 US gallons
	=	35 UK gallons
1 barrel per day	=	50 tonnes per year

Weight

1 grain	=	65 milligrams
15 grains	=	1 gram (g)
11 ounces (oz)	=	10 oz troy
1 ounce	=	28g
1 oz troy	=	31g
1 pound (lb)	=	454g
35 oz	=	1 kilogram (kg)
2¼lb	=	1kg
11 US tons	=	10 tonnes
62 UK tons	=	63 tonnes
100 UK (long) tons	=	112 US (short) tons

Gold

The purity of gold is expressed as parts of 1,000, so that a fineness of 800 is 80% gold. Pure gold is defined as 24 carats (1,000 fine). Dental gold is usually 16 or 20 carat; gold in jewellery 9–22 carat. A golden sovereign is 22 carat.

1 metric carat = 200 milligrams.

Gold and silver are usually measured in troy weights: 1 troy ounce = 155.52 metric carats.

A standard international bar of gold is 400 troy ounces; bars of 250 troy ounces are also used.

Metric units

Metric units not generally recommended as SI units or for use with SI are marked with an asterisk (eg Calorie*).

Length

10 angstrom	=	1 nanometre
1,000 nanometres	=	1 micrometre
1,000 micrometres	=	1 millimetre (mm)
10mm	=	1 centimetre (cm)
10cm	=	1 decimetre
1,000mm	=	1 metre (m)
100cm	=	1m
10 decimetres	=	1m
100m	=	1 hectometre
10 hectometres	=	1 kilometre (km)
1,000km	=	1 megametre
nautical: 1,852m	=	l int. nautical mile

Area

100 sq. mm	=	1 sq. cm
100 sq. cm	=	1 sq. decimetre
100 sq. decimetres	=	1 sq. m
100 sq. m	=	1 are
10,000 sq. m	=	1 hectare (ha)
100 ares	=	1 ha
100 ha	=	1 sq. kilometre

Weight (mass)

1,000 milligrams (mg)	=	1 gram (g)
1,000g	=	1 kilogram (kg)
100kg	=	1 quintal
1,000kg	=	1 tonne

Volume

1,000 cu. mm	=	1 cu. cm
1,000 cu. cm	=	1 cu. decimetre
1,000 cu. decimetres	=	1 cu. m

Capacity

10 millilitres (ml)	=	1 centilitre (cl)
10cl	=	1 decilitre (dl)
10dl	=	1 litre (l)
1l	=	1 cu. decimetre
100 litres	=	1hl
1,000l	=	1 kilolitre
10 hectolitres	=	1 kilolitre
1 kilolitre	=	1 cu. metre

Metric system prefixes

Prefix	Symbol	Factor by which unit is multiplied		Description
atto	a	10^{-18} =	0.000 000 000 000 000 001	
femto	f	10^{-15} =	0.000 000 000 000 001	
pico	p	10^{-12} =	0.000 000 000 001	million millionth; trillionth
nano	n	10^{-9} =	0.000 000 001	thousand millionth; billionth
micro	μ	10^{-6} =	0.000 001	millionth
milli	m	10^{-3} =	0.001	thousandth
centi	c	10^{-2} =	0.01	hundredth
deci	d	10^{-1} =	0.1	tenth
deca (or deka)	da[a]	10^{1} =	10	ten
hecto	h	10^{2} =	100	hundred
kilo	k	10^{3} =	1,000	thousand
myria	my	10^{4} =	10,000	ten thousand
mega	M	10^{6} =	1,000,000	million
giga	G	10^{9} =	1,000,000,000	thousand million; billion
tera	T	10^{12} =	1,000,000,000,000	million million; trillion
peta	P	10^{15} =	1,000,000,000,000,000	
exa	E	10^{18} =	1,000,000,000,000,000,000	

a Sometimes dk is used (eg, in Germany).

Miscellaneous units and ratios

Beer

small	=	half pint
large	=	1 pint
flagon	=	1 quart
anker	=	10 gallons

Champagne

2 bottles	=	1 magnum
4 bottles	=	1 jeroboam
20 bottles	=	1 nebuchadnezzar

Wines and spirits

	Proof (Sikes) (°)	Volume of alcohol (%)
Table wines	14-26	8-15
Port, sherry	26-38.5	15-22
Whisky, gin	65.5-70	37.5-40

tot (whisky, gin, rum or vodka)	=	25ml or 35ml (before end-1994, one-sixth to one-quarter gill; the larger size is mainly used in Scotland)
wine glass	=	125ml or 175ml
wine bottle or carafe (metric sizes)	=	25cl, 50cl, 75cl or 1l

Precious metals

1 metric carat	=	200mg
1 troy oz	=	155.52 metric carats

Water

1l weighs 1kg.
1 cubic m weighs 1 tonne.
1 UK gallon weighs 10.022lb.
1 US gallon weighs 8.345lb.

Energy

1 therm	=	29.3071 kilowatt hours (kW h)
1 terawatt hour (TW h)	=	1 thousand million kilowatt hours
1 watt second	=	1 joule
1 kilowatt hour	=	36 megajoules (MJ)
1 calorie (dieticians')	=	4.1855 kilojoules

Radioactivity

1 becquerel (Bq)	=	1 disintegration per sec.
1 rutherford	=	1m Bq

Dose of radiation

1 rad	=	10 millijoules per kg
1 gray	=	100 rad = 1 joule per kg
1 rem	=	1 rad, weighted by radiation effect
1 sievert (Sv)	=	100 rems

Background dose (UK) = 25 millisievert (mSv) per year

Energy is measured in kilowatt hours and power is measured in kilowatts. Energy is power multiplied by time, thus the kilowatt-hour is one unit of energy.

Crude oil

1 barrel	=	42 US gallons
	=	34.97 UK (imperial) gallons
	=	0.159 cubic m (159l)
	=	0.136 tonne (approx.)
1 barrel per day (b/d)	=	50 tonnes per year (approx.)

Clothing sizes (rough equivalents)
Men's suits

UK/US	32	34	36	38	40	42	44
Europe	42	44	46	48	50	52	54
Metric	81	86	91	97	102	107	112

Women's suits, dresses, skirts

UK	10	12	14	16	18	20	22
US	8	10	12	14	16	18	20
Europe	38	40	42	44	47	50	52

Men's shirts (collar sizes)

UK/US (in)	15	15.5	16	16.5	17	17.5
Europe (cm)	38	39.5	41	42	43	44

Shoes

UK	5	6	7	8	9	10
US men's	6	7	8	9	10	11
US women's	6.5	7.5	8.5	9.5	10.5	11.5
Europe	38	39	40.5	42	43	44.5

Paper sizes
"A" Series (metric sizes)
A0 = 841mm × 1,189mm (33.11 in × 46.81 in)
A3 = 297mm × 420mm (11.69 in × 16.54 in)
A4 = 210mm × 297mm (8.27 in × 11.69 in)
A5 = 148mm × 210mm (5.83 in × 8.27 in)
A6 = 105mm × 148mm (4.13 in × 5.83 in)
A7 = 74mm × 105mm (2.91 in × 4.13 in)

Conversion factors[a]

Multiply number of	by	to obtain equivalent number of
Length		
inches (in)	25.4	millimetres (mm)
inches	2.54	centimetres (cm)
feet (ft)	30.48	centimetres
feet	0.3048	metres (m)
yards (yd)	0.9144	metres
miles (land 5,280 ft)	1.609344	kilometres (km)
miles (UK sea)	1.853184	kilometres
miles, international nautical	1.852	kilometres
Area		
sq. inches (in²)	645.16	sq. millimetres (mm²)
sq. inches	6.4516	sq. centimetres (cm²)
sq. ft (ft²)	929.0304	sq. centimetres
sq. ft	0.092903	sq. metres (m²)
sq. yards (yd²)	0.836127	sq. metres
acres	4046.86	sq. metres
acres	0.404686	hectares (ha)
acres	0.004047	sq. kilometres (km²)
sq. miles	2.58999	sq. kilometres
Volume and capacity		
cu. inches (in³)	16.387064	cu. centimetres (cm3)
UK pints	34.6774	cu. inches
UK pints	0.5683	litres (l)
UK gallons	4.54609	litres
US gallons	3.785	litres
cu. feet (ft³)	28.317	litres
cu. feet	0.028317	cu. metres (cm³)
UK gallons	1.20095	US gallons
US gallons	0.832674	UK gallons

Multiply number of	by	to obtain equivalent number of
Length		
millimetres	0.03937	inches
centimetres	0.3937	inches
centimetres	0.03281	feet
metres	39.3701	inches
metres	3.2808	feet
metres	1.0936	yards
metres	0.54681	fathoms
kilometres	0.62137	miles (land)
kilometres	0.53961	miles (UK sea)
kilometres	0.53996	miles, international nautical
Area		
sq. millimetres	0.00155	sq. inches
sq. centimetres	0.1550	sq. inches
sq. metres	10.7639	sq. feet
sq. metres	1.19599	sq. yards
hectares	2.47105	acres
sq. kilometres	247.105	acres
sq. kilometres	0.3861	sq. miles
Volume and capacity		
cu. centimetres	0.06102	cu. inches
litres	61.024	cu. inches
litres	2.1134	US pints
litres	1.7598	UK pints
litres	0.2642	US gallons
litres	0.21997	UK gallons
hectolitres	26.417	US gallons
hectolitres	21.997	UK gallons
hectolitres	2.838	US bushels
hectolitres	2.750	UK bushels
cu. metres	35.3147	cu. feet
cu. metres	1.30795	cu. yards
cu. metres	264.172	US gallons

Multiply number of	by	to obtain equivalent number of
Weight (mass)		
ounces, avoirdupois (oz)	28.3495	grams (g)
ounces, troy (oz tr)	31.1035	grams
ounces, avoirdupois	0.9115	ounces, troy
pounds, avoirdupois (lb)	453.59237	grams
pounds, avoirdupois (lb)	0.45359	kilograms (kg)
short tons (2,000 lb)	0.892857	long tons
short tons (2,000 lb)	0.907185	tonnes (t)
long tons (2,240 lb)	1.12	short tons
long tons (2,240 lb)	1.01605	tonnes
Velocity and fuel consumption		
miles/hour	1.609344	kilometres/hour
miles/hour	0.868976	international knots
miles/UK gallon	0.35401	kilometres/litre
miles/US gallon	0.42514	kilometres/litre
UK gallons/mile[b]	282.481	litres/100 kilometres
US gallons/mile[b]	235.215	litres/100 kilometres
Temperature		
degrees Fahrenheit	5/9 after subtracting 32	degrees Celsius (centigrade)
-40°F	equals	-40°C
32°F	equals	0°C
59°F	equals	15°C

Multiply number of	by	to obtain equivalent number of
Weight (mass)		
grams	0.03527	ounces, avoirdupois
grams	0.03215	ounces, troy
kilograms	2.20462	pounds, avoirdupois
metric quintals (q)	220.462	pounds, avoirdupois
tonnes	2,204.62	pounds, avoirdupois
tonnes	1.10231	short tons
tonnes	0.984207	long tons
Velocity and fuel consumption		
kilometres/hour	0.62137	miles/hour
kilometres/hour	0.53996	international knots
kilometres/litre	2.82481	miles/UK gallon
litres/100 kilometres[c]	0.00354	UK gallons/mile
litres/100 kilometres[c]	0.00425	US gallons/mile
Temperature		
degrees Celsius	9/5 and add 32	degrees Fahrenheit
37°C	equals	98.6°F
50°C	equals	122°F
100°C	equals	212°F

a Between the UK and US systems, and the International System of Units (SI). As an example of the use of the table, 10 long tons (of 2,240lb each), multiplied by 1.12, is equal to 11.2 short tons (of 2,000lb each).

b Miles per UK gallon, divided into 282.481, gives litres per 100 kilometres; miles per US gallon, divided into 235.215, gives litres per 100 kilometres.

c Litres per 100 kilometres, divided into 282.481 gives miles per UK gallon; litres per 100 kilometres, divided into 235.215 gives miles per US gallon.

National accounts

These are the definitions adopted by the United Nations in 1968, but note that national accounts now refer to gross national product as gross national income (GNI).

See http://unstats.un.org/unsd/nationalaccount/ for more details.

Final expenditure

=   private final consumption expenditure ("consumers' expenditure")
+   government final consumption expenditure
+   increase in stocks
+   gross fixed capital formation
+   exports of goods and services

Gross domestic product (GDP) at market prices

=   final expenditure
−   imports of goods and services

Gross national income or product (GNI/GNP) at market prices

=   gross domestic product at market prices
+   net property income from other countries

Gross domestic product at factor cost

=   gross domestic product at market prices
−   indirect taxes
+   subsidies

North America administrative divisions

Here are the main administrative subdivisions of the United States and Canada. *See also* **countries and their inhabitants, placenames** in Part 1.

United States
States

Alabama (AL)
Alaska (AK)
Arizona (AZ)
Arkansas (AR)
California (CA)
Colorado (CO)
Connecticut (CT)
Delaware (DE)
Federal District of Columbia (DC)[a]
Florida (FL)
Georgia (GA)
Hawaii (HI)
Idaho (ID)
Illinois (IL)
Indiana (IN)
Iowa (IA)
Kansas (KS)
Kentucky (KY)
Louisiana (LA)
Maine (ME)
Maryland (MD)
Massachusetts (MA)
Michigan (MI)
Minnesota (MN)
Mississippi (MS)
Missouri (MO)

Montana (MT)
Nebraska (NE)
Nevada (NV)
New Hampshire (NH)
New Jersey (NJ)
New Mexico (NM)
New York (NY)
North Carolina (NC)
North Dakota (ND)
Ohio (OH)
Oklahoma (OK)
Oregon (OR)
Pennsylvania (PA)
Puerto Rico (PR)
Rhode Island (RI)
South Carolina (SC)
South Dakota (SD)
Tennessee (TN)
Texas (TX)
Utah (UT)
Vermont (VT)
Virginia (VA)
Washington (WA)
West Virginia (WV)
Wisconsin (WI)
Wyoming (WY)

a   DC is not a state.

Canada

Provinces

Alberta
British Columbia
Manitoba
New Brunswick
Newfoundland and Labrador

Nova Scotia
Ontario
Prince Edward Island
Quebec (Québec)
Saskatchewan

Territories

Northwest Territories
Nunavut

Yukon

O

Olympic games

Summer

I	Athens	1896	XVI	Melbourne	1956
II	Paris	1900	XVII	Rome	1960
III	St Louis	1904	XVIII	Tokyo	1964
IV	London	1908	XIX	Mexico City	1968
V	Stockholm	1912	XX	Munich	1972
VI	Berlin (cancelled)	1916	XXI	Montreal	1976
VII	Antwerp	1920	XXII	Moscow	1980
VIII	Paris	1924	XXIII	Los Angeles	1984
IX	Amsterdam	1928	XXIV	Seoul	1988
X	Los Angeles	1932	XXV	Barcelona	1992
XI	Berlin	1936	XXVI	Atlanta	1996
XII	Tokyo/Helsinki (cancelled)	1940	XXVII	Sydney	2000
			XXVIII	Athens	2004
XIII	London (cancelled)	1944	XXIX	Beijing	2008
XIV	London	1948	XXX	London	2012
XV	Helsinki	1952	XXXI	Rio de Janeiro	2016

Winter

I	Chamonix, France	1924	V	St Moritz, Switzerland	1948
II	St Moritz, Switzerland	1928	VI	Oslo, Norway	1952
III	Lake Placid, United States	1932	VII	Cortina d'Ampezzo, Italy	1956
IV	Garmisch-Partenkirchen, Germany	1936	VIII	Squaw Valley, United States	1960
	Cancelled	1940	IX	Innsbruck, Austria	1964
	Cancelled	1944	X	Grenoble, France	1968

XI	Sapporo, Japan	1972	XVII	Lillehammer, Norway	1994[a]
XII	Innsbruck, Austria	1976	XVIII	Nagano, Japan	1998
XIII	Lake Placid, United States	1980	XIX	Salt Lake City, United States	2002
XIV	Sarajevo, Yugoslavia	1984	XX	Torino (Turin), Italy	2006
XV	Calgary, Canada	1988	XXI	Vancouver, Canada	2010
XVI	Albertville, France	1992[a]	XXII	Sochi, Russia	2014

a Since 1994 the summer and winter Olympic games have taken place in alternate even-numbered years. Hence, the Albertville and Lillehammer winter games are only two years apart.

Organisations

These are the exact names and abbreviated titles of the main international organisations. Where membership is small or exclusive, members are listed too.

African Union formerly the Organisation of African Unity (OAU), founded in 1962, headquarters in Addis Ababa, Ethiopia.

Members

Algeria
Angola
Benin
Botswana
Burkina Faso
Burundi
Cameroon
Cape Verde
Central African
 Republic
Comoros
Congo (Brazzaville)
Congo, Democratic
 Republic of
Côte d'Ivoire
Djibouti
Egypt
Equatorial Guinea
Eritrea

Ethiopia
Gabon
The Gambia
Ghana
Guinea Bissau
Guinea
Kenya
Lesotho
Liberia
Libya
Madagascar
Malawi
Mali
Mauritania
Mauritius
Mozambique
Namibia
Niger
Nigeria

Rwanda
Saharawi Arab
 Democratic
 Republic
São Tomé and
 Principe
Senegal
Seychelles
Sierra Leone
Somalia
South Africa
Sudan
Swaziland
Tanzania
Togo
Tunisia
Uganda
Zambia
Zimbabwe

ALADI Asociación Latinoamericana de Integración (Latin American Integration Association), founded in 1980, based in Montevideo, Uruguay.

Members[a]

Argentina	Colombia	Paraguay
Bolivia	Cuba	Peru
Brazil	Ecuador	Uruguay
Chile	Mexico	Venezuela

a There are also 17 observer countries and 10 observer organisations.

Andean Community of Nations founded in 1969, headquarters in Lima, Peru.

Members

Bolivia	Ecuador
Colombia	Peru

APEC Asia-Pacific Economic Cooperation, founded in 1989, based in Singapore.

Members

Australia	Indonesia	Philippines
Brunei Darussalam	Japan	Russia
Canada	Malaysia	Singapore
Chile	Mexico	Thailand
China	New Zealand	United States
Chinese Taipei (Taiwan)	Papua New Guinea	Vietnam
Hong Kong, China	Peru	

ASEAN Association of South-east Asian Nations, established in 1967, headquarters in Jakarta, Indonesia.

Members

Brunei Darussalam	Malaysia	Singapore
Cambodia	Myanmar	Thailand
Indonesia	Philippines	Vietnam
Laos		

BIS Bank for International Settlements, the central bankers' central bank, founded 1930, based in Basel, Switzerland.

Members[a]

Algeria	Bosnia & Hercegovina	China
Argentina	Brazil	Croatia
Australia	Bulgaria	Czech Republic
Austria	Canada	Denmark
Belgium	Chile	Estonia

Finland	Latvia	Singapore
France	Lithuania	Slovakia
Germany	Macedonia	Slovenia
Greece	Malaysia	South Africa
Hong Kong SAR	Mexico	Spain
Hungary	Netherlands	Sweden
Iceland	Norway	Switzerland
India	Philippines	Thailand
Indonesia	Poland	Turkey
Ireland	Portugal	United Kingdom
Israel	Romania	United States
Italy	Russia	
Japan	Saudi Arabia	

a The European Central Bank is a shareholder.

CARICOM Caribbean Community and Common Market, formed in 1973, secretariat in Georgetown, Guyana.

Members

Anguilla[a]	Cayman Islands[a]	St Kitts-Nevis
Antigua and Barbuda	Dominica	St Lucia
Bahamas[b]	Grenada	St Vincent and the Grenadines
Barbados	Guyana	Suriname
Belize	Haiti	Trinidad and Tobago
Bermuda[a]	Jamaica	Turks and Caicos Islands[a]
British Virgin Islands[a]	Montserrat	

a Associate member.
b Member of the Community but not the Common Market.

Observer status

Aruba	Netherlands Antilles
Colombia	Puerto Rico
Dominican Republic	Venezuela
Mexico	

COMESA Common Market for Eastern and Southern Africa, founded in 1993, headquarters in Lusaka, Zambia.

Members

Burundi	Ethiopia	Seychelles
Comoros	Kenya	Sudan
Congo, Democratic	Libya	Swaziland
Republic of	Madagascar	Uganda
Djibouti	Malawi	Zambia
Egypt	Mauritius	Zimbabwe
Eritrea	Rwanda	

Commonwealth based in London, UK.

Members

Antigua and Barbuda	Jamaica	St Vincent and the Grenadines
Australia	Kenya	Samoa
Bahamas	Kiribati	Seychelles
Bangladesh	Lesotho	Sierra Leone
Barbados	Malawi	Singapore
Belize	Malaysia	Solomon Islands
Botswana	Maldives	South Africa
Brunei Darussalam	Malta	Sri Lanka
Cameroon	Mauritius	Swaziland
Canada	Mozambique	Tanzania
Cyprus	Namibia	Tonga
Dominica	Nauru[b]	Trinidad and Tobago
Fiji Islands[a]	New Zealand	Tuvalu
The Gambia	Nigeria	Uganda
Ghana	Pakistan	United Kingdom
Grenada	Papua New Guinea	Vanuatu
Guyana	St Kitts and Nevis	Zambia
India	St Lucia	

a Suspended on September 1st 2009.
b Member in arrears.

Dependencies and associated states

Australia

Ashmore and Cartier Islands	Coral Sea Islands Territory
Australian Antarctic Territory	Heard and McDonald Islands
Christmas Island	Norfolk Island
Cocos (Keeling) Islands	

New Zealand

Cook Islands	Ross Dependency
Niue	Tokelau

UK

Anguilla	Gibraltar
Bermuda	Isle of Man
British Antarctic Territory	Montserrat
British Indian Ocean Territory	Pitcairn Island
British Virgin Islands	South Georgia and South Sandwich Islands
Cayman Islands	St Helena, Ascension and Tristan da Cunha
Channel Islands	Turks and Caicos Islands
Falkland Islands	

Commonwealth of Independent States (CIS) founded by the former Soviet Socialist Republics in December 1991, based in Moscow, Russia.

Members

Armenia	Kazakhstan	Tajikistan
Azerbaijan	Kyrgyzstan	Turkmenistan
Belarus	Moldova	Ukraine
Georgia	Russia	Uzbekistan

ECOWAS Economic Community of West African States, founded 1975, secretariat in Abuja, Nigeria.

Members

Benin	Ghana	Niger
Burkina Faso	Guinea	Nigeria
Cape Verde	Guinea-Bissau	Senegal
Côte d'Ivoire	Liberia	Sierra Leone
The Gambia	Mali	Togo

EEA European Economic Area, negotiated in 1992 between the European Community and members of EFTA, came into force in 1994 and has been maintained because the three signatories – Iceland, Norway and Liechtenstein – wanted to participate in the Single Market without being full members of the EU.

EFTA European Free Trade Association, established 1960.

Members

Iceland	Norway
Liechtenstein	Switzerland

Euro area Name given to the economic region formed by the EU member countries that have adopted the euro as their currency. Also known as the euro zone.

Members

Austria[a]	Greece (2001)	Portugal
Belgium[a]	Ireland[a]	Slovenia (2007)
Cyprus (2008)	Italy[a]	Slovakia (2009)
Finland[a]	Luxembourg[a]	Spain
France[a]	Malta (2008)	
Germany[a]	Netherlands[a]	

a Joined in 1999 when the euro was introduced.

EU European Union, the collective designation of three organisations with common membership: the European Coal and Steel Community (ECSC, treaty expired in 2002), European Economic Community (EEC) and European Atomic Energy Community (EURATOM). They merged to become the European Community (EC) in 1967. In November 1993 when the Maastricht treaty came into force the EC was incorporated into the EU. Economic and Monetary Union (EMU) formed one of the articles of the Maastricht treaty, in which were set out the stages by which the EU would progress to full convergence, with a single currency, the euro. Headquarters in Brussels, with some activities in Luxembourg and Strasbourg.

Main institutions

European Parliament
Council of the European Union
European Investment Bank (EIB)
European Commission
Court of Justice of the European Communities
European Court of Auditors
European Ombudsman

European Data Protection Supervisor
European Central Bank
European Investment Fund
European Economic and Social Committee (ESC)
Committee of the Regions

Other bodies

European Agency for Safety and Health at Work (EU-OSHA)
European Agency for the Management of Operational Cooperation with External Borders (FRONTEX)
European Aviation Safety Agency (EASA)
European Centre for Disease Prevention and Control (ECDC)
European Centre for the Development of Vocational Training (CEDEFOP)
European Chemicals Agency (ECHA)
European Environment Agency (EEA)
European Food Safety Authority (EFSA)
European Foundation for the Improvement of Living and Working Conditions (EUROFOUND)
European GNSS Supervisory Authority (GSA)

European Maritime Safety Agency (EMSA)
European Medicines Agency (EMEA)
European Monitoring Centre for Drugs and Drug Addiction (EMCDDA)
European Network and Information Security Agency (ENISA)
European Railway Agency (ERA)
European Training Foundation (ETF)
European Union Agency for fundamental rights (FRA)
Community Fisheries Control Agency (CFCA)
Community Plant Variety Rights Office (CPVO)
Office for Harmonisation in the Internal Market (OHIM)
Translation Centre for Bodies in the European Union (CDT)

Members

Austria (1994)	Germany[a]	Netherlands[a]
Belgium[a]	Greece (1981)	Poland (2004)
Bulgaria (2007)	Hungary (2004)	Portugal (1986)
Cyprus (2004)	Ireland (1973)	Romania (2007)
Czech Republic (2004)	Italy[a]	Slovakia (2004)
Denmark (1973)	Latvia (2004)	Slovenia (2004)
Estonia (2004)	Lithuania (2004)	Spain (1986)
Finland (1994)	Luxembourg[a]	Sweden (1994)
France[a]	Malta (2004)	UK (1973)

a Founding member.
Note: Year of joining in brackets.

FTAA Free Trade Area of the Americas, set up in November 2002 to integrate the economies of the western hemisphere into a single free trade agreement.

Members

Antigua & Barbuda	Dominican Republic	Paraguay
Argentina	Ecuador	Peru
Bahamas	El Salvador	St Kitts & Nevis
Barbados	Grenada	St Lucia
Belize	Guatemala	St Vincent &
Bolivia	Guyana	the Grenadines
Brazil	Haiti	Suriname
Canada	Honduras	Trinidad & Tobago
Chile	Jamaica	United States
Colombia	Mexico	Uruguay
Costa Rica	Nicaragua	Venezuela
Dominica	Panama	

GCC Co-operation Council for the Arab States of the Gulf or Gulf Co-operation Council, established in 1981, headquarters in Riyadh, Saudi Arabia.

Members

Bahrain	Oman	Saudi Arabia
Kuwait	Qatar	United Arab Emirates

G7, G8, G10, G22, G26 In 1975, six countries, the world's leading capitalist countries, ranked by GDP, were represented in France at the first annual summit meeting: the United States, the UK, Germany, Japan and Italy, as well as the host country. The following year they were joined by Canada and, in 1977, by representatives of the European Union, although the group continued to be known as the G7. At the

1989 summit, 15 developing countries were also represented, although this did not give birth to the G22, which was not set up until 1998 and swiftly grew into G26. At the 1991 G7 summit, a meeting was held with the Soviet Union, a practice that continued (with Russia) in later years. In 1998, although it was not one of the world's eight richest countries, Russia became a full member of the G8. Meetings of the IMF are attended by the G10, which includes 11 countries.

G10 members

Belgium	Italy	Switzerland
Canada	Japan	United Kingdom
France	Netherlands	United States
Germany	Sweden	

IATA International Air Transport Association, head offices in Montreal and Geneva; regional offices in Miami and Singapore.

Members: most international airlines

International Seabed Authority an autonomous organisation in relationship with the UN, established 1996, based in Kingston, Jamaica
Members: 148 signatories to the Convention on the Law of the Sea.

Mercosur Mercado Común del Sur (Southern Common Market), founded in 1991, based in Montevideo, Uruguay.

Members	*Associate members*
Argentina	Bolivia
Brazil	Chile
Paraguay	Colombia
Uruguay	Ecuador
	Peru

NAFTA North American Free Trade Agreement, which came into force on January 1st 1994.

Members

Canada	Mexico	United States

NATO North Atlantic Treaty Organisation, an alliance of 26 countries from Europe and North America committed to fulfilling goals of North Atlantic Treaty signed on April 4th 1949; headquarters in Brussels, Belgium.

Members

Albania	Canada	Denmark
Belgium	Croatia	Estonia
Bulgaria	Czech Republic	France

Germany

Greece

Hungary

Iceland

Italy

Latvia

Lithuania

Luxembourg

Netherlands

Norway

Poland

Portugal

Romania

Slovakia

Slovenia

Spain

Turkey

United Kingdom

United States

OAS Organisation of American States, formed in 1948, headquarters in Washington, DC.

Members[a][b]

Antigua and
   Barbuda

Argentina

Bahamas

Barbados

Belize

Bolivia

Brazil

Canada

Chile

Colombia

Costa Rica

Dominica

Dominican Republic

Ecuador

El Salvador

Grenada

Guatemala

Guyana

Haiti

Honduras[c]

Jamaica

Mexico

Nicaragua

Panama

Paraguay

Peru

St Kitts-Nevis

St Lucia

St Vincent and the Grenadines

Suriname

Trinidad and Tobago

United States

Uruguay

Venezuela

a Has many permanent non-member observers.
b Cuba was excluded from participation in the OAS in 1962. However, on June 3rd 2009 it
   was decided that the 1962 Resolution excluding Cuba would no longer apply.
c Honduras was suspended from active participation on July 5th 2009.

OECD Organisation for Economic Co-operation and Development, capitalism's club, founded in 1961, based in Paris, France. The European Commission also takes part in the OECD's work.

Members

Australia

Austria

Belgium

Canada

Czech Republic

Denmark

Finland

France

Germany

Greece

Hungary

Iceland

Ireland

Italy

Japan

Luxembourg

Mexico

Netherlands

New Zealand

Norway

Poland

Portugal

Slovakia

South Korea

Spain

Sweden

Switzerland

Turkey

United Kingdom

United States

OPEC Organisation of the Petroleum Exporting Countries, established 1960, based in Vienna, Austria.

Members

Algeria	Iraq	Qatar
Ecuador	Kuwait	Saudi Arabia
Indonesia[a]	Libya	United Arab Emirates
Iran	Nigeria	Venezuela

a Indonesia suspended its membership from January 2009.

OSCE Organisation for Security and Co-operation in Europe, originally founded in 1972 as the Conference on Security and Co-operation in Europe (CSCE).

Members: 56, including European countries, Canada, the US and former republics of the Soviet Union

SADC Southern African Development Community, replaced the Southern African Co-ordination Conference in 1992, based in Gaborone, Botswana. Its aim is to work for development and economic growth in the region with common systems and institutions, promoting peace and security, and achieving complementary national and regional strategies.

Members

Angola	Malawi	South Africa
Botswana	Mauritius	Swaziland
Congo, Democratic	Mozambique	Tanzania
Republic of	Namibia	Zambia
Lesotho	Seychelles	Zimbabwe

The United Nations (UN) officially came into existence on October 24th 1945, based in New York, US.

Main bodies

General Assembly	International Court of Justice
Security Council	Secretariat
Economic and Social Council (ECOSOC)	Repertory of Practice of United Nations Organs
Trusteeship Council	

Secretaries-general

Sir Gladwyn Jebb (UK), acting, 1945-46

Trygve Lie (Norway), February 1946 to his resignation in November 1952

Dag Hammarskjöld (Sweden), April 1953 until his death in a plane crash in Northern Rhodesia (now Zambia), September 1961

U Thant (Burma, now Myanmar), November 1961-December 1971

Kurt Waldheim (Austria) 1972-81
Javier Pérez de Cuéllar (Peru) 1982-91
Boutros Boutros-Ghali (Egypt), January 1992 to the American veto of his
    second term in December 1996
Kofi Annan (Ghana, Africa), 1997–2006
Ban Ki-moon (South Korea), 2007–

Regional commissions		Head office
Economic Commission for Africa	ECA	Addis Ababa
Economic Commission for Europe	ECE	Geneva
Economic Commission for Latin America and the Caribbean	ECLAC	Santiago, Chile
Economic and Social Commission for Asia and the Pacific	ESCAP	Bangkok
Economic and Social Commission for Western Asia	ESCWA	Beirut

Other UN bodies and programmes

Department of Peace-keeping Operations	DPKO	New York
International Trade Centre	ITC	Geneva
Office for the Co-ordination of Humanitarian Affairs	OCHA	New York
Office of United Nations High Commissioner for Human Rights	OHCHR	Geneva
United Nations Capital Development Fund	UNCDF	New York
United Nations Children's Fund	UNICEF	New York
United Nations Conference on Trade and Development	UNCTAD	Geneva
United Nations Development Fund for Women	UNIFEM	New York
United Nations Development Programme	UNDP	New York
United Nations Drug Control Programme	UNDCP	Vienna
United Nations Environment Programme	UNEP	Nairobi
United Nations High Commissioner for Refugees	UNHCR	Geneva
United Nations Human Settlements Programme	UNHSP (UN-Habitat)	Nairobi
United Nations Institute for Research and Training	UNITAR	Geneva
United Nations Population Fund	UNFPA	New York
United Nations Relief and Works Agency for Palestine Refugees in the Near East	UNRWA	Gaza City, Amman
United Nations Volunteers	UNV	Bonn
World Food Programme	WFP	Rome

Specialised agencies within the UN system

Food and Agriculture Organisation	FAO	Rome
International Civil Aviation Organisation	ICAO	Montreal
International Fund for Agricultural Development	IFAD	Rome
International Labour Organisation	ILO	Geneva
International Maritime Organisation	IMO	London
International Monetary Fund	IMF	Washington, DC
International Telecommunications Union	ITU	Geneva
Multilateral Investment Guarantee Agency	MIGA	Washington, DC
United Nations Educational, Scientific and Cultural Organisation	UNESCO	Paris
United Nations Industrial Development Organisation	UNIDO	Vienna
Universal Postal Union	UPU	Berne
World Bank[a]		Washington, DC
World Health Organisation	WHO	Geneva
World Intellectual Property Organisation	WIPO	Geneva
World Meteorological Organisation	WMO	Geneva
World Tourism Organisation	UNWTO	Madrid

a Comprising the International Bank for Reconstruction and Development (IBRD), the International Centre for Settlement of Investment Disputes (ICSID), the International Development Association (IDA), the International Finance Corporation (IFC), and the Multilateral Investment Guarantee Agency (MIGA).

Related organisations

International Atomic Energy Agency	IAEA	Vienna
Preparatory Commission for the Nuclear-Test-Ban Treaty Organisation	CTBTO	Vienna
Organisation for the Prohibition of Chemical Weapons	OPCW	The Hague

WTO World Trade Organisation, the international organisation of the world trading system with co-operative links to the UN, established in 1995 as successor to the General Agreement on Tariffs and Trade (GATT), based in Geneva.

Members: 153 countries

Populations of the world

Here are the countries of the world with populations of at least 1m, showing their areas, capitals and GDP.

Country	Population (m), 2007	Area ('000 sq. km)	Capital	GDP ($bn), 2007
China	1,331.4	9,561	Beijing	3,205.5
India	1,135.6	3,287	New Delhi	1,176.9
United States	303.9	9,373	Washington, DC	13,751.4
Indonesia	228.1	1,904	Jakarta	432.8
Brazil	191.3	8,512	Brasilia	1,313.4
Pakistan	164.6	804	Islamabad	142.9
Bangladesh	147.1	144	Dhaka	68.4
Russia	141.9	17,075	Moscow	1,290.1
Nigeria	137.2	924	Abuja	165.5
Japan	128.3	378	Tokyo	4,384.3
Mexico	109.6	1,973	Mexico City	1,022.8
Vietnam	86.4	331	Hanoi	68.6
Philippines	85.9	300	Manila	144.1
Germany	82.7	358	Berlin	3,317.4
Ethiopia	81.2	1,134	Addis Ababa	19.4
Egypt	76.9	1,000	Cairo	130.5
Turkey	75.2	779	Ankara	655.9
Iran	71.2	1,648	Tehran	286.1
Thailand	65.3	513	Bankok	245.4
Congo-Kinshasa	61.2	2,345	Kinshasa	9.0
France	60.9	544	Paris	2,589.8[a]
United Kingdom	60.0	243	London	2,772.0
Italy	58.2	301	Rome	2,101.6
Myanmar	51.5	677	Rangoon	19.6[a]
South Korea	48.1	99	Seoul	969.8
South Africa	47.7	1,226	Pretoria	283.0
Colombia	47.0	1,142	Bogota	207.8

Country	Population (m), 2007	Area ('000 sq. km)	Capital	GDP ($bn), 2007
Ukraine	45.5	604	Kiev	141.2
Spain	43.6	505	Madrid	1,435.9
Tanzania	39.7	945	Dar es Salaam	16.2
Argentina	39.5	2,767	Buenos Aires	262.5
Poland	38.5	313	Warsaw	422.1
Sudan	37.8	2,506	Khartoum	46.2
Kenya	36.0	583	Nairobi	24.2
Algeria	33.9	2,382	Algiers	135.3
Canada	32.9	9,971	Ottawa	1,329.9
Morocco	32.4	447	Rabat	75.1
Afghanistan	32.3	652	Kabul	8.4[b]
Uganda	30.9	241	Kampala	11.8
Iraq	30.3	438	Baghdad	60.1[a]
Peru	28.8	1,285	Lima	107.3
Nepal	28.2	147	Kathmandu	10.3
Venezuela	27.7	912	Caracas	228.1
Uzbekistan	27.4	447	Tashkent	22.3
Malaysia	26.2	333	Kuala Lumpur	186.7
Saudi Arabia	25.8	2,200	Riyadh	382.7
Ghana	23.0	239	Accra	15.1
Taiwan	22.9	36	Taipei	383.3
North Korea	22.7	121	Pyongyang	40.0[a]
Yemen	22.3	528	Sanaa	22.5
Romania	21.5	238	Bucharest	166.0
Sri Lanka	21.1	66	Colombo	32.3
Australia	20.6	7,682	Canberra	821.0
Mozambique	20.5	799	Maputo	7.8
Syria	20.0	185	Damascus	37.7
Madagascar	19.6	587	Antananarivo	7.4
Côte d'Ivoire	18.8	322	Abidjan/ Yamoussoukro	19.8
Angola	16.9	1,247		61.4
Cameroon	16.9	475	Yaoundé	20.7
Chile	16.6	757	Santiago	163.9
Netherlands	16.4	42	Amsterdam	765.8
Niger	14.9	1,267	Niamey	4.2
Kazakhstan	14.8	2,717	Astana	104.9
Cambodia	14.6	181	Phnom Penh	8.4

Country	Population (m), 2007	Area ('000 sq. km)	Capital	GDP ($bn), 2007
Mali	14.3	1,240	Bamako	6.9
Burkina Faso	14.0	274	Ouagadougou	6.8
Ecuador	13.6	272	Quito	44.5
Malawi	13.5	118	Lilongwe	3.6
Guatemala	13.2	109	Guatemala City	33.9
Zimbabwe	13.2	391	Harare	3.4[b]
Senegal	12.2	197	Dakar	11.2
Zambia	12.1	753	Lusaka	11.4
Cuba	11.3	111	Havana	45.5[a]
Greece	11.2	132	Athens	313.4
Portugal	10.6	89	Lisbon	222.8
Belgium	10.5	31	Brussels	452.8
Chad	10.3	1,284	N'Djamena	7.1
Tunisia	10.3	164	Tunis	35.0
Czech Republic	10.2	79	Prague	175.0
Hungary	10.0	93	Budapest	138.4
Serbia	9.9	88	Belgrade	40.1
Guinea	9.8	246	Conakry	4.6
Belarus	9.6	208	Minsk	44.8
Bolivia	9.5	1,099	La Paz	13.1
Rwanda	9.4	26	Kigali	3.3
Dominican Republic	9.1	48	Santo Domingo	36.7
Sweden	9.1	450	Stockholm	464.3
Benin	9.0	113	Porto-Novo	5.4
Haiti	8.8	28	Port-au-Prince	6.7
Somalia	8.8	638	Mogadishu	2.5[a]
Azerbaijan	8.5	87	Baku	31.2
Austria	8.2	84	Vienna	373.2
Burundi	8.1	28	Bujumbura	1.0
Bulgaria	7.6	111	Sofia	39.5
Honduras	7.5	112	Tegucigalpa	12.2
Switzerland	7.3	41	Berne	424.4
Hong Kong	7.2	1	Hong Kong	207.2
El Salvador	7.1	21	San Salvador	20.4
Israel	7.0	21	Jerusalem	164.0
Tajikistan	6.7	143	Dushanbe	3.7
Togo	6.5	57	Lome	2.5

Country	Population (m), 2007	Area ('000 sq. km)	Capital	GDP ($bn), 2007
Paraguay	6.4	407	Asuncion	12.2
Laos	6.2	237	Vientiane	4.1
Libya	6.1	1,760	Tripoli	58.3
Papua New Guinea	6.1	463	Port Moresby	6.3
Jordan	6.0	89	Amman	15.8
Sierra Leone	5.8	72	Freetown	1.7
Nicaragua	5.7	130	Managua	5.7
Denmark	5.5	43	Copenhagen	311.6
Kyrgyzstan	5.4	199	Bishkek	3.7
Slovakia	5.4	49	Bratislava	75.0
Finland	5.3	338	Helsinki	244.7
Turkmenistan	5.0	488	Ashgabat	12.9
United Arab Emirates	4.8	84	Abu Dhabi	163.3[b]
Eritrea	4.7	117	Asmara	1.4
Norway	4.7	324	Oslo	388.4
Croatia	4.6	57	Zagreb	51.3
Costa Rica	4.5	51	San José	26.3
Georgia	4.4	70	Tbilisi	10.2
Singapore	4.4	1	Singapore	161.3
Ireland	4.3	70	Dublin	259.0
Central African Rep	4.2	622	Bangui	1.7
Congo-Brazzaville	4.2	342	Brazzaville	7.6
Moldova	4.2	34	Chisinau	4.4
New Zealand	4.1	271	Wellington	135.7
Puerto Rico	4.0	9	San Juan	77.4[a]
Bosnia	3.9	51	Sarajevo	15.1
West Bank and Gaza	3.9	6	Gaza City	5.3[b]
Lebanon	3.7	10	Beirut	24.4
Liberia	3.5	111	Monrovia	0.7
Uruguay	3.5	176	Montevideo	23.1
Lithuania	3.4	65	Vilnius	38.3
Panama	3.3	77	Panama City	19.5
Albania	3.2	29	Tirane	10.8
Mauritania	3.2	1,031	Nouakchott	2.6
Armenia	3.0	30	Yerevan	9.2

Country	Population (m), 2007	Area ('000 sq. km)	Capital	GDP ($bn), 2007
Kuwait	2.8	18	Kuwait City	112.1
Jamaica	2.7	11	Kingston	11.4
Mongolia	2.7	1,565	Ulaanbaatar	3.9
Oman	2.7	310	Muscat	35.7[b]
Bhutan	2.3	47	Thimphu	1.1
Latvia	2.3	64	Riga	27.2
Namibia	2.1	824	Windhoek	7.0
Macedonia	2.0	26	Skopje	7.7
Slovenia	2.0	20	Ljubljana	47.2
Botswana	1.8	581	Gaborone	12.3
Lesotho	1.8	30	Maseru	1.6
Guinea-Bissau	1.7	36	Bissau	0.4
Gambia, The	1.6	11	Banjul	0.6
Gabon	1.4	268	Libreville	11.6
Estonia	1.3	45	Talinn	20.9
Mauritius	1.3	2		6.8
Trinidad & Tobago	1.3	5	Port-of-Spain	20.9
Timor-Leste	1.1	15	Dili	0.4
Swaziland	1.0	17	Mbabane	2.9

a Estimate.
b Latest available year.
c Including French Guiana, Guadeloupe, Martinique and Réunion.
Source: *The Economist Pocket World in Figures*, 2010 Edition. Profile Books, London, 2010.

Presidents and prime ministers

Here are lists of presidents of America and prime ministers of the UK.

Presidents of the United States

Date	President	Date	President
1789–97	George Washington	1889–93	Benjamin Harrison
1797–1801	John Adams	1893–97	Grover Cleveland
1801–09	Thomas Jefferson	1897–1901	William McKinley
1809–17	James Madison	1901–09	Theodore Roosevelt
1817–25	James Monroe	1909–13	William H. Taft
1825–29	John Adams	1913–21	Woodrow Wilson
1829–37	Andrew Jackson	1921–23	Warren Harding
1837–41	Martin Van Buren	1923–29	Calvin Coolidge

Date	President	Date	President
1841	William Henry Harrison	1929–33	Herbert Hoover
1841–45	John Tyler	1933–45	Franklin D. Roosevelt
1845–49	James Polk	1945–53	Harry Truman
1849–50	Zachary Taylor	1953–61	Dwight Eisenhower
1850–53	Millard Fillmore	1961–63	John F. Kennedy
1853–57	Franklin Pierce	1963–69	Lyndon Johnson
1857–61	James Buchanan	1969–74	Richard Nixon
1861–65	Abraham Lincoln	1974–77	Gerald Ford
1865–69	Andrew Johnson	1977–81	Jimmy Carter
1869–77	Ulysses S. Grant	1981–89	Ronald Reagan
1877–81	Rutherford B. Hayes	1989–93	George H.W. Bush
1881	James Garfield	1993–2001	William J. Clinton
1881–85	Chester Arthur	2001–09	George W. Bush
1885–89	Grover Cleveland	2009–	Barack Obama

Prime ministers of the United Kingdom

Date	Prime minister
1721–42	Sir Robert Walpole
1742–43	Spencer Compton, Earl of Wilmington
1743–54	Henry Pelham
1754–56	Thomas Pelham-Holles, Duke of Newcastle
1756–57	William Cavendish, Duke of Devonshire
1757	James Waldegrave, 2nd Earl Waldegrave
1757–62	Thomas Pelham Holles, Duke of Newcastle
1762–63	John Stuart, Earl of Bute
1763–65	George Grenville
1765–66	Charles Wentworth, Marquess of Rockingham
1766–68	Earl of Chatham, William Pitt "The Elder"
1768–70	Augustus Henry Fitzroy, Duke of Grafton
1770–82	Lord North
1782	Charles Wentworth, Marquess of Rockingham
1782–83	William Petty, Earl of Shelburne
1783	William Henry Cavendish Bentinck, 3rd Duke of Portland
1783–1801	William Pitt "The Younger"
1801–04	Henry Addington
1804–06	William Pitt "The Younger"
1806–07	William Wyndam Grenville, Lord Grenville
1807–09	William Henry Cavendish Bentinck, 3rd Duke of Portland
1809–12	Spencer Perceval

Date	Prime minister
1812–27	Robert Banks Jenkinson, Earl of Liverpool
1827	George Canning
1827–28	Frederick Robinson, Viscount Goderich
1828–30	Arthur Wellesley, Duke of Wellington
1830–34	Earl Grey
1834	William Lamb, Viscount Melbourne
1834–35	Sir Robert Peel
1835–41	William Lamb, Viscount Melbourne
1841–46	Sir Robert Peel
1846–52	Earl Russell
1852	Earl of Derby
1852–55	Earl of Aberdeen
1855–58	Viscount Palmerston
1858–59	Earl of Derby
1859–65	Viscount Palmerston
1865–66	Earl Russell
1866–68	Earl of Derby
1868	Benjamin Disraeli
1868–74	William Ewart Gladstone
1874–80	Benjamin Disraeli
1880–85	William Ewart Gladstone
1885–86	Robert Arthur Talbot Gascoyne-Cecil, Marquess of Salisbury
1886	William Ewart Gladstone
1886–92	Robert Arthur Talbot Gascoyne-Cecil, Marquess of Salisbury
1892–94	William Ewart Gladstone
1894–95	Earl of Rosebery
1895–1902	Robert Arthur Talbot Gascoyne-Cecil, Marquess of Salisbury
1902–05	Arthur James Balfour
1905–08	Sir Henry Campbell-Bannerman
1908–16	Herbert Henry Asquith
1916–22	David Lloyd George
1922–23	Andrew Bonar Law
1923	Stanley Baldwin
1924	James Ramsay MacDonald
1924–29	Stanley Baldwin
1929–35	James Ramsay MacDonald
1935–37	Stanley Baldwin
1937–40	Neville Chamberlain
1940–45	Sir Winston Churchill
1945–51	Clement Richard Attlee

Date	Prime minister
1951–55	Sir Winston Churchill
1955–57	Sir Anthony Eden
1957–63	Harold Macmillan
1963–64	Sir Alec Douglas-Home
1964–70	Harold Wilson
1970–74	Edward Heath
1974–76	Harold Wilson
1976–79	James Callaghan
1979–90	Margaret Thatcher
1990–97	John Major
1997–2007	Tony Blair
2007–	Gordon Brown

Proofreading

Look for errors in the following categories:

1 "Typos", which include misspelt words, punctuation mistakes, wrong numbers and transposed words or sentences.
2 Bad word breaks.
3 Layout mistakes: wrongly positioned text (including captions, headings, folios, running heads) or illustrations, incorrect line spacing, missing items, widows (pages that begin with the last word or line of a paragraph – they have a past but no future), orphans (paragraphs that begin on the last line of a page – they have no past but they do have a future).
4 Wrong fonts: errors in the use of italic, bold, typeface (eg, Arial not Times New Roman), etc.

If the text contains cross-references to numbered pages or illustrations, the proofreader is often responsible for inserting the correct reference at page proof stage, and for checking cross-references.

The most effective way of proofreading is to read the text several times, each time with a different aim in mind, rather than attempting to carry out all checks in one go.

proofreading marks are illustrated on pages 239–41. (The full set of proofreading marks is defined by British Standard BS 5261 "Copy preparation and proof correction".) The intention of these marks is to identify, precisely and concisely, the nature of an error and the correction required. When corrections are extensive or complex, it is usually better to spell out in full the correct form of the text rather than leave the typesetter to puzzle over a string of hieroglyphs, however immaculately drawn and ordered. Mark all proof corrections clearly and write them in the margin.

word breaks It may be necessary to break words, using a hyphen, at the end of lines. Computer word-processing programs come with standard hyphenation rules but these can always be changed or overruled. Ideally, the aim should be to make these breaks as undisruptive as possible, so that the reader does not stumble or falter. Whenever possible, the word should be broken so that, helped by the context, the reader can anticipate the whole word from the part of it given before the break. Here are some useful principles for deciding how to break a word.

1   Words that are already hyphenated should be broken at the hyphen, not given a second hyphen.
2   Words can be broken according to either their derivation (the British convention) or their pronunciation (the US convention): thus, *aristo-cracy* (UK) or *aristoc-racy* (US), *melli-fluous* (UK) or *mellif-luous* (US). (*See* Part 2 for American usage.)
3   Words of one syllable should not be broken.
4   Words of five or fewer characters should not be broken.
5   At least three characters must be taken over to the next line.
6   Words should not be broken so that their identity is confused or their identifying sound is distorted: thus, avoid *wo-men*, *fo-ist*, *the-rapist*.
7   Personal names and acronyms (eg, NATO) should not be broken.
8   Figures should not be broken or separated from their unit of measurement.
9   A word formed with a prefix or suffix should be broken at that point: thus, *bi-furcated*, *ante-diluvian*, *convert-ible*.
10 If a breakable word contains a double consonant, split it at that point: thus, *as-sess*, *ship-ping*, *prob-lem*.
11 Do not hyphenate the last word on the right-hand page.

on-screen proofreading Proofreaders are increasingly being asked to proofread on screen, and there are various ways of doing this.

1   Print out the document or pdf, mark it up in the usual way, then scan it and save as a pdf to return by e-mail.
2   Mark up the pdf using the editing tools in a program such as Adobe Acrobat. This can be done in the traditional way

with a graphics tablet, using the pen to add proofreading marks, missing letters, and so on. Missing words or phrases, comments and queries can be typed in text or comments boxes or directly onto the pdf using the typewriter tool (available in Adobe Acrobat version 7 onwards). If the creator has "enabled" the pdf, it is possible to mark up changes and add comments using Adobe Acrobat Reader (version 8 onwards).

3   Mark up a text file (in, for example, Microsoft Word) using track changes. Changes and insertions are highlighted in a different colour, deletions and formatting changes are listed in the margin, and you can add comments and queries using the Comments facility.

INSTRUCTION	TEXTUAL MARK	MARGINAL MARK AND NOTES
Correction is concluded	None	Mark after each correction. Use the circled number to indicate the number of times the same change occurs in the same line without interruption.
Leave unchanged	• • • • • under characters to remain	
Insert in text the matter indicated in the margin	(caret mark)	New matter followed by or
Delete	through character(s) or through words	
Delete	through single character, rule or underline or through all characters to be deleted	
Close up – delete space		
Substitute character or substitute part of one or more words	through character or through all characters	new character or new characters
Wrong font. Replace with correct font	Circle character(s) to be changed	
Set in or change to italic	under character(s) to be set or changed	

INSTRUCTION	TEXTUAL MARK	MARGINAL MARK AND NOTES
Set in or change to capital letters	☰☰☰☰ under character(s) to be set or changed	☰
Set in or change to small capital letters	══ under character(s) to be set or changed	══
Set in or change to bold type	〰〰〰 under character(s) to be set or changed	〰
Set in or change to bold italic type	〰〰〰 under character(s) to be set or changed	└┘〰
Change capital letters to lower case letters	Circle character(s) to be changed	≠
Change italic to upright type	Circle character(s) to be changed	⊬
Turn type or figure	Circle type or figure to be altered. Use circled number to indicate the number of degrees of rotation.	↺ (180)
Substitute or insert character in "superior" position	╱ through character or ⅄ where required	⅄ or ⅄ under character eg 2⅄ or 2⅄
Substitute or insert full stop or decimal point	╱ through character or ⅄ where required	⊙
Substitute or insert comma	╱ through character or ⅄ where required	،

INSTRUCTION	TEXTUAL MARK	MARGINAL MARK AND NOTES
Substitute or insert colon	/ through character or ⟨ where required	⊙
Substitute or insert hyphen	/ through character or ⟨ where required	⊢-⊣
Substitute or insert semi-colon	/ through character or ⟨ where required	;
Insert or substitute space	⟨ or /	⟨
Make space equal	| between words or letters	⟨
Reduce space	⌒ between words or letters	⌒
Start new paragraph	⌐	⌐
Run on (no new paragraph)	⌒	⌒
Transpose characters or words	⎍ between characters or words, numbered when necessary	⎍
Transpose lines	⊰	⊰
Indent	⊏	⊏
Move to the left	|←[xxxx]	⊐
Insert single or double quotes	⟨ where required	' ' " "

Roman numerals

I	1	XX	20
II	2	XXI	21
III	3	XXX	30
IV	4	XL	40
V	5	L	50
VI	6	XC	90
VII	7	C	100
VIII	8	CC	200
IX	9	D	500
X	10	DCC	700
XI	11	DCCXIX	719
XII	12	CM	900
XIII	13	M	1000
XIV	14	MC	1100
XV	15	MCX	1110
XVI	16	MCMXCI	1991
XVII	17	MM	2000
XVIII	18	MMX	2010
XIX	19		

S

Solar system

	Distance from the sun			Diameter (equatorial)		
	au^a	km (m)	mi (m)	relative to Earth (=1)	km ('000)	mi ('000)
Sun	0	0	0	109.00	1,392.140	865.040
Mercury	0.39	58	36	0.38	4.880	3.032
Venus	0.72	108	67	0.95	12.103	7.520
Earth	1	150[b]	93[b]	1	12.756	7.926
Moon	–	150	93	0.27	3.475	2.159
Mars	1.52	228	142	0.53	6.794	4.221
Jupiter	5.20	778	483	11.21	142.984	88.846
Saturn	9.54	1,429	888	9.45	120.536	74.898
Uranus	19.19	2,875	1,786	4.00	51.118	31.763
Neptune	30.07	4,504	2,798	3.89	49.600	30.820

a Astronomical unit, roughly equal to the mean distance between Earth and the sun, approximately 150m km or 93m miles.
b Or 8.3 light minutes. Average distance; for the Earth the perihelion distance (at the point nearest to the sun) is 147.1×10^6 km = 91.4×10^6 mi = 8.2 light minutes, and the aphelion distance (at the point furthest from the sun) is 153.1×10^6 km = 95.1×10^6 mi = 8.5 light minutes.
Note: Pluto used to be included as one of the planets in the solar system, but it was downgraded in 2006. Some astronomers disagree with this decision.

Stockmarket indices

The following is a list of world stockmarket indices.

Americas

Argentina
Merval

Brazil
Bovespa

Chile
IGPA General

Colombia
IGBC Index

Mexico
IPC

Peru
Lima General

Venezuela
IBC

Canada
S&P/TSX Metal & Mining
S&P/TSX Comp
S&P/TSX 60

United States
DJ Industrial
DJ Composite
DJ Transport
DJ Utilities
FTSE Nasdaq 5000
S&P 500
NASDAQ Composite
NASDAQ 100
Russell 2000
NYSE Composite
Wilshire 5000

Asia & Australasia

Australia
S&P All Ordinaries
S&P/ASX 200
S&P/ASX 200 Res

China
Shanghai Composite
CSI 300

Hong Kong
Hang Seng
HS China Enterprise
HSCC Red Chip

India
BSE Sensex
S&P CNX 500

Indonesia
Jakarta Composite

Japan
2nd Section
Nikkei 225
S&P Topix 150
Topix

Malaysia
FTSE Bursa KLCI

New Zealand
NZSX 50

Pakistan
KSE-100

Philippines
Manila Composite

Singapore
FTSE Straits Times

South Korea
KOSPI
KOSPI 200

Sri Lanka
CSE All Share

Taiwan
WeightedPr

Thailand
Bangkok SET

Europe

Austria
ATX Index

Belgium
BEL 20
BEL Mid

Czech Republic
PX

Denmark
OMXC Copenhagen 20

Estonia
OMX Tallinn

Finland
OMX Helsinki General

France
CAC 40
SBF 120

Germany
M-DAX
TecDAX
XETRA Dax

Greece
Athens General
FTSE/ASE 20

Hungary
Bux

Ireland
ISEQ Overall

Italy
FTSE MIB
FTSE Italia Mid Cap
FTSE Italia All Share

Latvia
OMX Riga

Lithuania
OMX Vilnius

Luxembourg
Luxembourg General

Netherlands
AEX
AEX All Share

Norway
Oslo All Share

Poland
Wig

Portugal
PSI 20
PSI General

Romania
BET Index

Russia
RTS

Slovakia
SAX

Spain
IBEX 35
Madrid SE

Sweden
OMX Stockholm 30
OMX Stockholm AS

Switzerland
SMI Index

Turkey
IMKB Nat 100

UK
FTSE 100
FT30
FTSE All Share
FTSE4GoodUK
FTSE techMARK 100

Middle East & Africa

Egypt
EGX 30

Israel
Tel Aviv 100

Jordan
Amman SE

Morocco
MASI

Nigeria
SE All Share

South Africa
FTSE/JSE All Share
FTSE/JSE Res 20
FTSE/JSE Top 40

Cross-border indices

DJ Euro Stoxx 50
DJ Stoxx 50
DJ Global Titans
Euronext 100 ID
FTSE Multinationals
FTSE Global 100
FTSE4Good Global
FTSE E300
FTSE exT All Share
FTSEurofirst 80
FTSEurofirst 100
FTSE Latibex Top

FTSE Eurotop 100
FTSE Gold Min
FTSE All World
FTSE World
MSCI All World
MSCI ACWI Free
MSCI Euro
MSCI Europe
MSCI Pacific
S&P Global 1200
S&P Europe 350
S&P Euro

Source: *Financial Times*

Time of day around the world

Here is a list of countries of the world showing how many hours fast () or slow (-) they are relative to Greenwich Mean Time (GMT). The figures show the winter clock time; where summer time is normally observed, the hour is marked with*.

Algeria +1
Angola +1
Argentina -3
Australia
  New South Wales,
    Canberra,
    Tasmania,
    Victoria +10*
  Queensland +10
  South Australia
    +9.5*
  Northern Territory
    +9.5
  Western Australia
    +8
Austria +1*
Azerbaijan +4*
Bahamas -5*
Bahrain +3
Bangladesh +6
Belarus +2*
Belgium +1*
Bolivia -4
Brazil
  Fernando de
    Noronha -2
  Coast & Brasilia -3*
  West -4*
  Acre -5

Brunei +8
Bulgaria +2*
Canada
  Newfoundland
    Island -3.5*
  Atlantic -4*
  Eastern -5*
  Central -6*
  Mountain -7*
  Pacific -8*
Chile -4*
China (mainland) +8*
Colombia -5
Congo
  Katanga, Kivu +2
  Kinshasa +1
Costa Rica -6
Côte d'Ivoire GMT
Croatia +1*
Cyprus +2*
Czech Republic +1*
Denmark +1*
Dominican Republic
  -4
Ecuador -5
Egypt +2*
Estonia +2*
Ethiopia +3
Finland +2*

France +1*
Germany +1*
Ghana GMT
Greece +2*
Hong Kong +8
Hungary+1*
Iceland GMT
India +5.5
Indonesia
  Eastern +9
  Central +8
  Western +7
Iran +3.5*
Iraq +3*
Ireland GMT
Israel +2*
Italy +1*
Jamaica -5
Japan +9
Kazakhstan (West) +4
  Aktau, Atyrau,
    Aktyubinsk,
    Uraisk +5
  Almaty, Astana +6
Kenya +3
Korea, North & South
  +9
Kuwait +3
Latvia +2*

Lebanon +2*
Libya +2
Lithuania +2*
Luxembourg +1*
Malaysia +8
Malta +1*
Mexico, Mexico City
  −6*
Morocco GMT
Netherlands +1*
New Zealand +12*
Nigeria +1
Norway +1*
Oman +4
Pakistan +5
Panama −5
Papua New Guinea
  +10
Paraguay −4*
Peru −5
Philippines +8
Poland +1*

Portugal GMT*
Puerto Rico −4
Qatar +3
Romania +2*
Russia
  Moscow +3*
  Omsk +6*
Saudi Arabia +3
Serbia and
  Montenegro +1*
Sierra Leone GMT
Singapore +8
Slovakia +1*
Slovenia +1*
South Africa +2
Spain +1*
Sweden +1*
Switzerland +1*
Syria +2*
Taiwan +8
Tajikistan +5
Thailand +7

Trinidad & Tobago −4
Tunisia +1
Turkey +2*
Ukraine +2*
United Arab Emirates
  +4
United Kingdom
  GMT*
United States
  Eastern −5*
  Central −6*
  Mountain −7*
  Pacific −8*
  Alaska −9*
  Hawaii −10
Uruguay −3
Uzbekistan +5
Venezuela −4
Vietnam +7
Yemen +3
Zambia +2
Zimbabwe +2

index